ACCOUNTING IN TRANSITION:

Oral Histories of Recent U.S. Experience

THOMAS J. BURNS
Editor

COLLEGE OF ADMINISTRATIVE SCIENCE
THE OHIO STATE UNIVERSITY
COLUMBUS, OHIO
1974

College of Administrative Science
Monograph No. AA-9

Cover Design by Diane Poulton

ACCOUNTING IN TRANSITION:

Oral Histories of Recent U. S. Experience

of

Richard T. Baker

Michael N. Chetkovich

Sidney Davidson

Philip L. Defliese

Ernest L. Hicks

Charles T. Horngren

Ralph E. Kent

Donald J. Kirk

Robert K. Mautz

Herbert E. Miller

John H. Myers

A. Clarence Sampson

David Solomons

Arthur R. Wyatt

Stephen A. Zeff

Edited

by

THOMAS J. BURNS

This book

is

dedicated to

James R. McCoy

There is properly no History; only Biography

--Emerson

CONTENTS

ACCOUNTING IN TRANSITION: ORAL HISTORIES OF RECENT U.S. EXPERIENCE

Section	Title and Author	Page

PREFACE

This monograph of oral histories honors Dean James R. McCoy, who retires this year after a four-decade career at The Ohio State University--first as a student, then as a faculty member, later as chairman, and last as Dean. During this period, the major institutional arrangements for establishing the standards of U. S. accounting were changed several times; this publication is about these changes as viewed chiefly by fifteen prominent accountants.

Steve Zeff's 45-year chronology of U. S. standards serves as a general framework for the monograph. Each section in the volume constitutes a discussion typically with those who had played leading roles in bringing about the changes discussed. The fifteen discussants were: Richard T. Baker, Michael N. Chetkovich, Sidney Davidson, Philip L. Defliese, Ernest L. Hicks, Charles T. Horngren, Ralph E. Kent, Donald J. Kirk, Robert K. Mautz, Herbert E. Miller, John H. Myers, A. Clarence Sampson, David Solomons, Arthur R. Wyatt, and Stephen A. Zeff. For each section, a selection of background material was reprinted in section appendices. Many of the discussants have been associated with Jim McCoy over the years; for example, Richard T. Baker, Ernest L. Hicks, and Ralph E. Kent are O.S.U. alumni, and Herbert Miller and James McCoy earned graduate degrees in accounting during the same year at the State University of Iowa.

The years in which many of these institutional shifts occurred roughly parallel the years in which Jim McCoy made changes in his own career. When the Securities and Exchange Commission was established, he was a college student majoring in accounting, having started in 1930 and graduating first with a Bachelor's Degree in 1934 and later with a Master's Degree in 1936. When the AICPA's Committee on Accounting Procedure (CAP) was the chief rule-making group in the private sector, he progressed in his academic career, becoming a highly regarded professor of financial accounting and eventually Chairman of the Accounting Department. Except for a year at the State University of Iowa (1936-37) and military leave during World War II (1941-46), his entire career has been spent here. When the Accounting Principles Board (APB) was established in 1959, he became Dean of the College of Commerce and Administration. During the period in which the APB was reorganized, the university's academic reorganization occurred then, too; one result of that event was that the College of Commerce and Administration became the College of Administrative Science, with the same Dean. Last year, Jim McCoy announced his retirement; in the same year, the APB was discontinued, and the Financial Accounting Standards Board (FASB) was started.

The financial support for recording the histories was received from the following organizations: Anchor Hocking Corporation, Battelle Memorial Institute, Buckeye International, Columbus and Southern Ohio Electric Company, First Banc Group, Jeffrey Galion, Inc., Lazarus, and White Castle. Contributions were also made by the Columbus Chapters of the Financial Executives Institure and the Ohio Society of Certified Public Accountants. For the last organization, Jim McCoy has served as president, and he has had a long association with many executives of these firms. Funds for this publication were received from the Ohio Society of Certified Public Accountants, for whom Jim McCoy has been a Board Member.

Serving as discussion moderators were present or former accounting faculty colleagues of Jim McCoy: Paul E. Fertig, Orace E. Johnson, Richard V. Northrup, Harry C. Lyle, and myself. Also serving as discussion moderators were Beta Alpha Psi actives David Bond, Delbert Haney, Ralph Loretta, Terry Sternad, and Thomas Stober; James McCoy has long been active in the Omicron Chapter of this honorary, ever since he was initiated as an undergraduate over 40 years ago.

For all those named above (and for many not named) who contributed to this publication, I express my appreciation.

Columbus, Ohio
June, 1974

Thomas J. Burns
The Ohio State University

PROLOGUE

Chronology of Significant Developments in the Establishment of Accounting Principles in the United States, 1926-1972[1]

by

Stephen A. Zeff

In the last half-dozen years, a number of writers have proposed new approaches to the development of accounting principles in the United States. Yet little systematic research has been published on the process that has actually been used during the last several decades. For the practitioner or academician who has not closely followed the stages of evolution in this process, the succession of episodes, as related in the financial and accountancy press, must appear bewildering. Many events seem to be unrelated to one another, and very little published writing is available to place them in an understandable time frame. Nonetheless, there has indeed been an evolution, and it is important that practitioners and academicians alike acquire some appreciation of the train of events that form the record of achievement, such as it is, in the establishment of accounting principles. To this end, the following chronology is offered as an overview of the principal events that occurred between 1926 and 1972.[2]

1926 *New York Stock Exchange (NYSE), recognizing the need for more effective surveillance of financial reporting by listed companies, names J. M. B. Hoxsey to*

[1]Reprinted with permission from Journal of Accounting Research (Spring, 1972), pp. 217-227. An earlier version appeared in Corporate Financial Reporting: The Issues, The Objectives, and Some New Proposals, L. Revsine and A. Rappaport, Editors (Chicago: Commerce Clearing House, Inc., 1972), pp. 219-233.

[2]A historical study of this evolution is included in the author's monograph, Forging Accounting Principles in Five Countries: A History and an Analysis of Trends (Champaign, Ill.: Stipes Publishing Co., 1972), which formed the basis for the Arthur Andersen & Co. Lecture at the University of Edinburgh in November, 1970.

the new full-time position of Executive Assistant to the Committee on Stock List.

1926-27	*In three articles in The Atlantic Monthly and a book, Main Street and Wall Street, Harvard Economist William Z. Ripley accuses large corporations of, inter alia, deceptive and misleading financial reporting practices.*
1927	*Price Waterhouse & Co. becomes accounting adviser to the NYSE, being represented by George O. May.*
1930	*Hoxsey proposes that the American Institute of Accountants (AIA) and NYSE cooperate on improving corporate financial reporting.*
1931	*AIA Committee on Accounting Terminology compiles a 126-page book of definitions, Accounting Terminology, which is published as a preliminary report by the Institute.*
1932-34	*AIA Committee chaired by May and NYSE Committee on Stock List exchange proposals on unsettled accounting and auditing matters. AIA Committee proposes that within quite wide limits it does not matter which accounting methods are used by corporations, so long as they are used consistently and that full disclosure is made of the choices. AIA Committee suggests five accounting "principles or rules," which are accepted by the NYSE, communicated to NYSE-listed companies, and are approved (1934), together with a sixth, by the AIA membership. AIA Committee also recommends a standard form of the auditor's short-form report, which rapidly achieves wide acceptance, and introduces the term "accepted principles of accounting."*
1933	*NYSE, for the first time, threatens a listed company (Allied Chemical) with delisting unless it improves its financial disclosures. The company eventually complies.*
1933	*NYSE announces that henceforth it will require independent audits of companies seeking a listing. By this time, more than 90 percent of industrial companies already listed have independent audits.*
1933	*Enactment of the Securities Act, providing for "full and fair disclosure" in registration statements (prospectuses) accompanying large, interstate flotations of securities. Act is administered by the Federal Trade Commission.*

1934 *Enactment of the Securities Exchange Act which requires the filing of periodic reports by companies whose securities are listed on national securities exchanges. (Amended in 1964 to include over-the-counter companies having more than $1 million of assets and 500 or more stockholders.) 1934 Act also establishes the Securities and Exchange Commission (SEC), which will administer the 1933 and 1934 securities Act.*

1935 *Carman G. Blough first SEC Chief Accountant and urges (1935-38) the accounting profession to narrow the range of diversity in accounting practices. (Blough is succeeded by William W. Werntz in 1938, Earle C. King in 1947, and Andrew Barr in 1956.)*

1936 *AIA Committee issues Examination of Financial Statements, a document principally oriented to auditing procedures, but which also discusses accounting, and for the first time employs the term "generally accepted accounting principles."*

1936 *American Accounting Association (AAA), formerly the American Association of University Instructors in Accounting, issues a pamphlet entitled, "A Tentative Statement of Accounting Principles Underlying Corporate Financial Statements," which employs the deductive approach to developing accounting principles. (Revisions are published in 1941, 1948, and 1957.)*

1937 *SEC Chief Accountant issues first Accounting Series Release (ASR).*

1937-38 *Deadlock occurs among SEC Commissioners regarding the Commission's posture on accounting, which leads to the issuance by Blough of ASR No. 4, stating that accounting methods will be presumed to be misleading unless they have "substantial authoritative support" and the Commission has not previously issued a rule opposing such methods.*

1938 *AIA publishes A Statement of Accounting Principles, by Thomas H. Sanders, Henry Rand Hatfield, and Underhill Moore.*

1938 *AIA Council approves an enlargement of the Committee on Accounting Procedure (CAP) to 21 members.*

1939 *At the suggestion of the CAP, the AIA Council authorizes the CAP to issue pronouncements on accounting and establishes a research department. Thomas H. Sanders, of Harvard University, is appointed Director of Research, and is succeeded in 1941 by James L. Dohr, of Columbia University. The research directorship is a part-time position. Also in 1939, a Committee on Auditing Procedure is established within the Institute, with authority to promulgate Statements on Auditing Procedure.*

1939 *CAP issues first four Accounting Research Bulletins (ARB's).*

1940 *AAA publishes* <u>*An Introduction to Corporate Accounting Standards*</u> *by W. A. Paton and A. C. Littleton. Monograph elaborates upon the AAA's "Tentative Statement."*

1940 *AIA Committee on Terminology issues a report in the form of an ARB. Seven other Committee reports are issued later in the 1940's.*

1941 *CAP issues ARB No. 11 in which it recommends that stock dividends be recorded at fair value by the issuer. In 1943, the NYSE publicly supports the CAP position.*

1944 *AIA recognizes the need for more effective research and appoints Carman G. Blough as the first full-time Director of Research. Shortly after the appointment, the AIA research department begins to circulate exposure drafts of proposed ARB's to various interested groups.*

1944-45 *CAP issues ARB Nos. 23 and 24 on income-tax allocation and goodwill, respectively, which are followed by ASR Nos. 53 and 50 in which the SEC takes issue with portions of the two bulletins.*

1947 *Blough begins to edit a new department, "Comments on Accounting Procedures" (later "Accounting and Auditing Problems"), in* <u>*The Journal of Accountancy*</u>*, which he relinquishes in 1963.*

1947 *CAP issues ARB No. 32 in which it favors the "current-operating-performance" concept of the income statement, which the SEC Chief Accountant replies will not be enforced if it results in misleading financial statements.*

1947-48 *CAP hastily issues ARB No. 33, which recommends against the use of price-level depreciation. It is opposed by several large companies and some leaders of the accounting profession. As a result, the CAP's role in influ-*

encing the course of accounting practice is formally questioned, and sustained, within the Institute.

1947-52 *A Study Group on Business Income, largely guided by George O. May, issues several monographs and a final report (Changing Concepts of Business Income) on the nature and measurement of accounting net income in inflationary conditions. Study is jointly financed by the AIA and the Rockefeller Foundation.*

1949 *CAP proposes to compile a comprehensive statement of "generally accepted accounting principles," but later abandons the effort as infeasible.*

1949-50 *SEC proposes to incorporate Accounting Series Releases on accounting subjects into its Regulation S-X on disclosures, also to require the "all-inclusive" income statement of registrants. In response to adverse comments by the AIA and AAA, the SEC decides to incorporate the ASR's in Regulation S-X only by a single, general reference and agrees to a compromise on the matter of the all-inclusive vs. current-operating-performance concepts of the income statement.*

1952 *CAP issues ARB No. 11 (Revised) on stock dividends, which is publicly supported in 1953 by the NYSE.*

1953 *CAP issues ARB No. 43, a restatement and revision of the 34 ARB's on accounting, and the Committee on Terminology issues Accounting Terminology Bulletin (ATB) No. 1, which is a review and résumé of the eight ARB's on terminology. Three more ATB's are issued in the 1950's.*

1956 *Leonard Spacek, managing partner of Arthur Andersen & Co., begins to criticize the pace and direction of the accounting profession in establishing accounting principles.*

1956 *AIA Executive Committee proposes that the CAP prepare a comprehensive statement of basic accounting principles.*

1957 *Spacek charges that the CAP and the Institute's Committee on Relations with the Interstate Commerce Commission yielded to industry pressures on matters of accounting principle and auditing procedure. The AIA refers the charges to a special investigating committee which reports that they are groundless.*

1957-58 *Alvin R. Jennings, incoming AICPA (formerly AIA) President, recommends creation of a research foundation and appoints a Special Committee on Research Program, of which Weldon Powell is Chairman, to formulate a specific recommendation. The Committee's principal concern is the lack of research, understanding, and agreement on the basic postulates and principles underlying accounting practice.*

1959 *Council accepts the comprehensive recommendations of the Special Committee on Research Program, replaces the research department by an accounting research division having an expanded role, and replaces the CAP and the Committee on Terminology by the Accounting Principles Board (APB), of which Weldon Powell is to be Chairman. AICPA Executive Committee insists that the Big Eight firms be represented on the Board by their managing partners. The CAP issues ARB No. 51, on consolidations, its last bulletin.*

1959-60 *Two large subsidiaries of a public utility holding company seek to enjoin the CAP from issuing a clarifying letter to its ARB No. 44 (Revised) on income-tax allocation. The Federal District Court and Second Circuit Court of Appeals hold for the AICPA, and certiorari is denied by the U. S. Supreme Court. The letter is issued. In early 1960, the SEC issues Accounting Series Release No. 85, which forbids the designation of "deferred tax credit" as part of stockholder's equity.*

1959-60 *Perry Mason is named Acting Director of Accounting Research in November, 1959. On July 1, 1960, Maurice Moonitz becomes Director. (He is succeeded in 1963 by Paul Grady, as Acting Director, and in 1964 by Reed K. Storey, as Director.) During 1960, eight Accounting Research Studies are commissioned.*

1960 *Two-part article, "The Auditors Have Arrived," by Tom A. Wise, in the November and December issues of Fortune, does much to awaken interest in accounting and the accounting profession.*

1961-62 *AICPA publishes Accounting Research Studies 1 and 3, on postulates and principles, which are rejected by the APB as "too radically different. . .for acceptance at this time."*

1962-64 *By a bare two-thirds majority of 14 to 7, including a 4-4 split of Big Eight firms, the APB approves Opinion*

No. 2, which recommends that the "investment credit should be reflected in net income over the productive life of acquired property and not in the year in which it is placed in service." Prior to issuance, industry had vigorously objected to this treatment. Following issuance, three of the Big Eight firms make it known that they will not expect their clients to conform to the Opinion. In view of widespread opposition to Opinion, both in government and in the private sector, the SEC issues ASR No. 96, in which it allows both the deferral and flow-through methods of accounting for the investment credit. In early 1964, by a vote of 15 to 5, the APB issues Opinion No. 4, which acknowledges the "events and developments occurring since the issuance of Opinion No. 2" and declares that both the deferral and flow-through methods are "acceptable."

1962-Present *Controversies over the investment credit (1962-63 and 1967), product-line reporting (1966-68), and pooling of interests (1969-70), together with criticisms by the SEC, the Financial Executives Institute (FEI), and members of the profession, excite an almost continual interest by the financial press in accounting principles and the accounting profession.*

1963-64 *APB issues Opinion No. 3, which recommends that funds statements "be presented as supplementary information in financial reports." Shortly afterwards, the NYSE sends copies of the Opinion to the presidents of listed companies, strongly recommending that funds statements, preferably covered by the auditor's opinion and presented on a comparative basis, be included in annual reports to stockholders. In its first public endorsement of an Institute pronouncement, the Financial Analysis Federation (FAF) also urges companies to include funds statements in annual reports.*

1963-64 *APB, in a divided vote, asks Council to require that material departures from Board recommendations be disclosed in the financial statements or in the auditor's report. AICPA Executive Committee goes further, suggesting that Board Opinions be the only "generally accepted accounting principles." Council, in a compromise resolution following three days of intense debate, adopts the APB proposal in principle. Following a report by a special committee, Council in fall, 1964, implements the compromise proposal.*

1964 SEC amends proxy rule 14a-3 to require that any material differences in the application of accounting principles between reports filed with the Commission and reports sent to security holders must be reconciled or explained in the latter. As a result, the SEC asserts indirect surveillance over annual reports to stockholders issued by most companies under its jurisdiction.

1964 Clifford V. Heimbucher becomes APB Chairman, creates subcommittees to decentralize the Board's work, and supports establishment of an Administrative Division to provide staff support for the Board.

1964 Manuel F. Cohen, SEC Commissioner since 1961, becomes Commission Chairman, and begins to criticize the accounting profession for lack of progress in "narrowing areas of difference."

1964-66 Big Eight managing partners on the Board are gradually replaced by their senior technical partners.

1965 Publication of Paul Grady's Inventory of Generally Accepted Accounting Principles for Business Enterprises, as Accounting Research Study No. 7.

1965 SEC issues ASR No. 102 on the balance-sheet status of the deferred tax credit arising from installment sales --a controversial subject which had been included in an APB exposure draft but was later omitted from Opinion No. 6. This is one of the few instances in which the SEC has issued an ASR on accounting without exposing a draft or holding hearings.

1965 FAF establishes a Financial Accounting Policy Committee as liaison with the APB.

1965-70 Followed by several months an inquiry from the U. S. Senate's Subcommittee on Antitrust and Monopoly, SEC Chairman Cohen publicly calls for product-line reporting by conglomerates, APB issues Statement No. 2 encouraging voluntary disclosures, and the FEI and its research affiliate, the Financial Executives Research Foundation (FERF) take a strong interest in the subject. The FERF commissions R. K. Mautz to prepare a comprehensive research study, which appears in early 1968 under the title, Financial Reporting by Diversified Companies. The National Association of Accountants (NAA), also evincing its first serious research *interest in financial accounting, commissions two studies: External Reporting for Segments of a Business (1968), by Morton Backer and Walter B. McFarland, and A Framework for Financial Reporting by Diversified Companies (1969), by Alfred Rappaport and Eugene M. Lerner. The SEC gives consideration to these studies in formulating its guidelines in 1968-70.*

1966 *AICPA begins a series of financial writers' seminars designed to educate financial journalists about the accounting problems faced by the Board.*

1966 *A committee of the AAA issues a monograph entitled A Statement of Basic Accounting Theory.*

1966-67 *APB issues Opinion Nos. 8 (pensions), 9 (extraordinary items and earnings per share), and 10 (omnibus), which are endorsed by the NYSE. Numbers 9, 10 are supported by the American Stock Exchange (ASE). SEC expresses pleasure with the Board's resolution of several difficult problems.*

1966-67 *AICPA creates the full-time position of Executive Vice President to assume operating and policy supervision of Institute technical activities. Leonard M. Savoie, formerly a partner in Price Waterhouse & Co., is appointed and quickly becomes the Institute's spokesman on accounting and auditing matters.*

1967 *APB issues an exposure draft on accounting for income taxes, including a reassertion of its position of 1962 on the investment credit. As a result of an open letter of objection from Stanley S. Surrey, Assistant Secretary of the Treasury (Tax Policy), an expression by the SEC that it cannot promise support, and other communications, the ensuing Opinion No. 11, on income-tax allocation, is published without any recommendations on the investment credit. In 1969, the AICPA publishes a 70-page guidebook containing unofficial interpretation of the Opinion.*

1967-69 *Acting on the strong suggestion of the Investment Bankers Association of America that they are undesirable and unworkable, the APB temporarily suspends paragraphs 8 and 9 of Opinion No. 10, dealing with the imputation of debt discount to issues of convertible debt and debt issued with stock warrants. In Opinion No. 14, issued in 1969, the APB rescinds its recommendation as regards convertible debt, while reinstating the proposed treat-*

ment in the base of debt issued with detachable stock warrants.

1968 *FEI's Corporate Reporting Committee becomes an active collaborator on exposure drafts with the APB, sets up subject-area subcommittees as liaison with counterpart subcommittees of the APB.*

1968 *AICPA, FAF, FEI, and Robert Morris Associates jointly sponsor the Seaview Symposium on Corporate Financial Reporting, bringing together accounting practitioners, accounting educators, financial executives, financial analysts, and bank loan officers in a dialogue on accounting principles. The papers and proceedings are published by the AICPA in 1969 under the title, Corporate Financial Reporting: Conflicts and Challenges.*

1968-70 *Controversy over pooling-of-interests accounting becomes intense as the conglomerate merger movement reaches its zenith, then collapses. Direct and indirect pressure from the SEC, Congress, Federal Trade Commission, the Administration, financial analysts, and financial executives begins to bear down on the APB. Board issues an exposure draft, holds two symposia and numerous private meetings, agonizes during much of 1970 over various proposals and drafts, and finally issues Opinion Nos. 16 and 17 amid much dissent and criticism. Shortly after the Opinions' effective date of November 1, 1970, the NYSE and ASE send identical letters to the presidents of companies listed on their respective Exchanges, urging full support of both Opinions and giving notice that they will require letters from a company's independent auditor attesting to the company's compliance with Opinion No. 16 in connection with listing applications authorizing shares to be issued in poolings of interests.*

1968-71 *After considerable discussion between the banking industry and the Institute's APB and Committee on Bank Accounting and Auditing, the latter prepares and issues an audit guide, Audit of Banks, which, among other things, recommends that commercial banks provide for loan losses and securities' gains and losses prior to arriving at net income, contrary to industry practice. Complaints by bankers precipitate further meetings, following which the APB, in 1969, issues Opinion No. 13 in which it rescinds its exemption, in Opinion No. 9, of commercial banks, obliging them to adhere to the two controversial recommendations in the audit guide.*

Shortly thereafter, the NYSE announces that banks (and insurance companies) will no longer be exempt from submitting audited financial statements in listing applications. Later in 1969, the recommendations contained in the audit guide are made mandatory by the bank regulatory agencies. Bankers' criticisms of the recommendations continue into 1970. In ASR No. 121, issued in 1971, the SEC deletes the exemption from certification of the financial statements of banks.

1968–Present — *Abraham J. Briloff writes a series of articles for Barron's, calling into question the accounting and disclosure practices of numerous publicly-held corporations. While placing primary emphasis on abuses of pooling-of-interest accounting, Briloff also deals with the particular practices of computer leasing companies, land development companies, franchisers, and home builders. Briloff's articles generate increased stock-market sensitivity to the quality of financial reporting.*

1969 — *APB begins to hold a series of symposia on pre-exposure drafts of proposed Opinions. Participation is by invitation only, the Board inviting several organizations to all symposia and various other bodies to particular symposia, depending on the subject. Memoranda and brief oral presentations are requested of participants. The object of the symposium idea, which was suggested by the belated reaction of investment bankers to Opinion No. 10, is to inform affected groups of the Board's current thinking on subjects under consideration so as to secure reactions and suggestions before the Board reaches its conclusions. The symposium approach leads to a formalization of the Board's liaison with other interested groups.*

1969 — *AICPA announces a new Unofficial Accounting Interpretations service to clarify the APB's intent on specific questions arising from APB Opinions. Each interpretation requires the approval of the Executive Vice President and the APB Chairman.*

1969 — *For the first time, a practicing certified public accountant, James J. Needham, is named to the SEC.*

1969 — *APB issues 60-page Opinion No. 15 on earnings per share, modifying Opinion No. 9. Extensive detail in the Opinion provokes criticism that the Board is trying to impose a "cook-book" on the profession. Institute issues a 189-page guidebook of unofficial interpretations of the Opinion.*

1969 *APB issues Statement No. 3, proposing that the price-level adjustments explained and illustrated in Accounting Research Study No. 6 be presented as supplementary information to the basic financial statements.*

1969 *NAA forms a Management Accounting Practices Committee with authority to issue statements of opinion on accounting principles.*

1969-71 *Following a recommendation in its 1969 Disclosure Policy Study report, the SEC in 1970 amends its forms to require the presentation of audited funds statements in prospectuses and periodic filings. A week later, the NYSE announces that, effective with 1973 annual reports, all listed companies will be required to present comparative, audited funds statements. In 1971, the APB issues Opinion No. 19 which recommends that a "Statement of Changes in Financial Position," embodying a broadened concept of the funds statement be made part of the "basic financial statements."*

1970 *After five years of study and numerous drafts, the APB issues Statement No. 4, "Basic Concepts and Accounting Principles Underlying Financial Statements of Business Enterprises," the Board's first pronouncement on basic principles.*

1970-71 *In February, 1970, the APB issues an exposure draft on the subject of accounting changes, which proposes that prior years' financial statements be restated to reflect the new accounting principle or method of application. By mid-1970, support for that position deteriorates, and a second exposure draft on the same subject, issued in January, 1971, recommends against the restatement of prior years' financial statements and instead favors showing the cumulative effect of retroactive application of the new accounting principle or method immediately in the current period's income statement, together with the "pro forma" income of each period affected. Later in the year, the APB approves by a bare two-thirds majority, 12 to 6, including a 4-4 split of Big Eight firms, Opinion No. 20, which, with some exceptions, embodies the philosophy of the second exposure draft.*

1970-71 *On the heels of several recent Treasury decisions which permit taxpayers to change accounting methods for tax purposes if the taxpayer were to use the new method in all its reports for other purposes, the Treasury Department announces, in April, 1971, a study "to set forth more specifically the circumstances under which a new tax accounting method may be used by a taxpayer only if [also] used for financial accounting and reporting." After considerable debate within the profession, the AICPA Board of Directors (formerly the Executive Committee) advises the Treasury that it opposes such enforced conformity of tax accounting to financial accounting. A similar expression is approved by the AAA Executive Committee.*

1970-71 *Arthur Andersen & Co. petitions the Federal Power Commission (FPC) to require natural gas companies to use full-cost accounting for exploration costs incurred in working oil and gas reserves. Comments invited by the Commission are almost equally divided for and against full-costing. Accounting Research Study No. 11, published in 1969, had counseled against full-costing. The APB Chairman requests the Commission to postpone a decision until the Board can act on the subject. In November, 1971, the FPC decides in favor of full-costing accounting, which is to be applied on a nationwide basis.*

1971 *Responding to criticism both inside and outside the accounting profession, the AICPA commissions two major studies. One deals with the process by which accounting principles should be established, and the second concerns the objectives of financial statements. The first is chaired by former SEC Commissioner Francis M. Wheat, the second by former Institute President Robert M. Trueblood. The AAA, in an action by its Executive Committee, also calls for a blue-ribbon commission to make a comprehensive study of the way in which accounting principles should be established. In view of the Institute's study on the subject, the AAA decides to hold its proposal in abeyance.*

1971 *APB replaces the series of symposia by public hearings at which all interested parties may present their views on subjects being considered by the Board for prospective Opinions. The hearings are intended to meet three criticisms of the symposia, to wit: (1) participation was by invitation only, (2) the Board had already reached its conclusions before the symposia were held, and (3) presentations by participating groups were dog-*

matic and uncompromising, thus frustrating attempts at developing a dialogue. Three hearings are held in 1971, on the valuation of marketable equity securities, accounting for long-term leases, and accounting practices in the oil and gas industry. The prepared papers and hearing transcripts are published by the Institute.

1971 *Several weeks after President Nixon recommends that Congress revive the investment credit, AICPA representatives meet with Treasury officials to urge the Administration to refrain from expressing a view on the proper accounting treatment of the credit. The Institute receives a letter from the Treasury that it will remain neutral on the question. Following a meeting between AICPA representatives and the SEC Chairman, the APB prepares and issues an exposure draft again reasserting its 1962 preferred treatment of the investment credit. A letter of support is received from the SEC Chairman. Partly in response to industry pressures, the Treasury revises its neutrality stand and advises the Senate that it "strongly supports a continuation of the optional [accounting] treatment" of the credit and "will support a legislative resolution of this matter." Notwithstanding the eleventh-hour pleas of Institute leaders, Congress amends the tax bill, which later becomes law, to provide that taxpayers may freely choose which method of accounting for the credit they prefer. In the face of this Congressional dictum, the APB withdraws its exposure draft and issues a statement deploring Congressional involvement in the establishment of accounting principles.*

1972 *John C. Burton, a Columbia University accounting professor, is named SEC Chief Accountant. An era ends, as Andrew Barr, who is the last of four successive Chief Accountants who joined the Commission's staff in the 1930's, retires.*

1972 *The Wheat Study recommends that a seven-man, full-time Financial Accounting Standards Board be established under the auspices of a Financial Accounting Foundation, which is to be composed of representatives of the AICPA, FEI, NAA, FAF, and AAA. The Board's budget is proposed at between $2 1/2 and $3 million. A Financial Accounting Standards Advisory Council, made up of "persons conversant with and involved in the problems of communicating financial information," is suggested to keep the Board in touch with current thinking in the business and professional world. The entire recommen-*

dation receives the support of an overwhelming majority of the AICPA's Board of Directors and Council, and several Big Eight firms promise donations of $1 million to the Foundation. The APB continues its activities during 1972, but is to be replaced in early 1973 by the program recommended by the Wheat Study.

SECTION I

THE SEARCH FOR STANDARDS: U.S. AND ABROAD

INTRODUCTION

In this section, the two discussants range over a broad range of issues about the past and present institutional arrangements for setting U.S. accounting standards. Both are uniquely qualified to do so although for quite different reasons. As the last Chairman of the Accounting Principles Board (APB), and as Managing Partner of Coopers & Lybrand (a Big Eight firm), Mr. Defliese speaks out of first-hand experience and with great authority. His fellow discussant, a scholar who has studied accounting institutions in several countries, Professor Zeff, speaks with the perspective of an accounting historian.

As appendices to this discussion, the historic report of the AICPA Committee in 1959 that led to the establishment of the APB is included. Also, to emphasize the increasing need for international accounting standards, reports by two Canadians on the recent efforts to establish such are included.

--The Editor.

SECTION I

THE SEARCH FOR STANDARDS: U.S. AND ABROAD

1934 *Enactment of the Securities Exchange Act which requires the filing of periodic reports by companies whose securities are listed on national securities exchanges. 1934 Act also establishes the Securities and Exchange Commission (SEC), which will administer the 1933 and 1934 Securities Act.*

1937 *SEC Chief Accountant issues first Accounting Series Release (ASR).*

1939 *At the suggestion of the CAP, the AIA Council authorizes the CAP to issue pronouncements on accounting, and establishes a research department. The research directorship is a part-time position.*

1944 *AIA recognizes the need for more effective research and appoints Carman G. Blough as the first full-time Director of Research.*

1956 *Leonard Spacek, managing partner of Arthur Andersen & Co., begins to criticize the pace and direction of the accounting profession in establishing accounting principles.*

1957 *Spacek charges that the CAP yielded to industry pressures on matters of accounting principle and auditing procedure. The AIA refers the charges to a special investigating committee which reports they are groundless.*

-- Excerpts are from Stephen A. Zeff's "Chronology of Significant Developments in the Establishment of Accounting Principles in the United States, 1926-1972," <u>Journal of Accounting Research</u> (Spring, 1972), pp. 217-227.

THE DISCUSSANTS

Philip L. Defliese:

At the firm of Coopers & Lybrand (formerly Lybrand, Ross Bros. & Montgomery), Mr. Defliese is the Managing Partner and Chairman of the firm's International Executive Committee and U.S. Executive Committee. He was formerly the firm's National

Director of Accounting, Auditing, and SEC Services. He is a native New Yorker and received his Bachelor's and Master's Degrees from C.C.N.Y. In World War II, he was a U.S. Navy Lieutenant serving as executive officer of a destroyer escort and sub chaser. He is a former member of the New York State Board of CPA Examiners. Mr. Defliese is currently serving as a member of Council, which is the governing body of the AICPA. He has served on numerous committees of the AICPA, such as the Committee on Practice Review and the Committee on Personnel and Training, and he has chaired the Committee on Auditing Procedure. He is also an active member of the New York State Society of CPA's, the American Accounting Association, and the National Association of Accountants. Well-known for his co-authorship of Montgomery's Auditing, Mr. Defliese was chairman of the Accounting Principles Board (APB) for the three years preceding the formation of the Financial Accounting Standards Board (FASB). He is presently a member of the Advisory Council of that Board. In 1972 he received the American Institute's Gold Medal Award for distinguished service to the accounting profession.

Stephen A. Zeff:

At Tulane University, Dr. Zeff is Professor of Accounting. He received a Ph.D. from the University of Michigan in 1962. His research interests are principally the historical development of accounting thought and practice, and international comparisons of accounting standards and institutions. He was book review editor of The Accounting Review from 1962 to 1966 and was Director of Education of the American Accounting Association from 1969 to 1971. He was founder and editor, from 1968 to 1971, of the Boletin Interamericano de Contabilidad, and in 1972 he served as Senior Fulbright Scholar (honorary) at Monash University, Australia. A leading accounting historian, his recent work includes The American Accounting Association--Its First Fifty Years (AAA, 1966); Forging Accounting Principles in Five Countries: A History and an Analysis of Trends (Stipes, 1972); and, Forging Accounting Principles in Australia (Australian Society of Accountants, 1973). His current research includes a "forging" article on New Zealand, a critical historical study of the Accounting Principles Board, and a biographical study of Henry Rand Hatfield.

THE MODERATORS

The faculty moderator is Professor Paul E. Fertig, Chairman of the Accounting Faculty at The Ohio State University. With a Ph.D. from Ohio State, Professor Fertig has been a visiting professor at several universities. A member of the ASOBAT Committee, he has published in many professional periodicals; his co-authored text, Using Accounting Information, is in its second edition.

The student moderator is Thomas Stober, President, Omicron Chapter, Beta Alpha Psi. Winner of the National Beta Alpha Psi Essay Contest in 1973, Mr. Stober will enter the Ph.D. program at the University of Minnesota this Fall after graduating summa cum laude this Spring.

THE DISCUSSION

Reasons for Discontinuing APB:

FERTIG, Moderator: What were the conditions in accounting decision-making in the United States which made it imperative for many to decide to discontinue the Accounting Principles Board (APB) and to develop the Financial Accounting Standards Board (FASB) structure?

DEFLIESE: There was a rather booming stock market which precipitated many mergers. There was the emergence of the conglomerates with their emphasis on earnings per share and the use of alternative accounting principles to achieve operating results. These factors interacted so that accounting and the APB was felt to blame. The APB which was set up to narrow the alternatives in accounting was not doing its job either effectively or rapidly enough. Yet in some instances, certain segments of industry felt the APB was doing too effective a job. So you can make a case that the APB was doing too good a job, as well as for one that they weren't doing well enough. Finally, there was a great deal of agitation over the questions of pooling of interests and the earnings per share, which were not resolved satisfactorily for some.

Change was advocated on the ground that the APB was not independent (because it was made up of practitioners who were presumably serving the interests of their clients) and because it was not a full-time group (and therefore couldn't work at the job enough). The combination of these factors led to the conclusion by the Wheat Committee that there ought to be a change.

ZEFF: Certainly the tripping off mechanism for the setting up of the Wheat Committee were APB Opinions No. 16 and 17. There was a very fractious series of meetings about pooling that began with an exposure draft which disavowed entirely the pooling of interests, in accordance with the view of many academics and practitioners. Industry was wholly opposed to that solution. There was a tremendous amount of pressure brought to bear on the Board both from government and industry frequently arguing different positions. Some of the strongly held views of members of the Board caused it to have real difficulty in arriving at a majority position. The Board couldn't get 12 votes, which is the necessary two-thirds vote to pass anything--until the subject was eventually divided into two parts. The Board had actually reached a fragile 12-6 agreement on a unified position in June, but a month later, when one member of the majority decided he simply couldn't continue to hold to the view he had earlier supported, the Board was embarrassed. It again lacked a majority. This series of very difficult meetings was completely reported in the press. Moreover, the Financial Executives Institute (FEI) conducted a vociferous media campaign, sending its press releases all over the country. After the issuance of Opinions 16 and 17, which many found disappointing and probably nobody agreed with exactly, there was a widespread belief that the Board was ineffective. Whether or not it was true that the Board was actually ineffective, the appearance of these highly controversial opinions certainly encouraged this conclusion.

Also, there were those who were looking for an Opinion from the Board providing a broad framework of accounting principles. In October of the same year in which Opinions 16 and 17 were issued, they were disappointed when the Board opted for a Statement instead of an Opinion. In the middle of November, the leading partners of three big firms wrote to the President of the AICPA and in effect said that we need to have another look at the APB. This led to a conference chaired by Institute President Marshall Armstrong in Washington, D. C. in January, 1971. The three firms were Arthur Andersen, Arthur Young, and Touche Ross. All three letters were written within one week of each other. I haven't yet found out why they happened to be written in such close time proximity. The viewpoint of Bob Trueblood has subsequently been reported in The New York Times. He said in effect that his firm was reconsidering its support of the entire APB program and might in the future consider not accepting some pronouncements. This was a very strong statement and gave rise to alarm within the institute. These three letters were the immediate impetus for setting up the Wheat Committee. The Wheat Committee wasn't asked to say whether the APB had failed but only what could be done to improve the situation, so there was a presupposition that there existed certain defective elements in the APB structure.

But there are other points that could be mentioned. One was the lack of research support for the APB, as emphasized by many critics. After all, the idea behind the APB approach was to provide a research base for the kind of pronouncements which had been issued by the old Committee on Accounting Procedure (CAP). Yet the research base had been hardly more evident in the work of the APB than during the tenure of the CAP. Research was not being utilized. Not much research was even produced. The research that was produced didn't address the questions that the Board seemed to want to answer. The research frequently didn't utilize evidence that the Board would have found persuasive in reaching its conclusions. As the Board went along in years, its reliance on research became less and less.

Since research was an essential element in the APB concept, its absence or ineffectiveness in the APB operation caused many observers to become disenchanted. In particular, the absence of a guiding philosophy or a set of objectives and the issuance of APB Opinions 16 and 17 certainly provoked tremendous criticism. There was also a growing feeling that the FEI presented an insurmountable obstacle, unless this powerful body could be brought within the rule-making process.

DEFLIESE: What you have said is correct. You may have injected a bias concerning the opinions since only the passage of time will determine whether they were effective for the time, and whether some of the research that would be necessary in order to depart from the present historical cost concepts and the pooling concepts could have been accomplished in time to achieve any alternative rules. This subject is going to be reopened by the FASB. The research that may be necessary to achieve the reformulation of accounting concepts and objectives that are necessary as a prelude to getting anything done in that area will be found to be essentially the same for the FASB as it was for the APB. Without it, the FASB is not going to get much done.

I am restudying APB Opinion No. 16. I intend to recast some 68 mergers on a purchase basis rather than on a pooling basis. You can visualize what would have happened if the values under the purchasing concept would have been adopted a few years ago. Most of the share values today are probably a tenth of what they were then. If goodwill or any other intangibles would have been created on the basis of those values, our accounting today would be grossly inflated. So there is a real need for this type of research. We can't really begin to judge the results of those opinions until such research is done. Just as leaders can't always be judged until after they are gone, those opinions can't be judged yet.

The British and Other Experience:

ZEFF: Since 1970, the Accounting Standards Steering Committee (ASSC) in Great Britain has been issuing a series of exposure drafts--it is a body which represents all the major accountancy bodies in that country. In January, 1971, the ASSC issued an exposure draft No. 3 on Mergers and Acquisitions. This draft, which doesn't treat goodwill, is otherwise roughly identical to one of the earlier drafts of the APB on poolings, calling for a three-for-one size test. It is significant that this ASSC draft has still not been converted into an opinion or replaced by another draft, yet it is understood to be dead. Of the 11 that have been issued so far by the ASSC, the exposure draft on mergers and acquisitions has been the object of more criticism than any other draft. By the way, the ASSC did not use the terms "pooling of interest" and "purchase," but substituted "merger" and "acquisition" in order, one assumes, to get away from the stigmas attached to the former terms. But that device didn't seem to solve the problem. Britain simply didn't learn from the U.S. experience. They are discovering that the same fractiousness can occur there as has occurred here. Countries don't always learn from other countries.

FERTIG, Moderator: In the matter of accounting decision-making, how are other countries getting along compared to the United States?

ZEFF: That is a hard question because it is difficult to compare progress in different countries owing to the different institutional settings and social environments which one finds in those countries. For example, no country has such an open political system as we have. There is no country in the world that would have had anything like the Watergate hearings on television, and only few countries would have held hearings at all. The U.S. press is by far the most openly critical of institutions of any press in the world. Certainly the APB was subjected to greater scrutiny in the financial press than has any comparable body abroad.

This country is also the most litigious in the world. Many lawsuits on financial matters which are brought in the U.S. would in Britain be settled out of court through quiet negotiations in some club on London's Pall Mall Street.

In Canada, there has been less professional and public criticism of the rules-making process than in the U.S. even though Canada recently changed its process to follow rather closely the FASB approach. (Canada is much influenced by events in this country.) In Britain, there is not very much open criticism of rule-making. Matters tend to be settled behind the scenes. Nonetheless, when government wants something done, it makes its views known privately and can have tremendous impact on the final outcome. It was only as a result of some public criticism, rather rare in Britain, coupled with private representation by government, that the British changed their rule-making process in the latter part of 1969.

In studying different countries that have had some experience with establishing accounting standards, I find that the most significant single factor which forces the profession to change is public criticism in the financial press--particularly for a profession that conducts most of its affairs in confidential terms and is not accustomed to public scrutiny, let alone public criticism. Public criticism has done much to "move" the accounting profession. This is so in Canada, very much so in Great Britain, and also in Australia. Anywhere there has been sustained public criticism, there has been change in the system. This has been perhaps the most pervasive factor that one can discern in the experience of countries which have engaged in rule-making.

The main reason that the CAP was replaced by the APB and the APB was replaced by the FASB was the criticism from within the profession. In the case of the demise of the APB, criticism from within the profession had been fueled by public criticism. This kind of open criticism within the profession does not exist in most other countries. So in this sense it is somewhat hard to draw conclusions on a comparative basis.

DEFLIESE: There is no doubt that the demise of the APB is largely attributable to the criticism within the profession rather than by the press itself. But obviously the one stimulated the other. This is an American characteristic and it is in contrast to what we find in other countries.

<u>Effect of Litigation</u>:

FERTIG, Moderator: Neither one of you mentioned anything about the lawsuits or concern of the profession over litigation having any bearing on this matter particularly.

DEFLIESE: If you will examine the lawsuits very carefully, you will find that very few hinge upon accounting principles. Most involve a failure in auditing or disclosure or other elements of our profession. That is why the influence of litigation does not bear on the subject of accounting principles.

<u>Management and Other Participation</u>:

FERTIG, Moderator: Following up Steve Zeff's comment about the participation of management in the formulation of accounting standards, how do you feel about the adequacy of management participation under our new arrangement?

DEFLIESE: There is a limit on how much you can get management to participate in an exercise of this sort. We are fortunate to have at least one industry representative on the FASB. It would be difficult to get very many that would be qualified and would be willing to undertake that type of operation just as it is difficult to get many in the profession to disassociate themselves from firms to undertake the assignment. Also, everyone recognizes that management should participate but that it should be limited to a smaller segment because most standard-setting has to be within the professional area.

ZEFF: Aside from the chairman, the only member of the FASB who took a salary cut was the former financial executive. This suggests one reason why it may be difficult to persuade financial executives to take such a position. The important thing is that the FEI is part of this new operation by having two representatives serving as trustees of the Financial Accounting Foundation (FAF), and a former financial executive on the FASB. The severe test of the FASB will come when some of its pronouncements meet with general industry criticism. Such criticism may affect the continuing willingness of the FEI to be allied with this new program. Two or three former financial executives on the FASB would not necessarily implement this concept any more effectively than simply one. Yet in a number of ways the broader umbrella of the FASB is probably the most important innovative feature of this new approach. The APB, which was formally a part of the AICPA, counted as many as two financial executives among its members, but it did not have a direct link with the FEI. Certainly one man out of seven on the FASB is a larger percentage of representation of financial executives than one man (or even two men) out of eighteen for the APB.

Actually, I favored an economist on the FASB. One of the weaknesses of the APB was that it was unable or unwilling to anticipate the possible dislocations that some pronouncements would have caused in certain sectors of the economy. Possibly an economist on the APB might have sensitized the members to the possible implications of their opinions beyond those simply for investors. Life was very difficult for the APB because it did not appreciate the depth of government or industry interest when it was contemplating pronouncements.

DEFLIESE: It is unfortunate that the original membership of the APB, a 21-member Board which included three members of industry and three members of academia, was not continued. That membership provided a much broader representation. When that membership was reduced, the industry representation was considerably reduced. The results of the APB might have not been so different in the long run with more diffused membership. But the Board might have been better able to refute the charge that the Board was less effective because outside participation was inadequate.

ZEFF: David Norr, the only financial analyst member of the APB, testified before at the Wheat hearings that it is not essential that a financial analyst be represented on the APB. Of course, David Norr is not a typical financial analyst, as he is very knowledgeable about and interested in accounting.

DEFLIESE: Dave Norr is somewhat of a mixture of an accountant and a financial analyst. As a highly knowledgeable CPA, he is greatly influenced by his accounting background in his views on financial analysis; and even within his own fraternity, they recognize that influence. I would much prefer that there be a financial analyst among the seven.

FERTIG, Moderator: Given a seven-member FASB, would you agree that four accountants would be minimum?

DEFLIESE: Yes. At least four practitioners are needed to provide a reasonable cadre because that means there are going to be at least four different viewpoints.

FERTIG, Moderator: That isn't what I meant.

DEFLIESE: That may be a little facetious but I'm not so sure that that's not going to happen.

Statements Still Representations of Management:

FERTIG, Moderator: Is it fair to say that we have finally broken from the tradition that financial statements are the representations of the management?

DEFLIESE: No, I don't think we are ever going to depart from that responsibility which management has for financial representations. Auditors are closely associated with those representations. Periodically there is a need for a reexamination of the auditors' role in financial reporting but the prime responsibility will always be that of management.

Attempts to Codify Standards:

FERTIG, Moderator: For at least 25 years or perhaps longer, there have been attempts to codify accounting standards in writing to try to develop a short statement of concepts that would suffice as a rule book and almost invariably these efforts have fallen into disrepute. Do we now have machinery which you think would be better able to tackle the job than we have ever had or are we still where we have always been? APB Statement No. 4 for example, or ARS No. 7, the inventory? Or the inputs to the Trueblood Committee such as the objectives of financial statements? What about generalized statements of accounting standards?

DEFLIESE: I don't consider APB Statement No. 4 or ARS No. 7 represent failure to codify. I won't accept that because no one has been able to point out to me where they are failures now. They have been criticized for failing to point a direction for the future; that is an invalid criticism because that was not their objective. They were attempting to codify that which is, not that which should be; the objectives group was asked to direct itself to the latter and they have come through, in rather broad terms. Is their report sufficient for us to proceed to what we should design for the future? I don't know, but certainly the exercises we have been through in APB Statement No. 4 and in ARS No. 7 have pointed up all the inconsistencies that we have in our present accounting conventions. These exercises confirmed that we are backing conventions rather than principles. If we look at the evolution of accounting from its bookkeeping origins, we have to acknowledge that our discipline "grew like Topsy." There is a group of concepts that have been put together for a purpose. The important question is: Are they or are they not achieving that purpose or to what extent do they need to be modified in order to achieve that purpose?

About economics, the important thing to recognize is that the last thing a bookkeeper has ever thought about is economics. Bookkeepers are interested in recording the facts of transactions and they are not interested in the economic implications of these facts. Accountants have had a difficult time developing themselves beyond those origins. If we are going to revamp accounting to more closely pattern the economic effects, we have to get some new ideas. Many writers including myself are attempting this. Much more of this needs to be done before we attempt to formulate a pattern that would make it possible for us to depart from our historical cost concept and still produce meaningful financial statements quickly. This is a difficult task and it needs much work.

Utility of General Objectives Statement:

FERTIG, Moderator: Are generalized statements of objectives of financial statements useful in the promulgation of principles? Are the various firm statements on objectives prepared for the

Trueblood Committee helpful in deciding on the difference between a good and a bad accounting principle?

ZEFF: We have had much difficulty in agreeing on particulars, partially because certain precepts and assumptions are simply not expressed. Until we put them in print and discuss what basis there is for one versus the other, we are not going to reach agreement, except by accident, on a number of the final specific questions. To the extent that a determination of the objectives of the financial statements is essential to arriving at agreement on these assumptions, we are not going to make much progress until we agree what we are doing, why we are doing it, and for whom.

For this reason, it is important that the FASB take seriously the Trueblood report and the need for accounting objectives. It is more likely that the FASB will go further with this project than did its predecessors, as it is more removed from the world of industry and accounting practice. It is easier to generalize and deal with abstract questions if each member doesn't have to think of every issue in terms of the problems that his client-partners are currently facing or may soon be facing. The FASB members will be better able to work at the level of generalization which is required when one talks about objectives.

Let me make one side point. There has been an interesting evolution in the way we have used the very important phrase, "generally accepted accounting principles." In the days when that term was first used, in the early and middle 1930's, it was the prevailing belief, as espoused by George O. May, that we were primarily interested in trying to find out what is "best practice." From that, it was suggested we may determine what meets business needs. Who was to say that there is a better practice than those which were actually used in business? It was clearly stated in the Accounting Research Bulletins of the CAP that their authority rested on their general acceptability. One former member of that committee said not too long ago that every Accounting Research Bulletin carried its own apology for intruding on anyone's contrary ideas, in effect providing that readers might take it or leave it depending upon how acceptable the argument was. But as a result of the very difficult agreement reached by AICPA Council in 1964 regarding the authority of APB Opinions, the APB was told that it shouldn't limit its role to codifying extant practice. Yet Accounting Research Study (ARS) No. 7 reflects the older idea that perhaps if we find out what is done we will have a better vision of what we want to do. This conclusion does not necessarily follow. It is one thing to do an empirical study of what is being done, as opposed to prescribing what should be done. The former was ostensibly the basis of ARS No. 7, which was also based on Montgomery's Auditing to some extent. But I am not sure we get any necessary vision out of where we ought to go from simply reviewing where we are now. Both functions are important, but we should not assume that a knowledge of what is accepted inevitably leads to an identification of what should be accepted. I suspect that there is a growing realization of this point of view in practitioner circles.

"Accounting Power" or Politics:

FERTIG, Moderator: The opposing view is that the development of accounting principles are really the result of political forces. The SEC has a regulatory interest and corporate management has other interests in principles which would permit high flexibility and earnings per share that would be acceptable to management. Also accountants themselves constitute a pressure group. Accountants are interested in accounting principles that are capable of being audited. Financial analysts have their own interests. So the formulation of accounting principles is a matter of getting a resultant of a variety of political pressures. Are statements of accounting objectives really useful, if in fact the development of accounting principles is really a matter of what Bob Sterling calls political power or "accounting power," as he calls it?

DEFLIESE: There is a need to give cognizance to the views of all interested parties and this was the major complaint that the FEI and the financial analysts had against the APB. They felt that cognizance was not being given to their views on these matters. Yet in many cases the FEI and the financial analysts were at the extreme opposite ends of the spectrum in terms of position, with the APB somewhat around the middle. The academics were usually somewhere also at one extreme or the other depending on their particular views on the subject, which didn't always coincide. There was no doubt that someone had to referee this. The APB was trying to reconcile the varying views and the result was compromise, in many respects.

This is going to continue. The FASB is not going to suddenly have the light of God descend upon it so as to issue the fundamental truths of accounting that presumably exist someplace. Perhaps someone is going to have to make another trip to the mountain to get the stone tablets and come down in order to find where accounting should be. But these varying forces are going to have to come together and reach agreement. Until they do, we are not going to have anything that makes sense out of accounting. We may not come up with the best answer immediately; but as these things evolve, we may. The objectives, of course, are the framework which will serve as the basis for the refereeing. If we can agree on the objectives, and perhaps agreement could be reached on those more readily than on the specifics, then we can always try to fit the solutions within the framework of the objective.

FERTIG, Moderator: You don't see any conflict between the objectives and what you call refereeing them?

DEFLIESE: No.

ZEFF: The general objectives are necessary to help the Board crystallize its own thinking and perhaps to help the accounting profession and others understand why the Board has reached specific conclusions. The clarification of and an agreement on objectives will make it easier to gain consensus within the profession on certain solutions. The problem will still exist of having to sell specific conclusions to outside parties who may not be bound by the agreement within the profession on objectives. To a large degree, we have entered an era of accounting standards by negotiation. However, if you have a clearer conception of where you are heading and why you want to go there--than if you don't have any conception at all, which would seem to be the current case--it may be easier to sell solutions.

We have reached the point, as a couple of financial analysts wrote recently in The New York Times, where accounting has become too political. The SEC was involved at least once, if not twice, in the investment credit. The Treasury Department was involved at least twice, if not three times. Various industry groups have exerted their influence, directly to the APB, directly to the SEC, and even through Congress and the Administration.

We probably are going to have even more of it. I suspect that as soon as the FASB comes up with a recommendation that some individuals don't like, perhaps even some within the accounting profession, they will attempt to appeal their case directly to the SEC. Right now there is an environment of advocacy being generated. The accounting firms are gearing up to make presentations and submissions to the Board on their differing points of view. I am frankly fearful that once the major accounting firms commit themselves publicly to particular positions a pride of authorship will prevent them from acceding to contrary FASB conclusions, even if these conclusions were to be intellectually palatable. I am further afraid that some of them may even carry their arguments right to the SEC, effectively converting the SEC into an accounting court. This is a valid concern. If we develop too much of a climate of advocacy within the accounting profession, by making known our views in such uncompromising terms as we have seen recently, it is going to be very difficult for firms to say publicly that they have changed their position.

British Principles by Negotiation:

The most thoroughgoing example thus far of accounting principles by negotiation is going on right now in Great Britain. The British accounting profession has been trying, through the ASSC, to gain a broad base of acceptance for a pronouncement which essentially embodies the recommendations in APB Statement No. 3 on the general principles of inflation-adjusted accounting. Britain is a country where a ten percent rate of inflation has persisted for several years. In early 1971, the ASSC, which speaks for the profession subject to the final approval by the councils of five participating accountancy bodies, brought together the Department of Trade and Industry (DTI) (similar to, but more powerful than, our Department of Commerce), the Board of Inland Revenue (similar to our Internal Revenue Service), the Confederation of British Industry (CBI) (the spokesman for British Industry), the Stock Exchange, and the Bank of England, hoping to convince them of the merits of inflation-adjusted accounting. The ASSC had some difficulty in eliciting a response. It issued a discussion paper, similar to what the FASB intends to do even before taking a tentative position; it held a number of meetings with security analysts, as well as a series of private conferences with representatives of the DTI, Inland Revenue, the CBI, the Stock Exchange, and the central bank. Finally, in January, 1973, the ASSC felt bold enough to issue an actual exposure draft embodying its price-level recommendation. The ASSC exposure draft, in departing from its American prototype, provided for a <u>required</u> supplementary presentation of price-level financial statements in companies' annual reports to stockholders. In the same month, perhaps by pre-arrangement, an influential committee of the CBI largely endorsed the ASSC's proposed solution. (Eight months later, the CBI Council adopted this view as its own.) The Stock Exchange and Bank of England also signified a favorable reaction. Indeed, a few companies began to adopt the recommended accounting, anticipating that the draft would be enacted. The government hadn't said anything publicly up to this point. The ASSC had not been able to secure any kind of position from the government.

The exposure period was set at six months. During this time, the accounting profession was working behind the scenes, as only in England they can, with various groups that might be affected by such a pronouncement. A bare five days before the close of the six-month exposure period, on the last day of Parliament prior to the Summer recess, the Secretary of State for Trade and Industry announced that his department was going to inaugurate a major inquiry into the entire question of inflation-adjusted accounts. Since this was the last day of the Parliamentary session, no questions could be asked the next day. Nobody had any idea how extensive the study would be or whether the government was a priori favorably or unfavorably disposed toward the ASSC exposure draft. No one had any idea of the terms of reference of the study or of its likely membership. There was no opportunity to ask any questions, as Parliament had adjourned for the Summer. The accounting profession was made to look foolish because it had taken steps which were suggestive of success in negotiating an acceptable solution with all affected parties. Now the government abruptly announced that it was going to look into the matter and possibly delay the final issuance of an opinion for perhaps as long as two years. The accounting profession didn't know what to do. The ASSC finally resolved to push ahead with a recommendation to the various councils of the participating accountancy bodies for a pronouncement along the lines of the exposure draft. Owing to the government inquiry, the profession will probably delay the effective date of any pronouncement for two years. They will get an opinion out which will not take effect until the government has finally completed its inquiry. So here is a case where the accounting profession went to tremendous lengths, including behind-the-scenes meetings, a discussion paper and fact sheet, educational sessions, a six-month exposure draft, and other documents that were issued to educate all parties involved. They reached the threshold of finally taking the decisive step and were thwarted. This experience could as easily happen here, although probably with much more public posturing and bluster than in Great Britain.

DEFLIESE: Welcome to the club!

Safeguard of FASB from Special Interests and the AICPA:

STOBER, Moderator: What safeguards exist to keep the FASB from being controlled in the formulation of accounting standards by special interest groups?

DEFLIESE: The safeguard is that the FASB members are under contract, highly paid, and completely disassociated from all prior interests; and thus they are presumably independent. This is the main safeguard.

FERTIG, Moderator: Do you think the FASB separation from the AICPA will be effective?

DEFLIESE: Since the Institute does dominate in the selection of the board members, the FASB does have an umbilical cord to some extent to the Institute. But that is not a sufficient association to in any way detract from the independent aspect of these board members once they are selected.

Interdisciplinary Efforts:

STOBER, Moderator: What about the historical evolution of accounting principles bodies with respect to interdisciplinary efforts?

ZEFF: The question about the historical evolution of interdisciplinary efforts is a good one. But there hasn't been any on a world basis. Most countries look to what has happened in this country--they try to pattern the U.S. experience against their own environment--so really the principal experience is that of the U.S.A. It is interesting that less than four months after the Wheat Committee report was accepted by the AICPA Board of Directors and Council there was already on the agenda of the Board of Governors of the Canadian Institute of Chartered Accountants (CICA) a proposal for a Canadian Accounting Foundation drawn along the lines of the Wheat Report recommendations, except that only the chairman of the proposed standards committee would have been full-time. The latter was one of Philip Defliese's recommendations, namely that the chairman, at least, should be full-time.

It would take a great deal of time to trace the evolution of the process by which accounting principles are established in this country, but the experience in the United States has not been very long. It was not until 1959 that the AICPA finally had a senior technical committee making recommendations on accounting principles which had financial executives as members. The predecessor CAP was composed of only academics and practitioners. Such committees have always had members from the Big Eight firms; they have also had a small minority of academics as members.

Unfortunately, academics are often unable to do the required research to support their positions and seldom have practical experience with the particular problem areas facing the profession. Now, for the first time, there should be effective academic input. There have been excellent academic members but their participation has been impeded by not having the same kind of research and staff support within their universities as the partner-members, particularly those from the large firms, have had from within their firms. Each FASB member, however, enjoys the same research and staff support as his colleagues. In summary, except for the composition of the Wheat and Trueblood study groups, there hasn't yet been any significant interdisciplinary history in either this country or abroad.

Influence of the SEC

FERTIG, Moderator: Is the influence of the SEC on accounting principles over the years good or bad?

DEFLIESE: Well, it's good. It's had its good points and its bad points. Without the support of the SEC, there is no doubt, particularly in the latter stages of the APB, nothing would have been accomplished. From about 1965 on, the SEC largely supported the APB pronouncements once they saw the light of day. It was a great help and certainly it buttressed the 1964 council that made the APB pronouncements effective. On the other hand, in the early stages of the APB, the investment credit debacle with the SEC considerably diminished the influence of the APB as a result. This took a long time to overcome.

Unfortunately, too, in the latter stages, where the SEC would not go along with some of the things that the APB was doing, the APB attempting to avoid a confrontation compromised some of its views. Opinions Nos. 16 and 17 are good examples of the interaction of the views of the SEC, industry, and everybody else; the interaction resulted in the compromises reached in those opinions. For many years, the SEC was highly in favor of pooling. The SEC felt that the purchase method would create highly inflated balance sheets in many instances by recording intangibles which didn't exist. If in the poolings the share values had been used to apply the purchase method, the values generated were inflated in many cases. Since this was not good accounting, they espoused pooling to a large extent. But at the same time, the SEC insisted on amortization of goodwill. Therein lies the problem that the APB had in getting something out that was meaningful because many board members were not particularly disposed toward the concept that all goodwill had to be amortized over a maximum of forty years. So the SEC influence has been both good and bad. The FASB may find itself very much in the same posture as the APB did with the SEC.

STOBER, Moderator: Is the SEC working towards eliminating pooling of interest at the current time?

DEFLIESE: Well, there has been a change of personnel there and as a result, you get different views.

Usually the SEC view comes down to the view of the latest chief accountant for the SEC. At the moment, there is an anti-pooling feeling at the SEC because its present chief accountant is against pooling. Unfortunately, the general implications of extensive application of the purchase method have not been fully appreciated. Therefore, the research, particularly the applied research that is necessary in these instances, has to be done very carefully. Pooling is easy to criticize but when the purchase method is applied to what would otherwise be a pooling and that method is followed to its bitter end, sometimes you recognize that the pooling concept isn't that bad.

ZEFF: In the light of what Phil Defliese has said, it is ironic that the present chief accountant, prior to taking that post, was the author of a research study published by the Financial Executives Research Foundation which was intended to support the FEI position on poolings.

DEFLIESE: Yes, but don't overlook the author's personal views which were included in the study which were obviously anti-pooling; these views were very much to the chagrin of the FEI at the time.

ZEFF: If it were not for the SEC, the AICPA would not have started issuing pronouncements--at least not as early as 1939. This decision by the Institute was the result of an explicit message from the SEC to the accounting profession in 1937-38 that if the accounting profession did not provide the SEC with what it called substantial authoritative support, it would utilize its full statutory authority to decide what was proper accounting practice. This message was communicated to the AICPA, which gave the Committee on Accounting Procedure this new authority without any great enthusiasm. The AICPA has since warmed to the task.

I would agree with Phil Defliese that the SEC had both favorable and unfavorable influences on the development of financial reporting. For many years, the SEC had been a very reactionary body regarding any major innovation in accounting principle. The SEC has chiefly been preoccupied with closing loopholes and preventing abuses. It hasn't given constructive thought to fundamental changes in the nature and scope of accounting, including, for example, departures from traditional historical cost. In this latter regard, it has always been undeviatingly opposed to all departures from traditional historical cost.

To illustrate how negative the SEC has been, back in 1950 the CAP unanimously approved a bulletin authorizing quasi-reorganizations applied to instances where current values were higher than recorded values. But the issuance of this 1950 bulletin was delayed until the SEC chief accountant, who was present at the committee meeting, could find out from the SEC commission whether the SEC would go along with it. The message came back they would not, and the bulletin never was issued. So when one is criticizing the CAP for not going further in the 1950's, the object of the criticism might better be the SEC.

Sometimes the SEC experiences difficulty in assessing the political aspects of an issue, taking the form of pressure from the Treasury, from other regulatory agencies, or from the Congress which the SEC is not able to withstand. Furthermore, continuity in the SEC's policies cannot always be assured, as its membership changes and the chief accountants change.

The Canadian Situation

The situation in Canada is superior to that in the U.S. in that the Canadian profession is in a potentially stronger position to influence the future course of accounting practice than is the FASB in this country. (Of course, it must be conceded that the momentum and impetus for improvement in Canadian accounting practice would be measurably less in the absence of the U.S. example.) In December, 1972, for the first time, the ten provincial securities commissions* in Canada made it known through National Policy No. 27 that henceforth the generally accepted accounting principles which they accept in reports filed under the provincial securities acts will be those contained in the CICA Handbook, namely those that are recommended by the Canadian Institute's Accounting Research Committee (formerly the Accounting and Auditing Research Committee.) In this way, the CICA committee can ordinarily be assured in advance of the support of the ten provincial securities commissions. In the U.S., the FASB has the word of the SEC chief accountant that it is the intent of the SEC to support to every degree possible the pronouncements of the FASB. But this is not the assurance that the Canadian profession has been given by their provincial securities commissions. The FASB and the SEC must engage in a continuing dialogue in order that each can feel out the other on priorities and on the range within which compromise is feasible. This process is dangerously susceptible to mistaken and misunderstood signals, leading, perhaps, to an open rebuke.

DEFLIESE: We have seen in this country that when a pronouncement is ready to come out which may not be fully acceptable to the government or industry, there will be rumblings; this is likely to happen in Canada, too, once they reach one that may be so highly sensitive to provide the pressure groups to exert their influence. This is more readily to happen in Canada than Britain.

The British Situation and Nationalism:

ZEFF: It is more likely to happen in Canada. The Canadians are a canny lot; they frequently don't embark on a project that is

*No national securities commission exists in Canada.

controversial until they see what has happened in the U.S.A. first. Once they begin to sense the strengths and weaknesses of the U.S. solution, as well as the forces tending toward and against change in Canada, they will start to turn the wheels. They watch the experience in the U.S.A. very closely, while the British clearly haven't done this. Of course, the industrial and financial makeup of British society is very unlike ours, whereas one finds considerable similarity in institutional environment between the U.S. and Canada.

DEFLIESE: The British have been operating their institutional arrangements with a combination of naivete and smugness. But now with their inflation pronouncement, they have one that is going to give them trouble.

ZEFF: It is sometimes hard to compare the U.S. and Canada or the U.S. and Mexico, because the economic influence of the U.S.A. in both of those countries is enormous. As a result of subsidiaries of U.S. corporations operating in those countries, and the resulting work done for purposes of eventual consolidation with parent-company accounts by Canadian chartered accountants and Mexican contadores públicos, U.S. accounting practice has considerable impact. One can discern a flow of accounting recommendations from the U.S. to both Canada and Mexico. This is not to suggest, however, that the Canadian and Mexican professions slavishly follow U.S. precedent.

One result of the nationalistic drive that exists in any country is the belief that the country is in some sense distinctive or different so that on some accounting questions they will attempt to be different just to be different or to preserve a national identity. This national sensitivity permeates accounting no less than other subjects having international policy implications. For example, the Mexican Institute recently formally recommended the acceptance of direct costing for inventory accounting. The Mexicans are the first to have an accountancy body formally recommend direct costing for financial accounting purposes. The fact that the U.S. hadn't done so was more a source of pride than of concern to Mexico; here was an area where the Mexicans were able to affect accounting practice without simply following an American initiative.

DEFLIESE: They did it because they knew we wouldn't do it.

ZEFF: Yes, there is the natural desire to be different, but one also finds instances in which these countries are inescapably influenced by U.S. practice. Such an example is the Canadian oil and gas industry, which is effectively controlled in the U.S. In 1967 when both the Canadian Institute and the American Institute were considering pronouncements on income tax allocation, the APB, since it had a research study then in progress on extractive industries, decided to exclude, at least temporarily, the possible tax-allocation implications of intangible development costs. Since the Canadians had no such study in progress, they decided to cover intangible development costs in their pronouncement which, like APB Opinion No. 11, favored comprehensive tax allocation. But the oil and gas industry in Canada simply refused to comply; the companies were told, apparently by their home offices in the U.S.A., that "we're not subject to it and therefore you will not be subject to it." Canadian chartered accountants were told by the companies that they could issue all the qualified reports they liked, because there is no Canadian securities commission, unlike the case in the U.S.A., that insists upon unqualified reports in Canada. The large accounting firms in Canada got together and decided that it would be unwise to assure qualified reports for the entire industry. So they tacitly agreed that they wouldn't enforce the section of the Canadian pronouncement having to do with intangible development costs, as long as the companies gave full disclosure, until the Americans enact the same requirement.

Disclosure - Measurement Controversy with SEC:

FERTIG, Moderator: In recent years we have had some division of responsibility perhaps between the SEC and the accounting profession with regard to accounting principles, namely that the SEC would have primary responsibility for disclosure and the FASB would have primary responsibility for accounting measurement. Is there any possibility that you can see any redivision of duties there that would be along different lines?

DEFLIESE: I am afraid that I have difficulty disassociating disclosure from measurement. The two go hand-in-hand, and to say that the FASB will deal with measurement if the SEC will deal with disclosure just won't work. The FASB is going to have to deal with both.

ZEFF: Well, I don't have as much difficulty accepting this division of responsibility. The SEC chief accountant has said in a number of speeches recently that the SEC is attempting to enforce its primary preserve of authority, which is disclosure, while leaving measurement largely to the FASB. The SEC has traditionally acted unilaterally, sometimes not even consulting the accounting profession or, when it does, not necessarily accepting the profession's view, in matters of disclosure. After all, disclosure is what Regulation S-X is all about. There was a big battle in 1950 over whether all of the accounting series releases, some of which dealt with asset and income measurement, should be incorporated in that document. On the strength of forceful reorientations from the accounting profession to the contrary, the SEC implemented a compromise solution. Until now, no one has questioned the SEC primacy in questions of disclosure. It is due to the nature of the SEC's recent aggressiveness in this sphere that this dichotomy has come under attack. The companies act legislation found in British Commonwealth countries, such as Canada, the United Kingdom, New Zealand, and Australia, deals almost entirely with disclosure. The companies acts do not become involved with measurement questions.

The SEC chief accountant is historically correct when he says that the primary preserve of the SEC is disclosure. But he has recently gone into areas where the APB has had difficulty resolving measurement questions, apparently with the aim of utilizing disclosure as an interim solution. This is what has been different about his actions. In the past, disclosure issues haven't been as close to measurement issues as they have been, for example, in the area of leases.

DEFLIESE: The entire province of the SEC emanating from the 1933 and 1934 acts might be said to be disclosure. In other words everything they do is in the area of disclosure. They are really not attempting to regulate what companies can do and cannot do; the SEC is specifying what disclosures may be made in order to permit them to do what they want to do about issuing securities. But the disclosure of what is necessary to prepare a complete set of financial statements is still the province of the rule-making body of the accounting profession. Of course, there may be differences of opinion concerning the appropriate statements and the disclosure of those differences would be in the province of the SEC to specify. That has happened frequently where there might be an application of an accounting convention that is questioned by the SEC. The SEC has frequently satisfied itself by disclosure of a difference of opinion concerning the accounting treatment rather than the actual correction or changing of the financial statement. In that area, disclosure is their province and they could set up the determination of the degree of disclosure in order to satisfy their requirements. But basic disclosure is something you can't separate from the measurement process.

ZEFF: That lawsuit brings up the sensitivity of the profession to the recent aggressiveness of the SEC not only in disclosure but also in other areas, like SEC Accounting Release No. 146. This would not have occurred a few years ago.

It is also ironic that the suit, brought by Arthur Andersen & Co., was withdrawn when the SEC said it would hold hearings, because one of the firm's arguments was that the SEC had not held any hearings. But in 1965, the matter of dealing with the tax-allocation implications of using one method of recognizing the income from installment revenues for financial accounting purposes and another method for Federal income tax purposes was presented in a paragraph of an exposure draft, the one which eventually led to APB Opinion No. 6. It had to do with the "deferred tax credit" account, whether it should be a current or noncurrent liability where you have a current installment receivable. It finally was removed prior to issuance of the resulting opinion. Once the opinion was issued without the paragraph, Arthur Andersen & Co., which felt very strongly that the credit should be a current liability, as had been stated in the exposure draft, petitioned the SEC to take the action anyway. The SEC, in its Accounting Series Release No. 102, did so. Yet there were no public hearings, and Arthur Andersen & Co. did not complain that there were no public hearings on that particular matter. Moreover it was a matter of disclosure.

<u>Apprehension about CASB:</u>

STOBER, Moderator: What about the CASB? Is it possibly going to be taking over some formulation of financial accounting standards?

DEFLIESE: That is a good question and I don't know the answer. There is a great deal of speculation going on at the moment as to the impact of the CASB's influence on the FASB. Particularly inasmuch as the CASB has legislative authority far and beyond that which is available to the FASB and everyone is watching that development with a great deal of apprehension.

ZEFF: The chief accountant of the SEC and the staff of the CASB are both aware of the possible overlapping of their two spheres of authority. There have been a number of consultations between the two bodies to the point where the CASB was considering a couple of issues which the SEC thought more properly fell within the purview of the FASB, and the CASB was going to consider and has now deferred at the request of the SEC, awaiting some kind of advice from the FASB. So there is an attempt between the two to avoid conflict, but the CASB has undoubted statutory authority. The CASB can recommend something, and if Congress doesn't overrule it within 60 days, which in itself would be quite an event, it becomes law. The SEC could not interfere, and there is nothing anybody can do about it. So the implications for financial accounting of the work of the CASB are there; it all depends upon the CASB's intentions and patience.

DEFLIESE: The basic authority of the CASB only relates to government contracts and the pricing and such, and need not directly affect financial reporting. Obviously, there will be an influence just as in the regulated utility area, where the actions of commissions do ultimately affect the accounting.

The Future of the FASB and the Investment Credit:

STOBER, Moderator: Would you anticipate the same history for the FASB as the APB had?

ZEFF: In the sense that the APB finally concluded its history, the FASB will someday wind up its history. An interesting question is who would declare the FASB a failure. In the past it has been committees or officers of the AICPA. In the case of the FASB, the role of the AICPA is more remote. What factors might eventually lead to failure of the FASB? Is it simply that there would be bad research? Would it result from badly drafted and conceived pronouncements? If more than a few FASB pronouncements were opposed and overturned by the SEC? Will there be continual pressure on the FASB from Congress as a result of the initiatives of financial executives? Supposedly a declaration of failure would be up to the Financial Accounting Foundation (FAF). In effect, the FAF would have to declare itself out of business unless it were to replace the FASB with something else. The FASB is its only reason for existence, and if the FASB is not to be replaced, the trustees of the FAF must conclude that there is no longer any need for the FAF to continue in being. That has been a difficult decision for institutions to make. It will have to be fairly obvious that the FASB has failed or that the SEC consistently refuses to implement its recommendations or that the recommendations are palpably bad. I don't quite know who would have the courage to make that kind of statement. Also, it is not inevitable that, should the FASB be generally conceded to be a failure, that this outcome will be followed by governmental regulations, as some have suggested. This could, of course, be; it could have been true after the APB. It depends very much upon what the cause of the failure was, who is the SEC Chairman, and who is the SEC Chief Accountant.

FERTIG, Moderator: Do you think the FASB will be any more successful than the APB in responding to criticisms?

DEFLIESE: It depends upon which criticism you are talking about.

FERTIG, Moderator: With regard to narrowing financial statement alternatives.

DEFLIESE: It is bound to do that. It will be successful because it is going to have to come out and narrow some alternatives. It will do that. Whether it will do a good job of it or not depends on your own viewpoint. There are going to be differing views on just that point and as Steve Zeff has pointed out, the crucial test will be acceptance on the part of the SEC. If the SEC accepts what comes out, the FASB will be successful in narrowing the alternatives. It takes two to tango in this exercise. As the past has indicated, you can't tell which one is going to be the culprit and whether the FASB will be the culprit or the SEC. Also, Congress is another element. Industry need not be injected because industry will be in the influencing area, whether it is going to influence the SEC or Congress or the FASB.

I don't feel as pessimistic as some may feel about the FASB. The FASB will be as successful as the APB in doing some of its job. I believe the APB was successful in some areas although I may have a biased view along those lines. But the FASB will be in many respects even more successful. But it will have the same troubles in accomplishing its objectives as the APB had. They are not going to be able to solve them any more readily than the APB did. I just hope they survive their troubles.

ZEFF: While the FEI is formally allied with this new program, there is nothing that prevents individual companies or industries from stoutly disagreeing with anything the FASB wants to do. In this regard, there is nothing inherent in the FASB structure that makes the FASB any more likely to be successful than the APB in negotiating with its critics. They still have the old political pressures to deal with. They must try to resolve problems in the oil and gas industry with respect to full costing with the same pressures that fell upon the APB. If the FASB tries to move ahead in marketable securities, it will encounter the same resistance as did the APB. If it tries to urge the capitalization of leases on a larger scale by lessees, it may face another letter-writing campaign to Congress which was waged so successfully two years ago.

DEFLIESE: How about the Investment Credit?

ZEFF: The Investment Credit is unique. It came up three times, not twice. It first arose in 1962, when the behind-the-scenes efforts of a number of Federal agencies, including the Treasury, obliged the SEC to reflect views of those who were trying to persuade it rather than the genuine opinion of the chief accountant and perhaps even the view of the commission itself. It came up again in 1967 as part of the exposure draft that led to Opinion No. 11. It didn't appear in the final opinion because Stanley Surrey of the Treasury Department made known his views publicly that he was opposed to the allocation of the investment credit following which the SEC advised the APB it could no longer provide support. In 1971, it was enshrined in legislation. I have suggested that the next time this comes up, as I suspect it will, it will be made an amendment to the Constitution! This is the only step higher than Congressional legislation, for each time the matter has arisen it has escalated from before.

Need for Patience and Study of Record:

DEFLIESE: In summary, I make a plea for patience. As exhibited in this discussion, there should be recognition that solutions to our accounting problems are not going to come readily, or out of a hopper. These problems require a great deal of further research, a great deal of thought, and a great deal of exposure. All of this is going to take time.

Therefore, the FASB cannot immediately grind out pronouncement after pronouncement which can serve as a panacea for our problems. It will not happen and it should not happen because the FASB should take the time necessary to do the job. That should be recognized and everyone should not be impatient. The major problems of accounting and the auditing process exist in the judgmental selection of the accounting principles that are appropriate. Here the profession is going to have to take a greater responsibility than it has taken in the past concerning appropriate accounting by virtue of exercising the profession's auditing power.

ZEFF: One of the sloppiest portions of our accounting literature is that which comments on how accounting principles are established. There have been altogether too many speeches and articles, and perhaps even monographs and books, containing ostensibly empirical statements which have not been adequately researched, and recollections that have not been verified and checked against the record, which is available. As a result, inferences have been drawn and conclusions have been reached which would not emerge from a fair reading of the available evidence. Too many individuals believe that in this area one can simply stand up and say whatever he thinks, regardless of what has occurred or what appears in the record. In discussions of the development of accounting principles, a subject which is so important to the profession, while content is important, process is no less important, and at times even more important than content.

Occasionally I am astonished when I read articles that have been written as often by academics as by practitioners, financial executives, or security analysts to find statements that are palpably untrue when compared to the historical record. In writing about APB opinions, some writers indulge themselves by referring in vague terms to arguments for or against an abandoned proposition, without specifying who advanced such arguments, and when during the course of evolution of the opinion. I frequently can find no evidence whatever that such arguments were made. These writers are simply setting up "straw men" in order to propagandize their own argument. Until we compile a record, we are in a vulnerable position to assess the achievements of either the CAP or the APB. We haven't yet agreed on the criteria for evaluating these organizations. We should eschew that kind of contrived argument, where a certain conclusion is wanted and any available means is used to dignify that result. In recent years, we have become more careful of logical analysis and empirical validity both in our literature and in our discussion of most accounting topics; we should be more willing now to discipline ourselves when commenting on the process by which accounting principles are developed.

BIBLIOGRAPHY

PHILIP L. DEFLIESE:

Book:

(With Norman J. Lenhart), Montgomery's Auditing, Eighth Edition, Ronald Press, 1957.

Monographs:

A New Look at Utility Rate-Making, 1968.

The Accounting Principles Board and Its Recent and Pending Opinions, November 19, 1970.

The Prospects for Agreement on Accounting Principles, February 19, 1971.

Progress in the Development of Accounting Principles, May 18, 1971.

Statement Before the Study Group on Establishment of Accounting Principles, November 4, 1971.

Changing Accounting Objectives--What About Utilities?, May, 1972.

Forecasting--The Lybrand Position, December 12, 1972.

The Objectives of Financial Accounting, 1973.

Should Accountants Capitalize Leases? The Economic Case Against it at Present, 1973.

Poolings Revisited--A Temporary Defense of the Status Quo, March, 1974.

Published Speeches:

Professional Cooperation Between Financial Analysts and Certified Public Accountants (published by Coopers & Lybrand), May 18, 1965.

Public Utility Accounting--Comparable or Chaotic?, May 2, 1966.

Current Developments in the Accounting Principles Field, May 13, 1966.

Accounting Principles--Present and Prospective, October 14, 1966.

STEPHEN A. ZEFF:

Books and Monographs (Selected):

Uses of Accounting for Small Business, Bureau of Business Research, University of Michigan, 1962.

(Editor with T. F. Keller), Financial Accounting Theory: Issues and Controversies, McGraw-Hill Book Company, Inc., Vol. 1: 1964; 2nd Edition, 1973; Vol. 11: 1969.

The American Accounting Association--Its First Fifty Years, American Accounting Association, 1966.

(Editor with A. Rappaport and P. A. Firmin), Public Reporting by Conglomerates, Prentice-Hall, Inc., 1968.

(Editor), Business Schools and the Challenge of International Business, Tulane Graduate School of Business Administration, 1968.

Forging Accounting Principles in Five Countries: A History and an Analysis of Trends, Stipes Publishing Co., 1972.

Forging Accounting Principles in Australia, Australian Society of Accountants, 1973.

Articles (Selected):

"Right of Offset vs. Uniform Partnership Act in Winding-up Process," The Accounting Review, January, 1957.

"Standard Costs in Financial Statements--Theory and Practice," N.A.A. Bulletin, April, 1959.

"Legal Dividend Sources: A National Survey and Critique," The New York Certified Public Accountant, November and December, 1961.

"Replacement Cost: Member of the Family, Welcome Guest, or Intruder?," The Accounting Review, October, 1962.

"The Balance Sheet and Income Statement--Analytically Coordinate," N.A.A. Bulletin, February, 1964.

"Preparation for the Accounting Profession in the United States of America," Accountancy, April, 1964.

"Episodes in the Progression of Price-Level Accounting in the United States," The Accountants' Magazine, April, 1964; reprinted in several places.

(With W. D. Maxwell), "Holding Gains on Fixed Assets--A Demurrer," The Accounting Review, January, 1965.

(With R. L. Fossum), "An Analysis of Large Audit Clients," The Accounting Review, April, 1967.

"El Proceso de Desarrollo de Principios Contables en Mexico," Direccion y Control, February, 1971.

"Forging Accounting Principles in Canada," Canadian Chartered Accountant, May and June, 1971.

"1926 to 1971 Chronology of Significant Developments in the Establishment of Accounting Principles in the United States," Corporate Financial Reporting: The Issues, The Objectives and Some New Proposals, A. Pappaport and L. Revsine editors, (Commerce Clearing House, Inc., 1972); reprinted with updatings in Journal of Accounting Research, Spring, 1972.

(With M. S. Henderson), "Auditing the Auditor's Report," The Chartered Accountant in Australia, January, 1973.

"Comments by Directors on Auditors' Qualifications," The Australian Accountant, March, 1973.

"Developing Accounting Principles: A Summary Review and Analysis of the U.S. Experience," Journal of Contemporary Business, Spring, 1973.

(With T. R. Hofstedt), "Closing the Communications Gap: The Practitioner and the Researcher," The Accountant's Magazine, January, 1974. Spanish version appeared under the title, "Le Brecha de la Communicacion: El Investigador y el Profesionista," Contaduria Publica, May, 1973.

GENERAL BIBLIOGRAPHY (SELECTED)

Moonitz, Maurice, Obtaining Agreement on Standards in The Accounting Profession, Studies in Accounting Research No. 8, Sarasota, Florida: American Accounting Association, 1974.

Pattillo, James W., "Unity in the Accounting Profession," The Journal of Accountancy, July, 1974, pp. 50-58.

Stamp, Edward and Christopher Marley, Accounting Principles and the City Code: The Case for Reform, London: Butterworths, 1970.

Sterling, Robert R., editor, Institutional Issues in Public Accounting, Lawrence, Kansas: Scholars Book Co., 1974.

Storey, Reed K., The Search for Accounting Principles, New York: American Institute of Certified Public Accountants, 1964.

APPENDIX A TO SECTION I

1959 REPORT TO COUNCIL OF THE SPECIAL COMMITTEE ON RESEARCH PROGRAM*

Introduction:

Our committee was appointed in December, 1957, to consider a new approach to the means whereby accounting research should be undertaken, accounting principles should be promulgated, and adherence to them should be secured. This action followed an address by Alvin R. Jennings, now the President of the Institute, at the annual meeting in New Orleans in October, 1957, in which he cited some of the difficulties involved in the profession's present approach to this problem, and suggested a possible alternative.

One of our members, Marquis G. Eaton, was taken from us by death soon after the committee was organized. We wish to express our profound sorrow at his passing, and to acknowledge our great loss because of his absence from our deliberations.

We have reviewed the history and the work of the present committee on accounting procedure, and that of the Research Department (including what is now the Technical Services Department) of the Institute insofar as it concerns the committee on accounting procedure. We have studied several specific proposals, including that of Mr. Jennings, for the reorganization of the accounting research and related activities of the Institute. We have considered a number of comments and questions submitted to us by members of the Institute and others interested in our project. We have inquired into the organization of several other groups having research programs. We have exchanged views at some length among ourselves through correspondence. Finally, we have held three meetings--March 24-25, May 12-13, and August 1, 1958; these were attended by all of us, except that, because of illness, Carman G. Blough was not present on August 1, and by Perry Mason of the American Institute staff.

It should be understood that we have confined our attention largely to the field of financial accounting. The proposals in

*Reprinted by permission from The Journal of Accountancy, December, 1958.

this report are not intended to cover the fields of cost accounting and managerial accounting, for example, or auditing.

Basic Considerations:

Before presenting our proposals for the organization of the accounting research and related activities of the Institute in the field of financial accounting, it probably would be well to set forth some of the basic considerations we have had in mind in formulating them--what we think it is the American Institute of Certified Public Accountants should seek to accomplish in this direction.

The general purpose of the Institute in the field of financial accounting should be to advance the written expression of what constitutes generally accepted accounting principles, for the guidance of its members and of others. This means something more than a survey of existing practice. It means continuing effort to determine appropriate practice and to narrow the areas of difference and inconsistency in practice. In accomplishing this, reliance should be placed on persuasion rather than on compulsion. The Institute, however, can, and it should, take definite steps to lead in the thinking on unsettled and controversial issues.

The broad problem of financial accounting should be visualized as requiring attention at four levels: first, postulates; second, principles; third, rules or other guides for the application of principles in specific situations; and fourth, research.

Postulates are few in number and are the basic assumptions on which principles rest. They necessarily are derived from the economic and political environment and from the modes of thought and customs of all segments of the business community. The profession, however, should make clear its understanding and interpretation of what they are, to provide a meaningful foundation for the formulation of principles and the development of rules or other guides for the application of principles in specific situations. Also, the Institute should encourage cooperative study with other representative groups to determine that its understanding and interpretation of the postulates are valid and to provide a forum which will command sufficient respect to bring about a change in the postulates when any of them becomes outmoded.

A fairly broad set of coordinated accounting principles should be formulated on the basis of the postulates. The statement of this probably should be similar in scope to the statements on accounting and reporting standards issued by the American Accounting Association. The principles, together with the postulates, should serve as a framework of reference for the solution of detailed problems.

Rules or other guides for the application of accounting principles in specific situations, then, should be developed in relation to the postulates and principles previously expressed. Statements of these probably should be comparable as to subject matter with the present accounting research bulletins. They should have reasonable flexibility.

Adequate accounting research is necessary in all of the foregoing. Pronouncements on accounting matters should be based on thoroughgoing, independent study of the matters in question, during which consideration is given to all points of view. For this, an adequate staff is necessary, to carry out detailed investigations, evaluate data, formulate conclusions, and draft reports setting forth results. Research reports or studies should be carefully reasoned and fully documented. They should have wide exposure to both the profession and the public. This is an effective way to stimulate and crystallize thinking on accounting matters.

Initial attention, perhaps primary attention, should be given to the accounting problems in connection with the published financial statements of industrial and commercial corporations, including those subject to regulatory authority. But, in the long run, attention should not be confined to them. Equally important accounting problems exist in connection with the financial statements of small businesses, partnerships, individual proprietorships, associations, institutions, governmental bodies, and the like.

Thought should be given at the beginning and from time to time thereafter to the forward planning of the accounting research program and related activities, to the end that accounting procedures are evolved on a coherent and consistent basis and pronouncements are made in an orderly and timely manner.

The accounting research program should be one of the most important activities of the Institute. The work merits the attention of the Institute's ablest members.

The closest cooperation of others concerned with the results of this work should be enlisted. That of industry is especially important. That of governmental agencies, stock exchanges, and other professions is necessary also. Probably this cooperation can be effected best in connection with specific projects. It may be received not only from organized groups such as trade associations, regulatory commissions, and professional bodies, but *also from individual corporations, firms, and persons. Of course, other accounting organizations--the various national and state associations and societies--should be kept in close touch with the work and should be given every opportunity to present their views on matters under consideration.*

Summary of Proposals:

The following summarizes the highlights of our proposals. Various details relating to the organization and operation of the accounting research program and related activities as we envision them are discussed in a subsequent section of this report.

Organization for the Program:

The organization for carrying out the proposed accounting research program and related activities of the Institute would consist of an Accounting Principles Board and an accounting research staff.

The Board would consist of eighteen members of the Institute, selected primarily because of their ability. The members would be elected by the Council for three-year terms, upon nomination by the executive committee, which would designate one of the nominees to be the chairman. It would be designated a senior technical committee, and the sole group in the Institute having authority to make pronouncements on accounting principles.

Four members of the Board--three designated by the executive committee in making nominations, and the chairman of the Board, ex officio--would constitute a fiscal committee which would attend to the fiscal administration of the accounting research program, having responsibility for budgets, personnel, and similar matters. The executive director would have the privilege of the floor at its meetings.

The accounting research staff would comprise, on a permanent basis, a director of accounting research, three to five senior members, two to three junior members, and necessary secretarial assistance. It would be supplemented by temporary personnel, usually for specific projects, obtained from educational institutions, public accounting firms, or other sources.

The director of accounting research would be the administrative head of the accounting research staff, and would have active charge and direction of the carrying out of the accounting research program. He would be appointed by the executive committee upon the recommendation of the fiscal committee of the Board, and would be responsible to the fiscal committee in fiscal matters.

He would have the privilege of the floor at meetings of the Board and those of the fiscal committee. The position of director of accounting research is not intended to include the functions of the present position of director of research.

Operation of the Program:

The principal products of the proposed accounting research program and related activities would be a series of accounting research studies and a series of statements on generally accepted accounting principles.

Accounting research studies ordinarily would be published upon the completion of research projects by the accounting research staff, and would present a detailed, documented report on the work, give pro and con arguments on controversial points, offer conclusions or recommendations, and, where appropriate, illustrate and demonstrate the application of principles. They would be published under the name of the director of accounting research and those who had been associated with him in a project. They would indicate logical solutions to accounting problems in relation to basic postulates and broad principles. They would be informative, but tentative and not highly authoritative. They would furnish a vehicle for the exposure of matters for consideration and experimentation. Therefore, they should have wide distribution.

Immediate projects of the accounting research staff should be a study of the basic postulates underlying accounting principles generally, and a study of the broad principles of accounting. The results of these, as adopted by the Board, should serve as a foundation for the entire body of future pronouncements on accounting matters, to which each new release should be related. The further planning of the accounting research program would be undertaken by the director of accounting research and the chairman of the Board.

A small project advisory committee of Institute members, and, occasionally, others, under the chairmanship of a member of the Board, would work with the accounting research staff on each research project. There would be public announcement concerning work on research projects, and interested persons would be invited to submit memoranda for consideration.

Statements on generally accepted accounting principles would be issued by the Board and would be expected to be regarded as an authoritative written expression of what constitutes generally accepted accounting principles. They ordinarily would be based on accounting research studies previously prepared by the accounting research staff. As in the case of the accounting research studies, the statements on generally accepted accounting principles would be framed in relation to basic postulates and broad principles.

Upon the publication of an accounting research study, it would be considered by the Board, and accepted (as the basis of a statement on generally accepted accounting principles), rejected, or laid over for future attention, depending upon the circumstances, unless, of course, it consisted of a factual survey or something similar which did not require Board action. The Board, however, could itself initiate action on a particular matter, without waiting for the publication of an accounting research study; in this event it would instruct the director of accounting research to do what was necessary to prepare material for its consideration.

Drafting and similar work would be done for the Board by the accounting research staff. Drafts of proposed statements on generally accepted accounting principles would be widely exposed for comment before publication, to give interested persons opportunity to present additional memoranda for consideration by the Board.

Statements on generally accepted accounting principles would not be presented to the Council or to the membership of the Institute for approval, except in rare cases.

Reports to the Council:

The Council should receive regular semiannual reports from the Board, and in addition such special reports as it might require. The regular reports of the Board should comprise three parts--one relating to the technical work of the Board, one relating to the activities of the fiscal committee of the Board (over the signature of the chairman of the fiscal committee), and one relating to the activities of the accounting research staff (over the signature of the director of accounting research).

In his part of the report, the director of accounting research should give the reasons for abandoning any research project or for not publishing the results of any completed research project.

Financing the Research Program:

The annual cost of the program we propose would be considerable, of course. Eventually, it might be in the neighborhood of a quarter of a million dollars, although several years might elapse before this figure was reached, even if the funds were readily available, because time would be required to recruit and develop a staff of competent research personnel.

We believe the probable cost should not deter the Institute from proceeding with the program, although, manifestly, careful consideration should be given to means of financing the program before it is inaugurated. We suggest that the executive committee is the appropriate body to do this; we have not considered it within the scope of our assignment. We do believe, however, that the entire cost of the program should be borne by the profession.

Transition to the New Program:

The Board would succeed the present committees on accounting procedure and on terminology. The unfinished business of those committees at the time the accounting research program was inaugurated would be disposed of as agreed upon by the present committees, the Board, and the director of accounting research. This would not present too much of a problem, inasmuch as some time would be required to get the new program under way after its authorization by the Council, which could be used by the committees to wind up some projects and put others in shape for consideration by the Board or by the accounting research staff.

In the course of time, the Board would be expected to review all of the already existing accounting research bulletins and terminology bulletins of the present committees on accounting procedure and on terminology. In order to clarify the status of those bulletins meanwhile, the Board probably should make an announcement upon its organization, to the effect that they were to continue in force with the same degree of authority as before, but that the Board would reserve the right, as did the present committee on accounting procedure, to review and revise any of them from time to time.

The Technical Services Department and the present office of director of research presumably would continue to function as before, except that the Technical Services Department would not serve the Board as it has served the present committees on accounting procedure and terminology.

Review of the Program:

This or any other similar program which is adopted should be subject to review at more or less regular intervals, say every five years, so as to improve its organization and method of operation, and to reflect changing conditions in the Institute and in the profession. At some future time, other technical fields of activity of the Institute might be worked into the proposed new organization. There are now about twenty different committees dealing with such matters, served by the Technical Services Department.

Details of Organization:

The following supplements and amplifies the preceding summary of details of organization for and operation of the accounting research program and related activities.

Organization of the Board:

The Board would consist of eighteen members. It has been suggested that a smaller group might operate more effectively, but we believe that a reasonably large group would be desirable, and we feel that a Board of eighteen working along the lines indicated in this report would be manageable.

All of the members of the Board would be selected from the membership of the Institute.

The ability of the individuals would be the primary consideration in selecting the members of the Board. Effort would be made to seek out the best qualified persons. Competence and interest are more important than representation of particular groups or geographical areas.

The members of the Board would be nominated by the executive committee and elected by the Council of the Institute. This is the procedure followed with respect to certain other agencies of the Institute, for example, the trial board. Its application here would recognize the importance of the Board and would provide an effective method of securing qualified personnel.

The term of service would be three years. However, initially, six members would be elected for three years, six for two years, and six for one year; thereafter, six would be elected each year. The executive committee would have discretion as to the nomination of any member to succeed himself. This procedure is intended to provide continuity in the work of the Board, which is important. In presenting nominations to the Council, the executive committee would designate one of the nominees to be chairman of the Board for a three-year term.

The executive committee would also designate which nominees would be members of the fiscal committee of the Board and would select one of them to be its chairman. Initially, one member of the fiscal committee would be designated from among the six mem-

bers of the Board to be elected for three years, one from among those to be elected for two years, and one from among those to be elected for one year; thereafter, one would be designated from among the six to be elected each year. The normal term of service, both for the chairman and the other members of the fiscal committee, would be three years.

In the case of a vacancy in the Board, a new member would be nominated by the executive committee and elected by the Council for the unexpired term of the retiring member.

The Board would adopt its own rules of procedure. These should provide, among other things, as the rules of procedure of the present committee on accounting procedure provide, that pronouncements on accounting matters have the approval of at least two-thirds of the members of the Board, and that such pronouncements be issued timely. The director of accounting research would have the privilege of the floor at meetings of the Board.

The Board would report to the Council. Its regular report would comprise three parts--one relating to the technical work of the Board, one relating to the activities of the fiscal committee of the Board (over the signature of the chairman of the fiscal committee), and one relating to the activities of the accounting research staff (over the signature of the director of accounting research).

The Board would be designated a senior technical committee, as the committee on accounting procedure has been, and the sole group in the institute having authority to make pronouncements on accounting principles.

The Board would rely on the accounting research staff for drafting work and the like.

The Chairman of the Board would participate with the director of accounting research in the planning of the accounting research program. Members of the Board would serve on project advisory committees for research projects.

The fiscal committee of the Board would attend to the fiscal administration of the accounting research program. The magnitude of the program, considered in relation to other activities of the Institute, which are constantly expanding, is such that responsibility for its administrative problems preferably should be lodged elsewhere than with the executive committee of the Institute. The plan outlined in this report is comparable to that adopted for the continuing education program recently inaugurated.

The fiscal committee would consist of four members: the chairman of the Board, ex officio, and three other members of the Board selected as explained above, one of whom would act as the chairman. The term of service would be three years.

The fiscal committee would adopt its own rules of procedure. The executive director and the director of accounting research would have the privilege of the floor at meetings of the fiscal committee.

The fiscal committee would report to the Council through the Board, its report (over the signature of its chairman) being one part of the regular report of the Board to the Council, as explained above.

The responsibilities of the fiscal committee would comprehend the approval of budgets for the accounting research program, for consideration by the Council; follow-up on budgets after their adoption by the Council, to see that they are adhered to; selection of the director of accounting research, and recommendation to the executive committee of the Institute concerning his appointment; determination of personnel policy with respect to the accounting research staff; and general jurisdiction over the expenditure of monies for the accounting research program.

Organization of the Research Staff:

Good staff work is fundamental in any soundly organized research program. We propose the creation of an effective staff under competent direction.

There would be assigned to the accounting research staff on a permanent basis, the director of accounting research, three to five senior members, two or three junior members, and perhaps two secretaries.

The director of accounting research should be a person of substantial attainments and high reputation in accounting. He should have a good educational background, preferably including a graduate degree. He should be a certified public accountant. He should have had considerable experience and have demonstrated his ability as a writer and an administrator. His salary should be commensurate with his qualifications--probably at least $25,000 a year.

The senior staff members should be capable of carrying on research projects with a minimum of supervision. They should be highly qualified individuals. Creative thinking, demonstrated research and writing ability, some accounting experience, and *preferably a certified public accountant certificate perhaps are the basic requirements. A salary scale of from $15,000 to $20,000 probably would be necessary to attract the kind of talent needed.*

The junior staff members should be able to assist the senior staff members on research projects, perhaps assume major responsibility themselves for some projects, assist in drafting accounting research studies and statements on generally accepted accounting principles, and prepare minutes of meetings of the Board and related committees. They should be young men and women with outstanding academic records and demonstrated writing ability. Since work with the Institute presumably would not be counted in qualifying them for the certified public accountant examination, individuals of this type ordinarily would not be available until after they had fulfilled the experience requirements for the certificate. A salary scale of from $6,000 to $12,000 probably would be appropriate at this level.

The permanent staff would be supplemented as occasion required and opportunity arose, by personnel engaged on a temporary basis, perhaps usually for specific research projects. This might well be done especially during the time it would take to build up an adequate permanent staff. Thereafter, it would serve to give the accounting research program some flexibility, and would help to meet the need for specialized technical assistance on some projects. Also, it could be a means towards the important end of keeping the staff in reasonably close touch with practical business affairs.

Temporary staff personnel could be drawn from universities and colleges, from public accounting firms, or from other sources. Teachers could be used for part-time work, or for full-time work if on leave from their faculties. Staff members of public accounting firms could be used to great advantage on some assignments; we earnestly hope the partners of a number of the larger firms would be willing to make themselves and members of their staffs available occasionally for work with the Institute. The same applies, but to a lesser extent, in the case of experienced employees of commercial, industrial, financial, and other organizations. Temporary staff members might be employed at either the senior or junior level, and their salaries would vary accordingly.

It has been suggested that perhaps some research projects could be assigned to doctoral candidates at universities and colleges as the basis for dissertations. We doubt that this would be practicable. The work would be expected to require more background and experience than most graduate students have, and would involve more supervision and cooperation from other members of the research organization than would be appropriate for independent graduate research.

The director of accounting research would be the administrative head of the accounting research staff. He would be appointed by the executive committee upon the recommendation of the fiscal committee of the Board. He would be responsible to the fiscal committee in fiscal matters such as the employment of staff members, both permanent and temporary. He would participate with the chairman of the Board in the planning of the accounting research program. He would select and appoint the other research staff personnel. He would have active charge and direction of the carrying out of the program, including the assignment of research projects and the supervision of work. He would have authority to approve accounting research studies for publication, but would be expected to consult with and to rely heavily upon the views of project advisory committees as to the suitability of such studies for publication. He would report to the Council on the work of the accounting research staff, his report (over his signature) being one part of the regular report to the Council, as explained above.

The director of accounting research would have the privilege of the floor at meetings of the Board and those of its fiscal committee and would provide effective liaison between those bodies and the accounting research staff. He would undertake studies for the Board, and would provide the Board with assistance in drafting and similar work on request.

The position of director of accounting research is not intended to include the functions of the present position of director of research. The director of accounting research would devote himself exclusively to matters of financial accounting, and his activities would not comprehend, for example, the fields of management services and auditing. While he would be expected to maintain contact with certain government agencies and others outside the Institute, and to make some public appearances, his activities in this connection should be in furtherance of the accounting research program. He would not be expected to conduct a department or edit a column for The Journal of Accountancy.

We have assumed in this report that the accounting research staff would be in effect a separate division of the Institute organization. It could, of course, be incorporated as a subsidiary of the Institute or as an Institute foundation.

Accounting Research Studies:

The principal end product of the work of the accounting research staff would be a series of accounting research studies. These ordinarily would be published upon the completion of research projects by the accounting research staff. They would be in the form of pamphlets or monographs presenting detailed, documented reports on the work, giving pro and con arguments on controversial points, offering conclusions or recommendations, and, where appropriate, illustrating and demonstrating the application of principles. They would be published under the name of the director and those who had been associated with him in a project, and should bear a clear statement to the effect that they had not been approved or disapproved by the Board or by the Institute, and did not necessarily reflect their views.

The accounting research studies would provide the profession and the public with a reasonably complete discussion and documentation of accounting problems, and would indicate logical solutions to the problems in relation to basic postulates and broad principles. They would be informative, but tentative and not highly authoritative. They would furnish a vehicle for the exposure of matters for consideration and experimentation prior to the issuance by the Board of a statement on generally accepted accounting principles. They would be expected to contribute substantially toward the development of sound accounting practices, especially as to unsettled and controversial matters, and toward the recognition and acceptance of later pronouncements by the Board. In order to accomplish these ends, their distribution should be as wide as possible among accountants, both public and private, students and teachers, and others who would be interested. Publication of a summary and the conclusions of each accounting research study in The Journal of Accountancy *would assist in calling attention to the studies.*

An immediate project of the accounting research staff should be a study of the basic postulates underlying accounting principles generally, and the preparation of a brief statement thereof. There should be also a study of the broad principles of accounting, and the preparation of a reasonably condensed statement thereof, similar in scope to the statements of the American Accounting Association. The results of these, as adopted by the Board, should serve as the foundation for the entire body of future pronouncements by the Institute on accounting matters, to which each new release should be related.

The further planning of the accounting research program, that is, the selection of the research projects and decision as to the order in which to take them up, would be undertaken by the director of accounting research and the chairman of the Board. If they could not agree, they would refer the matter to the Board for decision. In planning the work, consideration would be given to requests or instructions from the Board for the study of matters of particular interest to it, and to suggestions from any other source for the investigation of particular problems. There should be borne in mind the desirability of developing pronouncements on accounting matters in a coherent, consistent series rather than as unconnected articles on isolated matters. Effort should be made to avoid restricting research projects to matters upon which the Board would be expected to take action immediately by incorporating the results of an accounting research study in a statement on generally accepted accounting principles; encouragement should be given to the exploration of unsettled and controversial matters as to which the Board might not be expected to make a pronouncement for some time. Due regard, of course, should be had for the necessity of keeping the program within budget allowances, as to both funds and talent.

Upon the reaching of a decision to undertake a research project, the director of accounting research would make the necessary staff assignments. With the approval of the chairman of the Board, he also would appoint a project advisory committee for the project and designate the chairman thereof.

A project advisory committee would consist of a small group, usually five to seven, of individuals especially qualified in the area under study, to consult from time to time with the director of accounting research and the staff members assigned to the project. The project advisory committee ordinarily would be selected partly from the Board, with a member of the Board acting as the chairman, and partly from the general membership of the Institute. Occasionally, however, it might be desirable to invite individuals from industry and other sources outside the Institute to be guest members.

The project advisory committee would be expected to provide the accounting research staff with a means of keeping in close touch with business practice. Its members would be available during the progress of the work, to suggest sources of information, to review conclusions reached by the staff members, and, ultimately, to review the draft of the report and to advise as to its suitability for publication as an accounting research study.

At an appropriate time, public announcement would be made to the effect that the accounting research staff was studying, or was about to begin studying, a particular matter, and that persons who desired to have their views considered should submit memoranda to the director of accounting research. In some cases the announcement might be more effective if it were withheld until after some preliminary work had been done, as this would permit the listing of specific questions or phases of the topic on which comments were especially desired. Such announcement would include notices in The Journal of Accountancy and in The CPA, and letters to organizations and individuals who customarily cooperate with the Institute in its accounting research program and related activities and to any others thought to be interested in the project. The material received in response to this invitation would be given careful consideration. Unless restricted by the contributor, it would be considered as available to all interested persons.

The director of accounting research, the staff members assigned to the research project, and the project advisory committee would work together as a team. The director of accounting research would exercise administrative supervision at all times, and would have authority to publish the results as an accounting research study. As to the latter, however, he should give due consideration to the views of the project advisory committee, and ordinarily would be expected not to proceed contrary to the strong opposition of the group.

If the results were not published by the Institute, a staff member would be permitted to publish them under his own name in some circumstances, as where a university or college professor had done the work as a temporary member of the accounting research staff. It seems unlikely that publication of a rejected study would be desirable where the work had been done by a permanent member of the accounting research staff.

Each accounting research study published by the Institute would carry the names of the director of accounting research, the staff members who made the study, and the project advisory committee. Any of these persons, except possibly some of the staff members, who disagreed with the conclusions expressed in the study would be expected to have an explanation of his position included in the published document.

Statements on Accounting Principles:

It is expected that these statements, to be issued by the Board, would be regarded as an authoritative written expression of what constitutes generally accepted accounting principles.

The statements on generally accepted accounting principles ordinarily would be based on accounting research studies previously prepared by the accounting research staff and, in some cases, others, with emphasis on the conclusions expressed in them. The finished product of the accounting research staff thus would become the principal raw material of the Board. In view of the prior publication of the accounting research studies, in most cases, statements on generally accepted accounting principles would be expected to receive wide recognition and acceptance upon their issuance.

As in the case of the accounting research studies, the statements on generally accepted accounting principles would be framed in relation to basic postulates and broad principles.

Upon the publication of an accounting research study, it would be considered by the Board, and accepted (as the basis of a statement on generally accepted accounting principles), rejected, or laid over for future attention, unless, of course, it dealt with a subject (for example, a factual survey of prevailing practice with respect to the accounting treatment of a given item) which would not be expected to be acted upon by the Board.

It would be rejected if the Board disagreed with its conclusions or thought the subject inappropriate for treatment in a statement on generally accepted accounting principles. If the Board disagreed sharply with the accounting research study, it should make its dissent public, together with its reasons therefor, so that the profession and others concerned would be warned that the previously published document did not have authoritative support. Possibly, the most effective way for the Board to do this would be to proceed promptly with the preparation of a statement on generally accepted accounting principles which would approve a contrary position. Alternatively, the Board could arrange to have an announcement of its views published in The Journal of Accountancy and The CPA. We hope that instances of this kind would be rare.

The accounting research study would be laid over for future attention if the Board believed that a waiting period would be desirable, in which to let a given matter settle down. For example, if an accounting research study dealt with a new problem or with a problem as to which there was considerable difference of opinion (and we hope that a number of them would deal with such problems), it might be in order to allow time for public reaction to its reasoning and experimentation with its recommendations before releasing the statement on generally accepted accounting principles. An extended waiting period might be needed in some cases to demonstrate the acceptability or nonacceptability of an accounting research study. During this period, members of the Institute would have an excellent opportunity, on the basis of the documented material contained in the published accounting re-

search study, to lead thinking in the direction of a sound solution to the problem involved.

Although the statements on generally accepted accounting principles usually would be based on previously published accounting research studies, this would not necessarily be the case. The Board could itself initiate action with respect to a particular matter. In this event it would instruct the director of accounting research to undertake any necessary research work and prepare the draft of a pronouncement for its consideration without waiting for publication of the accounting research study.

Drafting and similar work in connection with statements on generally accepted accounting principles would be done by the accounting research staff. The Board should avoid detail of this kind, and should devote its efforts to the substance of the material presented for its consideration.

Drafts of proposed statements on generally accepted accounting principles would be exposed for comment before publication, under a plan similar to that followed by the present committee on accounting procedure with respect to its accounting research bulletins. This would permit the submission of additional memoranda in support of or in opposition to the position proposed to be taken by the Board. Every effort should be made to improve the effectiveness of this cooperative procedure.

Routine questions concerning statements on generally accepted accounting principles would continue to be handled as they now are. Substantive questions would be referred to the Board, which would issue a series of interpretive rulings.

The proposal of Mr. Jennings, which led to the appointment of our committee, suggested that pronouncements of the research organization should be presented to the Council for approval or rejection, and that upon receiving the approval of two-thirds of the members of the Council voting upon any particular pronouncement, they should be considered binding upon the members of the Institute. We have concluded that only rarely should a pronouncement be given the degree of finality represented by adoption of the principle by the Council or possibly by the membership of the Institute. The Board would be expected to review its past pronouncements from time to time, and in a few instances might decide that a particular statement was of such great significance and had received such general support and acceptance, that it should be given formal recognition and become mandatory upon the membership of the Institute. In such cases the Board would include recommendations for such action in its report to the Council. We feel that the best method of enforcing most of the

Board's pronouncements would be to secure their acceptance as high authority by professional accountants in advising clients and in preparing reports on financial statements.

Respectfully submitted,

Andrew Barr
Carman G. Blough
Dudley E. Browne
Arthur M. Cannon
Paul Grady
R. K. Mautz
Leonard Spacek
William W. Werntz
Weldon Powell, Chairman

September 1958

APPENDIX B TO SECTION I

TOWARDS AN INTERNATIONAL ACCOUNTING PROFESSION*

by

Gordon H. Cowperthwaite

The organization of professional accounting bodies in individual countries began over a century ago and today many countries in the world have a well-developed accounting profession responsible for standards, ethics, and the education and training of members. Since the growth of the accounting profession was in response to a need created by changing social and economic conditions, the profession in each country developed at a pace set by that country's expanding economic environment. This phenomenon set the stage not only for cooperation between accounting bodies developing at a comparable rate but also for assisting countries developing at a slower pace.

Initially, regional conferences were held periodically for the exchange of information in the hope of finding solutions to mutual problems. These conferences resulted in the accounting bodies in Europe becoming linked through the medium of the Union d'Experts Comptables, those of North and South America through the Inter-American Accounting Conference, and those of Asia and the Pacific through the Confederation of Asian and Pacific Accountants.

Substantial technical aid has been extended by many countries directly to other countries and includes the promotion of existing accountancy bodies and the formation of new ones; examination facilities; provision for practical experience; and the development of educational services. Technical information in the form of numerous professional journals, research bulletins, and other material is published by various accounting bodies and the exchange of complimentary copies of this material, as well as information regarding an organization, its policies and practices, has become customary.

Inter-country cooperation

Several important steps towards international understanding have taken place in recent years, including the formation in 1966

*Reprinted with permission from CA Magazine, June, 1974, pp. 36-40.

of the Accountants' International Study Group, comprising representatives of the United States, United Kingdom, and Canada. In the eight years since its formation, this group has studied several important issues affecting the countries represented and has published studies on a variety of subjects.

In the last few years several other countries, particularly in Europe, have developed comparable study groups as trading patterns have evolved into new blocks such as the European Common Market.

From a foundation of cooperation among accountancy organizations, the aid given to one another and the spontaneous exchange of information on a unilateral basis, a newer and potentially major development--likely to affect the profession internationally --occurred in November, 1972 when the International Coordination Committee for the Accountancy Profession (ICCAP) was formed. This article outlines the steps that preceded the formation of ICCAP, its objectives, how it is now organized, and its hopes for accomplishment in the future.

International Congresses of Accountants

The first International Congress of Accountants was held over fifty years ago and since that time, with gaps during World War II, Congresses have been held at five-year intervals. The Tenth, held in Sydney, Australia in October, 1972, was attended by over 3,500 members from 60 participating countries.

Frequently, and particularly in the past 15 years, the theme of conferences has centered on harmonization of accounting standards, international standards of accounting, and other topics which go beyond the boundaries of any one country. The subjects tend to reflect the development of multinational corporations, the complexity of our society today, and the concern of the professional accountant with such topics as inflation accounting, financial statement preparation, and comparable matters.

International Working Party (1967-1971)

At the Ninth International Congress of Accountants held in Paris in 1967, an International Working Party was formed, comprising 14 individuals from a variety of countries. Among the terms of reference given to the Working Party was the request:

> *To review the part played by the periodic International Congresses in the continuing and progressive development of accounting thought and understanding; and in that con-*

text to consider the scope and frequency of such Congresses and the objectives to which they should be directed.

Three meetings of the Working Party were held following its formation in 1967 and a final report was issued in December, 1971.

Several important recommendations were made, including the suggestion that ICCAP be formed. It could be said, therefore, that the Working Party was the first attempt to consider how the accounting profession could be organized on an international level.

The decision taken at the Tenth International Congress of Accountants at Sydney in October, 1972

Although the Congress in Paris in 1967 stressed the need for international cooperation and the importance of the accounting profession adjusting to the needs of the international community, the 1972 Congress exhibited a stronger note of urgency concerning the development of a world organization to address international problems relating to world trade, as well as a strong desire to strengthen cooperation among the various accounting bodies. Prompted by this sense of urgency and cooperation, the heads of the delegations of 60 countries attending the Congress in Sydney unanimously approved the adoption of the International Working Party's Final Report and the "International Coordination Committee for the Accountancy Profession" (ICCAP) was formed.

ICCAP--What is it?

In a world of abbreviations, ICCAP may well have more meaning than its full name--which in some languages has an unwieldy flavour. In spite of this, it reflects the important objective of obtaining international coordination within the many branches of the accountancy profession throughout the world.

While ICCAP delegates have a common purpose--the internationalization of the accountancy profession, and a common basis--all are accountants, there are barriers which must be overcome, including those of language and customs. It could be said that in its own way ICCAP is a replica of the United Nations since it has international representation, problems, and objectives. One difference, however, is that from the beginning ICCAP was fortunate in that the meetings have been held in a spirit of considerable harmony and understanding.

ICCAP has eleven members, one each from Australia, Canada, Federal Republic of Germany, France, India, Japan, Mexico, The Netherlands, Phillipines, United Kingdom, and the United States.

Each country is entitled to one delegate who represents the total accounting profession in his particular country. It is anticipated that delegates will be rotated over a period of years. Canada's delegate, Gordon Cowperthwaite, FCA, Managing Partner of Peat, Marwick, Mitchell & Co., Toronto, represents the CICA, the Society of Industrial Accountants, the Certified General Accountants Association, and the Financial Executives Institute. To facilitate coordination between ICCAP and the various accounting bodies, each delegate is accompanied to meetings by a representative of the permanent staff of one of the professional accounting bodies in the country.

The first Chairman of ICCAP is Dr. R. Goerdeler, from the Federal Republic of Germany. Germany has been selected to act as host of the Eleventh International Congress of Accountants, to be held in Munich in October, 1977.

Since its formation in November, 1972, ICCAP has met in plenary session twice--in Dusseldorf, Germany in April, 1973, and Mexico City in October, 1973. The third meeting is scheduled for San Francisco, June 25 and 26 of this year. In addition to these plenary sessions, Working Parties have been formed on special subjects and considerable work has been done in developing the objectives and the approach that appears best suited to permit ICCAP to advance towards the accomplishment of its tasks.

The need for a permanent secretariat to take over the administration of ICCAP was one of the first considerations of the Working Party responsible for Structure, but an interim decision was made not to form one at this time. Rather, ICCAP will work with and provide leadership from individual countries' permanent staff in the development of the required standards and the completion of research and other backup activities.

The objectives of ICCAP

The objectives of ICCAP, as adopted in Mexico City in 1973, were defined as follows:

> *The long-term objective of ICCAP as established at the Tenth International Congress of Accountants in Sydney in 1972 should be the development of a coordinated world-wide accounting profession with uniform standards. ICCAP should accept responsibility to give leadership towards the achievement of this objective and should take the following action:*
>
> - *Initiate, coordinate, and guide work that has as its goal the achievement of international techni-*

cal, ethical and educational guidelines for the accounting profession and reciprocal recognition of qualifications and work towards this purpose by establishing appropriate committees as well as working through the regional organizations for implementation.

- *Encourage and promote the development of regional organizations with common objectives and formulate guidelines for the structure and constitution of such regional organizations.*

- *Review ICCAP's role, functioning and constitution and propose changes necessary to achieve its objectives.*

The most important factor, however, is the firm decision of this eleven-member body to accept leadership for the development of a coordinated world-wide accounting profession with common standards. Achievement of this objective will not be easy, given the various cultural and economic backgrounds of the participating countries, but the goal is common to all presently involved in ICCAP and hopefully is shared by individual accountants around the world.

ICAAP's organization

So that progress can be made on a rapid basis, five standing committees were formed at the October 1973 meeting in Mexico City and are now at work. They are:

Regional Bodies

This committee, made up of representatives from The Netherlands, Mexico, and Australia, is charged with formulating guidelines on the creation, objectives, and constitution of regional bodies. Its terms of reference are:

- *To consider and make recommendations to ICCAP:*

  (a) in what regions the formation and the development of regional organizations should be encouraged and the practical steps to be taken.

  (b) on the objectives, constitution and activities which should be suggested to such regional organizations.

- *To carry out ICCAP policy regarding the formation of regional bodies as may be approved by ICCAP from time to time.*

Ethics Committee

The encouragement and development of regional organization must be accompanied by the development of national bodies with common standards. ICCAP therefore considered that it was necessary to formulate guidelines on the ethical principles to be adopted by professional bodies in framing their ethical rules.

The specific terms of reference for the Ethics Committee, consisting of representatives from Australia, The Netherlands, Japan, and the USA, are:

- *To consider and recommend to ICCAP a model code of ethics and/or cardinal ethical principles which should be observed in the formulation of any code for the profession, including the practice of the profession internationally; the extent to which such a code or parts of it should be applicable to accountants not in public practice and to formulate and promulgate guidelines from time to time on various aspects of ethics arising from changing economic or social conditions.*

- *To give advice to professional accountancy bodies, where this is sought, on the drafting of ethical codes, and to support, where practicable, the introduction and enforcement of higher ethical standards.*

- *To facilitate the exchange of information on ethical matters between member bodies.*

Professional Education and Training Committee

The terms of reference for this committee, with representation from France, UK, India, and the Philippines, in their efforts to formulate guidelines for minimum standards of professional education and training for professional accountancy bodies are:

- *To consider and recommend to ICCAP the minimum standards of professional education and training (including the range and depth of knowledge and the intellectual level of professional examinations) to be required by professional accountancy bodies of persons as a condition of membership.*

Future international organization

In October, 1973, ICCAP examined the type of organizational structure most likely to commend itself to participating bodies of International Congresses. It concluded that the type of structure to be developed and defined should be an international organization of accounting bodies with an executive committee responsible to the members in general meetings for the carrying out of policies and the day-to-day administration of affairs. A committee, comprised of delegates from the UK, USA, France, Canada, and Germany, has been formed to make a submission outlining the details of the structure to the Heads of Delegations meeting in Munich in 1977.

The specific terms of reference for this committee are:

- *To consider and make recommendations to ICCAP on the constitution, membership, financing, structure, and functions of an international organization of accounting bodies incorporating the agreed objectives of ICCAP.*

A draft constitution for what is tentatively being called the "International Federation of Accountants"--to replace "ICCAP" --was approved by the delegates to the Structures Committee which met in London on April 5. This draft will be submitted to the ICCAP meeting in San Francisco and subsequently the definitive proposals will be submitted to the Eleventh Congress in Munich.

Publicity

A positive publicity program is to be developed by the Canadian representative, in consultation with Germany, to ensure that the objectives and proposals of ICCAP are understood internationally in the period prior to 1977.

International Accounting Standards Committee (IASC)

An immediate response to the expressed desire at Sydney in 1972 was the formation in June, 1973, of IASC which has autonomy for the promulgation of accounting standards. IASC has nine founding member countries and invitations have been extended to all countries attending Congresses to become associate members. If ICCAP is to achieve its objective of the development of a coordinated worldwide accounting profession with uniform standards, it becomes apparent that the work of IASC is of paramount importance. . . .

APPENDIX C TO SECTION I

INTERNATIONAL STANDARDS*

by

R. D. Thomas

In June 1973, a significant step was taken by the accounting profession when representatives of professional bodies in Australia, Canada, France, Germany, Japan, Mexico, the Netherlands, the United Kingdom and Ireland, and the United States signed an agreement in London which brought into being the International Accounting Standards Committee (IASC). . . . Since accountants regard annual reporting an integral part of stewardship, it is appropriate to review what has happened during the first year of the Committee's existence and, as part of the increasing trend to providing a forecast of the near future, to take a look at its immediate plans and long-term prospects.

While the heavy commitments undertaken by the nine accounting bodies which founded the IASC were set out in the special review carried in this journal last September, they are so significant and so necessary to an understanding of the ongoing responsibilities of the Committee, that they are repeated here.

(a) to support the standards promulgated by the Committee;

(b) to use their best endeavors:

(i) to ensure that published accounts comply with these standards or that there is disclosure of the extent to which they do not and to persuade governments, the authorities controlling securities markets and the industrial and business community that published accounts should comply with these standards.

(ii) to ensure that the auditors satisfy themselves that the accounts comply with these standards. If the accounts do not comply with these standards the audit report should either refer to the

*Reprinted with permission from CA Magazine, June, 1974, pp. 48-49.

disclosure of non-compliance in the accounts, or should state the extent to which they do not comply;

(iii) to ensure that, as soon as practicable, appropriate action is taken in respect of auditors whose audit reports do not meet the requirements of (ii) above;

(c) to seek to secure similar general acceptance and observance of these standards internationally.

Joining forces

If the IASC is successful and the participating professional bodies are able to fulfill these commitments (and, based on the first year's experience, there is every reason to be optimistic about both of these prospects), the accounting profession will be among the first--if not the first--professional group to attempt to establish international standards on its own initiative and entirely from its own resources. However, consider for a moment some of the substantial gains we stand to make as a profession by joining forces internationally:

- *We will substantially reduce duplication in the use of the time and talents of those engaged in accounting and auditing research. This is a very scarce commodity.*

- *The accounting profession will begin to coalesce on common standards rather than the (usually slightly) different results invariably produced by research carried on independently in many countries--often at the same time (see point above).*

- *The advantages to the international business community of not having to recast financial statements according to differing standards, coupled with the greater usefulness of statements based on common standards, are hard to exaggerate.*

It may be premature to try to forecast whether any or all of these advantages will, in fact, be gained through the creation of the IASC but, in the short time that the Committee has been in existence, three things have been clearly demonstrated:

- *The accounting bodies which founded the IASC are solidly behind the commitments they made in establishing it.*

• *Many other countries are anxious to be part of this international effort to develop uniform standards.*

• *The initial schedule (which many people thought was very tight indeed) has been maintained and there is every reason to believe that, with minor exceptions, this will continue.*

First Exposure Draft released

At the end of its first year, the Committee has its first Exposure Draft (on "Disclosure of Accounting Policies") out for comment together with a proposed "Commentary on Statements of International Accounting Standards." The Commentary is intended to be the general introduction to the series of International Accounting Standards (IAS's) and is similar to the Introduction to Accounting Research and Auditing Standards Sections of the CICA Handbook *(for example, IAS's are not intended to be retroactive, to apply to immaterial items, and are issued only with the affirmative vote of seven of the nine countries represented on the IASC).*

The first Exposure Draft is based on the work of one of the Steering Committees established to work on individual projects. At present, Steering Committees are made up of the representatives of three of the countries on the IASC (similar to the geographic working Sections of the Accounting Research Committee and Auditing Standards Committee); they do the detailed preparation and drafting of proposed IAS's for consideration by the full Committee. In addition to the Steering Committee responsible for the first Exposure Draft, the following Steering Committees are now at work:

• *Valuation and Presentation of Inventories (Canada, Japan, and Mexico)*

• *Consolidated Financial Statements and the Equity Method of Accounting (Australia, Germany, and the United States)*

• *Basic Disclosure in Financial Statements (Germany, Mexico, UK, and Ireland)*

• *Depreciation of Fixed Assets (Australia, Canada, and France)*

• *Translation (Conversion) of Foreign Accounts in Financial Statements (Japan, The Netherlands, and the US).*

In addition, a new Steering Committee on "Accounting for Inflation" was established at the committee's April meeting, with Israel being asked to join Britain, Canada, and The Netherlands to work on this major project.

Future plans

The Committee's plans are to issue between three and four Exposure Drafts a year--with a standard exposure period of four months for comments to be received on each Exposure Draft. Because of the usual problems of getting a new organization going, the second Exposure Draft (on the "Presentation and Valuation of Inventories") will likely be approved at the July Committee meeting with further Exposure Drafts following at approximately three-month intervals.

Detailed procedures have been arranged in all of the countries represented on the IASC for the committees responsible for each country's research activities to review IASC Exposure Drafts and to comment on them. In Canada, once an IAS has been approved by the IASC, either (or both) the Accounting Research or the Auditing Standards committees will immediately consider the action, if any, it (or they) must take in order to include the substance of an IAS in the CICA Handbook.

While, initially at least, the imprimatur of accounting bodies in the various countries will be essential to establish the authority of an IAS, if Statements of International Accounting Standards become widely accepted they will, of themselves, begin to have their own intrinsic authority which accountants, businessmen, and governments throughout the world will come to recognize.

An invitation to join

The IASC has issued invitations to all of the accounting bodies recognized as being part of the international Accounting Congress to join the Committee's work on international standards. Annual membership fees have been established, ranging from £100 a year for accounting bodies with a membership of 1,000 or less, up to £1,000 a year for those whose membership is over 5,000. Accounting bodies which accept this invitation must satisfy the IASC that they are prepared to accept, and are capable of undertaking, the obligations that each of the Founding Member bodies undertook when they established the Committee. Many countries throughout the world have either accepted this invitation or have indicated their intention of doing so and hopefully, by this time next year, we should be able to report that many accounting bodies throughout the world are actively participating in and supporting the IASC's programs.

The International Accounting Standards Committee

Australia
E. H. Burgess
R. F. Munro

Canada
P. H. Lyons
R. D. Thomas

France
H. F. A. Cordoliani
A. Henrot
R. Mazars

Germany
Krafft V. D. Tann
H. Kaminski
Hans Havermann

Japan
J. Kawaguchi
S. Nakajima
S. Tasumi

Mexico
J. Freyssinier
M. Galvan

The Netherlands
P. C. Louwers
H. C. Treffers
H. Volten

United Kingdom and Ireland
Henry Benson (Chairman)
A. I. MacKenzie
J. D. Winters

United States
J. P. Cummings
R. N. Sempier

Secretariat
Paul Rosenfield, Secretary
R. J. Simmons, Assistant Secretary

SECTION II

THE APB EXPERIENCE: 1959-1973

INTRODUCTION

In this section, two former members of the APB discuss, in an unbuttoned fashion, the successes and failures of this institution. Both are leaders of the academic profession (whose textbooks have made them accountant household names) although one, Dr. Herbert E. Miller, joined a Big Eight accounting firm several years ago. Although they agree on many aspects of the APB, it should be remembered that Dr. Miller served in the early relatively peaceful years of the Board while Dr. Charles T. Horngren's membership was during the last strife-ridden years. Supplementing Professor Horngren's comments is a letter he wrote to the Wheat Committee about U.S. rule-making institutions; also included in the appendices are a list of the APB's thirty-one Opinions and four Statements, and a list of APB members and the Opinions on which each member voted.

-- The Editor.

SECTION II

THE APB EXPERIENCE: 1959-1973

1959 *Council accepts the comprehensive recommendations of the Special Committee on Research Program, replaces the research department by an accounting research division having an expanded role, and replaces the CAP and the Committee on Terminology by the Accounting Principles Board (APB), of which Weldon Powell is to be chairman. AICPA Executive Committee insists that the Big Eight firms be represented on the Board by their managing partners.*

1962-64 *By a bare two-thirds majority of 14 to 7, including a 4-4 split of Big Eight firms, the APB approves Opinion No. 2, which recommends that the "investment credit should be reflected in net income over the productive life of acquired property, and not in the year in which it is placed in service." Following issuance, three of the Big Eight firms made it known that they will not expect their clients to conform to the Opinion. In view of widespread opposition to the Opinion, in both government and the public sector, the SEC issues ASR No. 96, in it allows both the deferral and flow-through methods of accounting for the investment credit. In early 1964, by a vote of 15 to 5, the APB issues Opinion No. 4, which acknowledges the "events and developments occurring since the issuance of Opinion No. 2" and declares that both the deferral and flow-through methods are "acceptable."*

1962-Present *Controversies over the investment credit (1962-63 and 1967), product-line reporting (1966-68), and pooling of interests (1969-70), together with criticisms by the SEC, the Financial Executives Institute (FEI), and members of the profession, excite an almost continual interest by the financial press in accounting principles and the accounting profession.*

1963-64 *APB, in a divided vote, asks Council to require that material departures from Board recommendations be disclosed in the financial statements or in the auditor's report. AICPA Executive Committee goes further, suggesting that Board Opinions be the only "generally accepted accounting principles." Council, in a compromise resolution following three days of intense debate,* adopts the APB proposal in principle. Following a report by a special committee, Council in Fall, 1964, implements the compromise proposal.

1966 A committee of the AAS issues a monograph entitled A Statement of Basic Accounting Theory.

1968 FEI's Corporate Reporting Committee becomes an active collaborator on exposure drafts with the APB, sets up subject-area subcommittees as liaison with counterpart subcommittees of the APB.

1968 AICPA, FAF, FEI, and Robert Morris Associates jointly sponsor the Seaview Symposium on Corporate Financial Reporting, bringing together accounting practitioners, accounting educators, financial executives, financial analysts, and bank loan officers in a dialogue on accounting principles. The papers and proceedings are published by the AICPA in 1969 under the title, Corporate Financial Reporting: Conflicts and Challenges.

1968-Present Abraham J. Briloff writes a series of articles for Barron's calling into question the accounting and disclosure practice of numerous publicly-held corporations. While placing primary emphasis on abuses of pooling-of-interest accounting, Briloff also deals with the particular practices of computer leasing companies, land development companies, franchisers, and home builders. Briloff's articles generated increased stock-market sensitivity to the quality of financial reporting.

1969 APB begins to hold a series of symposia on pre-exposure drafts of proposed Opinions. Participation is by invitation only, the Board inviting several organizations to all symposia and various other bodies to particular symposia, depending on the subject. Memoranda and brief oral presentations are requested of participants. The object of the symposium idea. . .is to inform affected groups of the Board's current thinking on subjects under consideration so as to secure reactions and suggestions before the Board reaches its conclusions. The symposium approach leads to a formalization of the Board's liaison with other interested groups.

1969 APB issues Statement No. 3, proposing that the price-level adjustments explained and illustrated in Accounting Research Study No. 6 be presented as supplementary information to the basic financial statements.

1969-70 Controversy over pooling-of-interests accounting becomes intense as the conglomerate merger movement reaches its zenith, then collapses. Direct and indirect pressure from the SEC, Congress, Federal Trade Commission, and Administration, financial analysts, and financial executives begins to bear down on the APB. Board issues an exposure draft, holds two symposia and numerous private meetings, agonizes during much of 1970 over various proposals and drafts, and finally issues Opinion Nos. 16 and 17 amid much dissent and criticism.

1970 After five years of study and numerous drafts, the APB issues Statement No. 4, "Basic Concepts and Accounting Principles Underlying Financial Statements of Business Enterprises," the Board's first pronouncement on basic principles.

1971 In 1971, the APB issues Opinion No. 19 which recommends that a "Statement of Changes in Financial Position," embodying a broadened concept of the funds statement, be made part of the "basic financial statements."

1971 APB replaces the series of symposia by public hearings at which all interested parties may present their views on subjects being considered by the Board for prospective opinions. The hearings are intended to meet three criticisms of the symposia, to wit:

(1) participation was by invitation only,
(2) the Board had already reached its conclusions before the symposia were held, and
(3) presentations by participating groups were dogmatic and uncompromising, thus frustrating attempts at developing a dialogue.

1971 Several weeks after President Nixon recommends that Congress revive the investment credit, AICPA representatives meet with Treasury officials to urge the administration to refrain from expressing a view on the proper accounting treatment of the credit. The Institute receives a letter from the Treasury that it will remain neutral on the question. Following a meeting between AICPA representatives and the SEC chairman, the APB prepares and issues an exposure draft again reasserting its 1962 preferred treatment of the investment credit. A letter of support is received from the SEC Chairman. Partly in response to industry pressures, the Treasury revises its neutrality stand and advises the Senate that it "strongly supports a continuation of the optional *(accounting) treatment" of the credit and "will support a legislative resolution of this matter." Notwithstanding the eleventh-hour pleas of Institute leaders, Congress amends the tax bill, which later becomes law, to provide that taxpayers may freely choose which method of accounting for the credit they prefer. In face of this Congressional dictum, the APB withdraws its exposure draft and issues a statement deploring Congressional involvement in the establishment of accounting principles.*

--Excerpts are from Stephen A. Zeff's "Chronology of Significant Developments in the Establishment of Accounting Principles in the United States, 1926-1972," Journal of Accounting Research (Spring, 1972), pp. 220-226.

THE DISCUSSANTS

Charles T. Horngren:

Professor Horngren was a member of the Accounting Principles Board (APB) from 1968 until its termination in mid-1973. He is the Edmund W. Littlefield Professor of Accounting at Stanford University. He has taught at Marquette University, the University of Wisconsin, Milwaukee, and was on the University of Chicago faculty for ten years. In addition, he was in public accounting practice in Wisconsin and has been a consultant for various organizations. He was given an Outstanding Educator Award by the American Accounting Association in 1973, the first year such awards were given.

A frequent contributor to the periodical literature, Professor Horngren has authored several textbooks, including Cost Accounting: A Managerial Emphasis (Prentice-Hall, 3rd edition, 1972); Accounting for Management Control: An Introduction (Prentice-Hall, 3rd edition, 1974). Co-author: CPA Problems and Approaches to Solutions (Prentice-Hall, 4th edition, 1974).

Professor Horngren has a bachelor's degree from Marquette University, an MBA from Harvard, a Ph.D. from the University of Chicago, and a CPA from the state of Wisconsin. Active in many professional organizations, he was formerly the Director of Research of the American Accounting Association and has been chairman of several AAA committees. In addition, he has been a member of the Research Planning Committee, National Association of Accountants; Executive Committee, College of Measurements, Institute of Management Sciences; and the Professional Development Board, American Institute of CPA's.

Herbert E. Miller:

Dr. Miller was a member of the APB from its start in 1959 into 1962. He has been a partner in Arthur Andersen & Co., Chicago, since 1970. Previously he had been a Professor of Accounting at several universities, including the University of Michigan (1946-1961) and Michigan State University (1961-1970). He has received both the Elijah Watts Sells Gold Medal Award on the CPA examinations and the William A. Paton Medal.

A frequent contributor to the periodical literature, Dr. Miller was co-author of the Finney & Miller textbook series (Prentice-Hall) and editor and a contributor to CPA Review Manual (Prentice-Hall, Inc., 4th edition, 1972).

Dr. Miller has a bachelor's and master's degree from the University of Iowa, a Ph.D. from the University of Minnesota, and a CPA from the states of Iowa, Michigan, and Illinois. Active in many organizations, he was formerly president of the American Accounting Association and also formerly president of the Beta Alpha Psi National Council. He was a member of the Council, AICPA, for 1966-1970. He has been chairman of committees both for the AICPA and the AAA.

THE MODERATORS

Faculty moderator is Professor Thomas J. Burns, Director of the Ph.D. Program in Accounting and Beta Alpha Psi Faculty Advisor at The Ohio State University. A Ph.D. and CPA, he has numerous publications. Student moderator is Mr. Ralph Loretta, Beta Alpha Psi Vice President and honors student. After graduation this June, he will earn the MBA degree at Indiana University before starting a public accounting career.

THE DISCUSSION

The APB Obituary:

LORETTA, Moderator: The APB was born in September, 1959, and died in June, 1973, after a life of almost 14 years.

But it really started back in October, 1957, at the annual meeting of the AICPA, when the AICPA President Alvin Jennings recommended the creation of a research foundation; he appointed Weldon Powell as chairman of a special committee to investigate a research program. The committee was to recommend procedures that would produce research and provide for the understanding of and the agreement about the underlying accounting postulates.

In September, 1958, the special committee report was issued. It recommended the establishment of the APB to replace both the CAP and the Committee on Terminology. The establishment of a new accounting research division to replace the old research department was also recommended.

The need for fundamental research upon which Board pronouncements would be based received considerable emphasis in the report. To carry out these research studies, a research staff was to be assigned exclusively to the APB. In explaining the approach to be taken in attacking broad problems of financial accounting, the report indicated such studies should begin with a statement of the accounting postulates derived from the economic and political environment, including the business community. Further, a broad set of accounting principles was to be formulated on the basis of the postulates; finally, rules or guides for the application of accounting principles were to be developed in relation to these postulates and principles. Also, adequate research was to be undertaken in all stages of this process.

It was requested that an immediate project of the accounting research staff be the development of the basic postulates and broad principles of accounting. Such would serve as the foundation of the entire body of future pronouncements of the Institute on accounting matters. In the Spring of 1959, the Institute's Executive Committee Council approved the recommendations of the special committee; by September 1, of the same year, the APB and the Accounting Research Division came into existence. The twenty-member board was headed by Weldon Powell. Over three years later, in November, 1962, the APB issued its first opinion.

By January, 1971, or nine years later, due to the mounting concern over the inability of the APB to deal effectively with the issues before it, the institute held a special conference to discuss the establishment of accounting principles. In April, 1971, as a result of this conference, Francis Wheat was named chairman of a study group appointed to examine the establishment of accounting principles and Robert Trueblood was designated chairman of a study group that sought to define the objectives of financial statements. In March, 1972, the Wheat study group recommended that a seven-man full-time financial accounting standards board be established, the FASB, which eventually replaced the APB in 1973. This recommendation was adopted by the Institute. The Trueblood group made its report in 1973. In June, 1973, the APB concluded its activity with the issuance of Opinion No. 30 and No. 31, leaving a publication record of 14 research studies, 4 statements, and 31 opinions.

In all, 57 individuals served as members to the APB in its 14-year history. This membership includes 40 representatives from CPA firms, 8 business executives, 7 representatives from the academic community including Dr. Herbert Miller who served as a board member for four years from 1959 to 1962, and Professor Charles Horngren who has served as a board member from 1968 through 1973. Also, one member was from the government and one, Carman Blough, a former SEC chief accountant, was an AICPA staff member at the time of his appointment.

The APB and Member Authority and Responsibility:

BURNS, Moderator: Would you explain your authority and your responsibilities as an APB member.

MILLER: Since I am neither historian or scholar, I must rely entirely on my memory which may at times be less precise than this occasion deserves. As to authority, I didn't feel as though I had any particular individual authority and I do not recall that I visualized the APB as an entity as having any great authoritative status initially.

I had been on the Committee of Accounting Procedure (CAP), which I didn't feel was a particularly authoritative body either. The CAP operated under a philosophy that was then widespread in the profession, namely, if the committee pronouncements had merit, then those pronouncements would be followed and thereby achieve authoritative status. This view was held by then AICPA Director of Research, Carman Blough. It wasn't their origin that determined their status but the quality of the pronouncements, that is, whether they served a useful purpose in resolving accounting controversies. So I didn't view my role or the APB's role as one of great authority. Our output had to earn an authoritative status.

Now as to responsibilities. At that time I was a university professor. As you know, the university professor feels a great responsibility and a loyalty to his subject matter, rather than per se to a business school or university. Thus I perceived that my responsibilities related to the subject matter of accounting. I was to try to see that accounting evolved as quickly and as responsibly as possible to the changing conditions, a circumstance that will always exist with a subject such as accounting.

In the early years, the Board was in a formulative period; while we were waiting for the research to be done, we established our own procedures. At the time, my impression was that it would have been out of order for the APB to start issuing opinions before a consensus was established on postulates and principles. Otherwise the Board might have issued an opinion that would have been inconsistent with the basic principles that presumably would be forthcoming from research. Any frustrations of the Board and myself during this period were natural ones and attributable to this inevitable waiting period. Of course, with our second pronouncement on the investment credit, plenty of other frustrations developed but that came about later.

BURNS, Moderator: Those early waiting years for the APB would seem to have been the happy ones. In the last years of the APB, (to Horngren) what was your authority and responsibility and that of the Board's?

HORNGREN: I joined the Board on January 1, 1968, just after Opinion No. 11 on the interperiod allocation of income taxes and Opinion No. 12, an omnibus opinion, were issued. So I joined a going concern whose authorities and responsibilities had largely crystallized. The role of the Board was most clearly to quench fires as they arose and to keep ahead of Jimmy Ling and other clever corporate entrepreneurs who were coming up with some imaginative accounting maneuvers. The greatest responsibility of the Board seemed to be to try to maintain the credibility of accounting reports. There were very close relationships with the SEC and other government agencies with respect to agenda priorities and other things of that sort.

The Board was down to 18 people at that time and the division of labor was handled through committees. As far as being orderly and thoughtful concerning the way we did our work, the general plan, which was adhered to for the most part (with some exceptions), was to have a research study commissioned. When the commissioned research study was published, comments were welcomed. The comments were evaluated and the research study, of course, was evaluated by the members of the Board.

If the Board thought an opinion should be issued, a committee was formed. A committee would vary in size, but typically it was from four to six people. They would evaluate all this input; then they would formulate a questionnaire on various aspects of the topic. After the Board members were polled for their reactions to the questionnaire, the committee would formulate an outline on the pros and cons of the issues involved. After the outline was formed, the entire Board would discuss it. The whole procedure was very orderly. While the outline was being drafted, we started to invite industry participation in our deliberations. We would also communicate with key committees of various groups, most notably the FEI but also committees of other groups. In our later years, we would hold public hearings; so there was a very elaborate procedure for getting input. Afterwards, an exposure draft was prepared. In order to expose the draft, we needed a two-thirds vote. We would get additional reactions and keep working out an opinion, tailoring it to reflect what we felt were justifiable objections or suggestions. Finally the opinion document would be forthcoming from this 18-man-elephant of a Board.

So far as my personal feelings were concerned, I remember when I was appointed to the Board, I got a congratulatory letter from Reed Storey, then Director of Research; he said in the letter you will find the experience educational and frustrating. I think that was a very good prediction. While I found it very educational, it was frustrating at times because of the nature of the task. It was a very complicated job. When there are many decision-makers trying to reach a consensus, there is bound to be cause for some frustrations.

However, there was a sense of accomplishment, too. If you look at the Board's output over the 14 years, and where accounting was then versus where it is now, undoubtedly progress was made. Not, of course, nearly the progress that was foreseen when the Board was originated. Then we had these expectations which now we understand were incredibly naive. Nowadays, our expectations just have to be much less both in terms of the output of the Board and also in terms of grandiose schemes for accounting research. The nature of accounting research is such that massive efforts such as the one that was originally launched are not going to bring forth light where there is darkness. This is not the era of accounting miracles. It is not in the nature of the accounting world nor in the nature of accounting researchers.

Frequency of APB Meetings:

BURNS, Moderator: How often did the Board meet?

HORNGREN: Board meetings typically would be three days long and the subcommittees would meet for a couple of days in between the regular Board meetings. From 1968 on, the regular Board meeting was being held roughly eight or ten times a year.

BURNS, Moderator: I gather in the early years of the Board, it didn't meet as often.

MILLER: Quarterly, and at the most, they were two-day meetings.

Board Efforts to Establish General Principles:

LORETTA, Moderator: Why was the Board unable to adhere to its charge in its early years, namely, to establish a statement on the postulates of accounting, or a fairly broad set of coordinated accounting principles?

MILLER: Many forces were at work that led to this inability. I concur that to some extent the plan in retrospect seems naive. But I do remember one time cautioning Alvin Jennings that he and the profession were placing too much hope on research as a way to enlightenment.

In the area of postulates, the accounting research study on postulates was excellent. I don't know of anyone who could have done a better job than Maurice Moonitz. I was a member of one of the project advisory committees for the postulates and principles studies. This gave me an opportunity to review each of the several drafts that developed. As I recall, Maurice wasn't so sure himself about how self-evident these postulates should be. You can go down to the grass roots to where the assertions stated are self-evident almost to the point where they are so obvious that you can't see any relevance to them. In his early drafts, Maurice Moonitz went down on the scale to almost saying that in the beginning there was Adam and Eve. He didn't go that far, of course, but they were very obvious statements. So then in subsequent drafts he became less basic. Even so, on balance practitioners tended to view this document with a kind of "so what" attitude. By implication they were asking "What do I know now that I didn't know before?" and "How will this statement of postulates help me?" They couldn't really see that this document would help them with their problems. It was received and accepted with thanks, and that was that. If this was the kind of document that research was going to produce, there was some early apprehension that perhaps the Board members were going to be disillusioned.

Although the APB did not feel that ARS No. 1 was of poor quality, some of the Board members did wonder why the special committee wanted to start with postulates because they couldn't see how they would be of help.

The Board reaction to Accounting Research Study No. 3 on principles was quite different. The reaction was about things that it considered as substantive and had many implications. The principles that Sprouse and Moonitz derived had perceivable consequences that were disturbing. Since the positions taken by Sprouse and Moonitz were not traditional in some areas, many APB members worried because these positions weren't generally accepted. The Board had in mind something more like that which eventually came out in APB Statement No. 4. They probably had never envisioned anything as detailed as APB Statement No. 4 since they were still hoping there were some broad principles that with the help of professional judgment could be applied in such a way that good financial reporting would result and the profession would not be straight-jacketed with a lot of detailed rules. I felt that a detailed set of principles was not the way to go then and I continue to think that way now.

ARS No. 3 mentioned such ideas as appraisals, replacement costs, and holding gains. If this study were adopted, Board members felt that financial reporting would be losing some objectivity. Some of the content of this study was unfamiliar and had an aura of newness; the Board had been expecting something quite traditional which it could feel very comfortable with, accept and build on. But ARS No. 3 gave the Board no familiar foundation or traditional structure on which to build its subsequent opinions. Meanwhile since the financial reporting problems had stacked up, the APB quite naturally and understandably fell back into the "putting out fires" posture or the old style plan of operation used by the CAP. Afterwards the pressures got so great on so many problems, such as leasing, income taxes, mergers, and poolings, that the Board never really had a good chance again to implement the charter directive.

LORETTA, Moderator: Do you feel APB Statement No. 4 fulfilled the APB charter requirement for a set of principles?

HORNGREN: First, we should not only characterize the Board as merely quenching brush fires as they arose because we have not described all its activities. After all, it did turn out fundamental research in APB Statements Nos. 3 and 4. The former was on general price level adjustments and the other one, admittedly, was an inventory of generally accepted accounting principles as they are perceived and practiced today. The latter was a description of practice but it was responsive to the charter. To that extent at least the Board did issue official documents.

These statements reflect the many hours put in discussing those statements. Each statement received just as much discussion as any opinion did. In fact, APB Statement No. 4 sopped up many days of discussion on the part of the Board members. Even if they were not considering the fundamental accounting principles that many professors would like to see codified by 1984, the Board felt that this at least was the first step. If we are going to depart from historical cost, we will at least depart from the APB Statement No. 4 rather than just nothing.

MILLER: Why was it necessary to use the category of a statement rather than an opinion? The charter envisioned that basic principles were so fundamental and important that they were to have the most authoritative status. Yet a statement has a second-class status.

HORNGREN: That is correct. But I, as a Board member, viewed the statement as a transitional document, really as a semi-official opinion.

To answer your question point blank, the reason it was not brought out as an opinion rather than a statement is that there was no hope of getting sufficient votes for an opinion. But you can get 12 votes for a statement easier than you can for an opinion.

After Investment Credit, Approach Changes from Persuasion to Compulsion:

MILLER: But conceivably a statement can do as much good or harm as an opinion.

HORNGREN: Yes, except that earlier we talked about persuasion versus authoritarianism in regard to authoritative support. In the late 60's opinions had achieved through the AICPA Council the stamp of authority. You must abide by them or depart from them at your peril. But the statements are recommendations and they had about as much impact as a feather on a lagoon. When APB Statement No. 3 was published, there were three publicly-held companies in the United States who were printing price-level adjusted statements; now, there is only one.

BURNS, Moderator: You reminded us that the charter provision stated that the purpose was to be accomplished by persuasion. Yet, by the later years of the Board, purposes were accomplished on a compulsory basis. How would you comment on this change from persuasion to compulsion?

MILLER: It was the investment credit episode that stimulated that change. The investment credit was an important turning point that got the Board from a simple world of never being recognized in The Wall Street Journal into one where the Board became highly visible. The investment credit was the first major opinion. For it, the Board really ran out of time so that the exposure process was very abbreviated. Even the high quality research input from Perry Mason and Maurice Moonitz was limited.

I had the feeling at the time, shared by some of my associates on the Board, that a Board that was created to narrow the areas of difference must not end up with an opinion that would hold that there were two or more permissible ways. In short there was a very strong feeling that the Board ought to come out with one solution. And it did. But when the reactions came in from APB Opinion No. 2 it was clear that some major firms and the SEC would not support the opinion.

The Board felt that the rug had been pulled out from under it so before it would engage in any more thoughtful discussion and heated debate it desired to have assurances that what it said would be followed. Otherwise the Board members would lose interest in the whole exercise. This kind of feeling swept through the Board when the second opinion was undermined. The individual members of the profession were very reluctant to ever give the APB any status which would take away from the individual practitioner his right to exercise his own judgment. But the reaction within the Board to the undermining of the second opinion was strong and generated a feeling that without some kind of authoritative status there was little use in all of the effort expended to reach an opinion. I believe that this change in attitude by the Board members accounts for the switchover of policy by the accounting profession.

The Formal Research Study Approach:

LORETTA, Moderator: Why did the Board seem to abandon the formal research study approach? Also, what was the general significance of research in the Board's deliberations?

HORNGREN: In later years, there weren't as many research studies being commissioned as in earlier years. That was partially attributable to the fact that the output of studies had slowed down considerably. The first three or four studies came out in a reasonable length of time, and then it seemed to take forever to get a study out. We continued to commission those studies, but they weren't coming out of the pipeline. If you look at the agenda of research-in-process, the inventory was staggering. So we didn't abandon the idea of the research studies; the output was not forthcoming in time in some cases.

In other instances, however, every research study that was published, at least if my memory serves correctly, was discussed and was the first thing considered when an opinion was about to be launched. Of course, the extractive industries opinion never did make it. But certainly the Board gave it a good try. It delayed until the research study came out. The "research study would be ready six months from now." That kind of talk apparently went on for four or five years before the study finally came. When it did, the Board went to work and started to grind out an opinion on the subject.

So the research studies were regarded as important. They were still being commissioned at the end. When they came out, they were the first basis for deliberation and did serve as a starting point. There was a lot of respect for the research that was available. Sometimes you couldn't wait for two or three years on a topic that was so important that something ought to be done immediately.

One that comes to mind, of course, is APB Opinion No. 15 on earnings per share. There wasn't much research on convertible securities and all the "funny money" securities that were issued in the 60's. Even financial analysts couldn't understand annual reports. I remember a Professor of Finance who looked at a Ling Temspo's new security registration statement; he couldn't understand what kind of security it was. So I don't think research would have helped very much. As a result, APB Opinion No. 15 is arbitrary and not very defensible from a scholarly point of view but it was a response to a need that was perceived by the Board and the SEC.

Research played a very important role as a starting point in the Board's deliberations. For example, the Board discussion of the Wyatt study on business combinations and the Catlett and Olson study on goodwill would have been very respectable in any doctoral seminar in any institution in the world. Yet you may say when you look at the opinions, where did research influence them? But there is so much more to getting out an opinion than just getting out research studies!

BURNS, Moderator: Did the Board continue to commission research studies in the last years of its life, in 1971, 1972, and 1973?

HORNGREN: As I recall, in 1972 and 1973 we didn't commission any research studies. Yet in 1971, the Board had commissioned a research study on accounting valuations and income determination. Near the end, the Board was also still considering commissioning another Sprouse and Moonitz type of research study as a follow-up for APB Statement No. 4.

MILLER: Remember that I wasn't on the Board after the first few research studies were completed. My limited experience was that they were very thoughtfully received and very seriously considered. That the APB didn't agree always with the researcher is something any of us would expect to happen.

BURNS, Moderator: Are there detailed minutes of these meetings of the APB when they were deliberating on these research studies?

HORNGREN: The minutes which are public documents that are available from the AICPA office, did summarize the deliberations. Moreover, many large public accounting firms that were represented on the Board took their own minutes which must be available at least to the members of the firm. I don't know whether they would be available to those outside the firm. Also all letters of comment that were received on all exposure drafts are also public documents, unless the writer specifically requested that his document be considered confidential (that was exceptional).

Relationship Between SEC and APB Changed:

BURNS, Moderator: What was the relationship of the Board to the SEC in the early years of the Board?

MILLER: It wasn't as active a relationship as I gather prevailed in the latter years of the APB. There was general recognition that you will have a much better chance of having a successful opinion if the SEC supports it. But I don't recall that at any time the SEC ever treated the APB in any way that would be less than a full or equal partner. I never felt then that the SEC was quarterbacking the APB. I had no such impressions. We really hadn't developed much of an exposure process then either. Back in the CAP days, drafts were exposed with hardly any reactions. It was just an exercise in courtesy with Carman Blough serving as an evaluator of the few comments that came in.

This was also the experience in the early days of the APB as well. I think the relationship between the SEC and the APB was a healthy and helpful one. At that time, I can recall no serious problems. After APB Opinion No. 2 was issued and the SEC announced that it would accept an alternative view, there was a change in the relationship.

BURNS, Moderator: I believe that Carman Blough was the SEC chief accountant before he went with the AICPA. Didn't his experience create a special kind of relationship between the APB and the SEC in those early days?

MILLER: Well, that is true. It was also a fact that the chairman of the CAP for many years was William Wertz who had also been the SEC chief accountant. So the relationship between the Institute's activities in the accounting principles area and the SEC was naturally close. However, there was no formal arrangement to my knowledge. As I recall, Carman Blough, as the first chief accountant, had on his staff every chief accountant that the SEC had until John Burton. Consequently there was a special relationship between Blough and the SEC chief accountant. We never had any hesitation in approaching the SEC or exchanging views with the chief accountant.

BURNS, Moderator: What about the Board's relationship with the SEC in the latter years of the Board?

HORNGREN: As I mentioned earlier, the Board membership was an educational experience for me. As each year went by from 1968 through 1973, I became increasingly convinced that my initial impression that the APB was the supreme authority in regulating the public accounting profession on accounting principles was incorrect. I had believed that it was really a private sector arrangement; I had read such publicity in the Journal of Accountancy, and it was what most accountants seemed to prefer to believe. But as we hammered out various opinions I saw the interaction, even if always an informal one, between the SEC and the APB. I became increasingly convinced that the APB was a subordinate to the SEC. Now I don't mean subordinate in the sense that it was the janitor in a factory run by some despotic plant manager. I don't mean that at all.

I mean a highly decentralized operation where the SEC had veto power. The record does show that the SEC has interfered and that they do have veto power. When the SEC suggests that the Board had better do something quickly about lessors because if the Board doesn't the SEC is going to do something, the Board does something quickly even if it has to realign its priorities. Quite often the Board's priorities were realigned on what the SEC felt was important. Now I stress decentralization here; there was relative freedom to make decisions and there was mutual respect for each body--but to pretend that the APB acted as an almost independent body is false. In reality there was an informal decentralized organization here developing accounting principles. Under this new arrangement with the FASB, they are continuing that arrangement. But there was no question about it that the SEC had quite a bit to say, if indirectly, about how the APB operated.

MILLER: Wouldn't you say that this relationship which is continuing and which you described so clearly could change only if the SEC assumed an even more responsible role?

HORNGREN: I wholeheartedly agree with that. The APB and the FASB really serve at the pleasure of agencies such as the SEC.

MILLER: Yet, in the early stages of the APB, I don't think that I felt that the APB was existing at the pleasure of the SEC. This was something that has evolved during the history of the APB.

HORNGREN: This is my perception. It is not a unanimous perception of the 18 members of the APB. Some of what I have just said might be quite violently disagreed with by some of my APB compatriots.

Let me add a footnote about how the Board operated in the five and one-half years that I was on it. I could not believe how well the Board members got along personally. Personalities played a very minimal role. You would fight in the morning and enjoy lunch together. I miss that now. It was a wonderful group who really tried to do a careful job under rather difficult circumstances.

Allegation that APB Members Represented the Positions of Their Clients:

BURNS, Moderator: Would you comment on the allegation that the APB members represented the positions of their clients.

MILLER: When I was on the APB, I was not affiliated with an accounting firm. I don't really know any way that I would have been aware of it for sure if indeed any such relationship of undue pressure by clients on the APB members did in fact exist. I had no impression that the clients had any such relationship. Maybe I wasn't perceptive but I didn't perceive it.

HORNGREN: There is a difference between form and substance here. That question was raised about the APB repeatedly throughout its existence particularly before it started turning out many opinions each year. But it was the perception that was important and this perception is a major reason why the APB died. The situation is perceived as these Board members are beholden to their clients and are, therefore, *ipso facto* not independent. If the public believes this, regardless whether it is true or not, something must be changed. In substance it never bothered me in the least. I did not think it was a major factor. I am sure that in the 31 Opinions, clients got their views through to the members of public accounting firms who were voting. But consider how they got through, not through a threatening phone call, but through a formulation of a point of view on the part of a technical partner who served on the Board. Who do technical partners in firms talk to throughout their careers? By and large they talk to their fellow partners and they talk to clients and they get a general philosophy and attitude regarding accounting principles through those conversations. Who do professors talk to through their lives? Most of the time they talk to fellow professors and students; the result is that the academician therefore has a different point of view. But if you talk to clients and partners for 20 to 30 years, your point of view is going to be influenced in the aggregate by those conversations and by those experiences. And so to that extent, these Board members were not independent. But, there are so many clients being served by the same firm that if it is a spokesman for one client's point of view it might lose two other clients who are on the other side of the question. So I have always viewed that as a phony issue in substance, although it is a very important point in perception.

The FEI Opposed the Board:

BURNS, Moderator: Can you think of any other political institution besides the SEC and management that may have impinged on the Board?

HORNGREN: The FEI as an institutional body representing management, by and large, was opposed to the Board, particularly in the latter years, on almost every issue. I hesitate here because I may be exaggerating, but the FEI seemed in favor of scrapping the APB; to the extent that it could be an institutional force it helped in its termination. They felt, and you can accept their point of view or reject it depending on how you size it up, that they should have more of a direct voice in the formation of accounting principles.

The Media and the U.S. Congress:

BURNS, Moderator: What about any impact of the media on the Board during your term on it?

HORNGREN: I don't recall the media per se having any impact on the Board. There was nothing like the input on the Board that the financial executives, the SEC, and the representatives of the investment banking industry had. But the Board had become most conscious that the media spotlight was on what they were doing and so to that extent they felt most sensitive to public reaction. Beyond that, I don't think there was an influence.

MILLER: While I wasn't on the Board at the time I have the impression that toward the latter stages of the Board's life that you occasionally heard from senators and representatives. Is that another myth?

HORNGREN: It is well documented that we heard from senators on the investment tax credit fiasco. In the investment tax credit situation of 1971, there was clearly a political hammering out of accounting principles. Both the SEC and the APB were united there; they went down in flames together.

MILLER: Now we have precedent, and I am apprehensive that might be easy to revive in the future even under the FASB. If any accounting issue gets sufficiently sensitive, it is very likely that the political repercussions may come much more rapidly or more readily than in the past.

HORNGREN: We can expect that. When we were worrying about leases, we got a flurry of letters from Congressmen on leases. A letter from the Secretary of Transportation was received indicating we were going to destroy American industry and transportation because the Board was going to capitalize leases on the balance sheet. In a democratic society, there must be acceptability in order to establish an accounting principle. We must learn to contend with it. I hope the FASB is able to cope with this.

When you use the term "political influence," it has evil connotations; yet in a democratic country, all regulatory agencies, private or public, are subject to inquiries and suggestions from Congressmen to managers to the investing public and any other segment of society. This is so for the SEC and the CASB too. I don't think that that is bad. The important thing is how all regulatory agencies are equipped to deal with these political influences.

Consensus Approach in Writing Opinions:

LORETTA, Moderator: Would you detail the process by which the Board issued an opinion when you were a member and also possibly explain why so many opinions were criticized on the grounds that they lacked coherence and logic.

MILLER: In the first few years of the APB, it was pretty informal. First drafts were generally written by Maurice Moonitz or Perry Mason, more than likely it was Perry Mason during the period Maurice Moonitz was busy with ARS Nos. 1 and 3. The Board members would also get into the drafting. They would change sentences and even words as necessary to resolve arguments and secure the required majority vote. When you get this kind of deliberative democratic process going on in preparing a document, it's awfully hard to have it earn an A grade for excellence in writing. That is just not possible.

This was the same approach used in preparing bulletins for the CAP. Everybody got into the act of drafting. We would sit there all day writing and rewriting. Somebody would ask: "How does this wording sound?" Somebody might respond with an encouraging comment. Somebody else would say "Well, I would change it to read as follows . . . how about that?" Then we would drop that point. Later somebody would get to worrying about it so we would return to the point and change the wording again. Under this method of drafting the final product often lacked a uniform style. The APB was not supposed to get involved in drafting pronouncements as the CAP had because a staff had been provided. Even so the APB did engage in similar "joint" drafting in its early years. Even in the latter days of the APB, I suspect members were writing and drafting even though they had the research director, Reed Storey, an excellent writer, doing much of the initial drafting for the Board. It seems to be inevitable that in committee pronouncements excellent writing does not emerge.

HORNGREN: I would reinforce these comments on writing opinions. The opinions of both the APB and probably the FASB are never going to read like Ernest Hemingway novels. They are the product of consensus and the description given as to how the final draft is formed is a very accurate one. You sit there and you go down line by line and see if everybody approved and if not, let us put in this phrase. The chairman is working to get twelve votes for approval; once he gets them, he isn't going to do any substantial editing. At that point, when he gets the votes, it is beyond editorial improvement except in the most minor fashion. One reason why research was not produced, to the extent that many wanted in the latter years, is that Reed Storey, who was Director of Research, was drafting opinions for the Board. He would draft many of the first drafts and the second drafts. Since Reed is a very good writer, it hung together very well. For example, if you look at the first part of APB Opinion No. 16, you will find some very good writing describing the overall problem. He did some very good writing for the Board, but it was mangled in the latter stages of drafting opinions.

The Lasting Accomplishments of the APB:

BURNS, Moderator: In your opinion what will be the lasting accomplishments of the APB?

MILLER: It is difficult to competently respond to that question. Yet, I do not want to duck the question.

In the aggregate the APB served a very useful function of accommodating to changing conditions in financial reporting. Among these changes were a much greater public awareness of financial reporting problems and considerably more influence being exerted by the regulatory agencies. Without the APB, the credibility that has been lost in financial reporting would have been much more extensive. The APB's lasting accomplishments should not be judged in terms of a particular opinion or a particular statement as such, or whether useful contributions to the literature and appropriate guidelines were produced. I don't believe that trying to decide now whether the APB's output will have a lasting influence is of greatest relevance. However, I don't intend for my attitude to imply that the APB activity was a waste of time. After all, some power remains over financial reporting standards in the private sector in 1974, so the APB deserves some credit.

HORNGREN: Again I agree. On the matters of this complexity, I don't think we should have great expectations for such organizations. Inherent complexity and great expectations are mutually contradictory terms. But progress has been made considering the constraints that the Board worked under.

However, speaking as an accounting professor, APB opinions did result in definite improvements in accounting. For example, APB Opinion No. 21, interest on receivables and payables, is a definite accomplishment, because it emphasizes present value concepts that were not in the AICPA authoritative literature previously.

The fund statement, Opinion No. 19, the statement of all changes in financial position, represented progress even though practitioners with small clients may not agree. APB Opinion No. 18, valuing investments on the equity method, was an improvement. The extinguishment of debt opinion, which aroused a lot of controversy on the Board, was certainly an example of narrowing the number of acceptable accounting alternatives. Given generally accepted accounting principles as they exist, that opinion represented an improvement. The general theory that is stated in the nonmonetary items opinion is also a progressive step. Also, APB Statements Nos. 3 and 4 were definite contributions to the literature.

While on the Board, my greatest frustration personally was the opinion on business combinations. APB opinion No. 16, to which I dissented, was not an improvement.

Predicting the Future of the FASB:

LORETTA, Moderator: Recognizing that many have predicted that the FASB will not be able to complete its mission any more successfully than the APB fulfilled its objectives, what is your prediction and why?

MILLER: It is too soon to make a prediction. I have thought a lot about it. There is no reason to believe that they are going to have a bed of roses but then there is nothing to indicate that the FASB is going to go under within 18 months or six years. One reason for believing this is that I'm not sure if anybody else wants to take it over.

The initial support accorded the FASB is so extensive that there will have to be major and widespread dissatisfaction with its efforts before its existence will be in jeopardy. Many believe that the FASB, while perhaps not the ultimate organizational rule-making structure for the private sector, is rather close to the final design for such input. I wouldn't know what else one could do in the organizational design area. Of course, small refinements to any plan can be expected to occur. But I can think of no obviously better plan than that embodied in the FASB. There are enough accountants and others that want to keep this input from the private sector functioning so that the FASB is going to have to make many more mistakes than the APB made, before the FASB will be terminated.

HORNGREN: That question, to predict the future of the FASB, has been asked me on and off for the last few months, and my stock answer is: it depends.

There are no feasible alternatives. Either this FASB plan works or the private sector is shut out of rule-making either entirely or almost entirely. Before this time, there were always thoughts of how are we going to realign the APB in some way or another, but those thoughts were confined to keeping authority within the private sector. Now it is either private sector or public sector. When you talk about it in those general terms, everybody says, of course, it's got to be under private sector. Yet when a specific issue comes up that is really controversial, we will readily see how much support that the FASB gets.

In the aggregate sense, every accountant is for the FASB, but when the FASB is going to impinge on the way he does accounting in his firm, that's a different story. Then he is going to write to his congressman and straighten him out. Well, if that develops, the outlook is truly gloomy.

But I am optimistic for a few years because I think everybody will go along even though some of the opinions are viewed by many people as perhaps not as good as they should be. The FASB will have a life at least as long as the APB. Who can predict beyond that, with so many changing forces in our democracy and in the world of accounting?

BIBLIOGRAPHY

CHARLES T. HORNGREN:

Books and Monograph:

(Editor with S. Davidson, D. Green, and G. Sorter), Readings in Accounting Theory, Prentice-Hall, 1964.

(With J. Demski, G. Feltham, R. Jaedicke, and R. Sprouse), Cost Concepts and Implementation Criteria--An Interim Report, AICPA, 1969.

Cost Accounting: A Managerial Emphasis, Prentice-Hall, Inc., 3rd Edition, 1972.

(Editor with J. A. Leer), CPA Problems and Approaches to Solution, two volumes, Prentice-Hall, Inc., 4th Edition, 1974.

Accounting for Management Control: An Introduction, Prentice-Hall, Inc., 3rd Edition, 1974.

Articles (Selected):

"The Funds Statement and its Uses by Analysts," The Journal of Accountancy, January, 1955.

"Security Analysis and the Price Level," The Accounting Review, October, 1955.

"Stock Dividends and the Entity Theory," The Accounting Review, July, 1957.

"Flow of Funds, Depreciation, and the Price Level, Analysts Journal, August, 1957.

"Disclosure: 1957," The Accounting Review, October, 1957.

"Disclosure: What Next?," The Accounting Review, January, 1958.

"Increasing the Utility of Financial Statements," The Journal of Accountancy, July, 1969.

(With G. Sorter), "Direct Costing and External Reporting," The Accounting Review, January, 1961.

(With G. Sorter), "Asset Recognition and Economic Attributes--The Relevant Costing Approach," The Accounting Review, July, 1962.

"Choosing Accounting Practices for Reporting to Management," N.A.A. Bulletin, September, 1962.

(With G. Sorter), "An Evaluation of Some Criticisms of Relevant Costing," The Accounting Review, April, 1964.

"A Discussion of Inventory Measurement," The Accounting Review, July, 1964.

(With N. Churchill and P. Firmin), "Common Body of Knowledge for CPA's," Journal of Accountancy, December, 1964.

"How Should We Interpret the Realization Concept?," The Accounting Review, April, 1964.

"Reliability and Accounting Measurements," Research in Accounting Measurement, Y. Ijiri, R. Jaedicke, and O. Nielson, editors, AAA, 1966.

"Analysis of the Utilization of Capacity: A Contribution to Margin Approach," The Accounting Review, April, 1967.

"Motivation, Coordination, and Management Control Systems," Management Accounting, June, 1967.

"Capacity Utilization and the Effect of Variance," The Accounting Review, January, 1969.

"Effects of Managerial Decision Models on Accounting," The Journal of Accounting, June, 1969.

"Accounting Discipline in 1999," The Accounting Review, January, 1971.

"What is Next for Accounting Principles?," Financial Executive, February, 1971.

"Useful Numbers and Historical Costs," A Symposium on Historical Costs, B. Zaidi, editor, Sacramento State College, 1971.

"Accounting Principles: Private or Public Sector?," <u>The Journal of Accountancy</u>, May, 1972.

"Accounting Objectives Need Cost-Benefit Analysis," published by Ernst & Ernst, September, 1972.

"Marketing of Accounting Standards," <u>The Journal of Accountancy</u>, October, 1973. Also published in <u>Institutional Issues in Public Accounting</u>, R. R. Sterling, editor, Scholars Book Co., 1971.

HERBERT E. MILLER:

Books:

(With H. A. Finney), <u>Principles of Accounting, Introductory</u>, 1953, 1957, & 1963 editions; Also <u>Intermediate</u>, 1951, 1958, & 1965 editions; Also <u>Advanced</u>, 1952 & 1960 editions; <u>Principles of Financial Accounting</u>, 1968; <u>The Accounting Process</u>, 1963 & 1971 editions; Prentice-Hall, Inc.

(Editor and Contributor), <u>CPA Review Manual</u>, Prentice-Hall, Inc., 4th edition, 1972.

Articles (Selected):

"Accounting Statements for Publication," <u>The Accounting Review</u>, July, 1942.

"Reserves for War Contingencies and Post-War Adjustments," <u>The Accounting Review</u>, July, 1944.

"Surplus Reviews," <u>The Accounting Review</u>, April, 1947.

"Quasi-Reorganization in Reverse," <u>The Accounting Review</u>, April, 1948.

"The 1948 Revision of the American Accounting Association's Statement of Principles," <u>The Accounting Review</u>, January, 1949.

"After There is Agreement on Broad Accounting Principles--What Then?," <u>The Texas Certified Public Accountant</u>, September, 1961.

"How Much Income Tax Allocation?," <u>The Journal of Accountancy</u>, August, 1962.

"Interpreting the Basic Accounting Postulates," The Ohio CPA, Spring, 1963.

"Audited Statements--Are They Really Management's?," The Journal of Accountancy, October, 1964.

"The Environment of the Accounting Profession," The Journal of Accountancy, January, 1966.

"Accounting Principles--The Academician's Viewpoint," Accounting Papers of the Twenty-Sixth Annual Conference of Accountants, The University of Tulsa, April, 1972.

"Collectivization of Judgment," The Arthur Andersen Chronicle, No. 1, 1974.

GENERAL BIBLIOGRAPHY (SELECTED)

Gerboth, Dale L., "Middling Through with the A.P.B.," The Journal of Accountancy, May, 1972, pp. 42-49.

_______________, "Research Intuition and Politics in Accounting Inquiry," The Accounting Review, July, 1973, pp. 475-482.

Moonitz, Maurice, "Some Reflections on the Investment Credit Experience," Journal of Accounting Research, Spring, 1966, pp. 47-61.

Rodney, Earl, "The Accounting Beehive," Financial Executive, July, 1973, pp. 36-37.

Savoie, Leonard M., "Accounting Attitudes," Financial Executive, October, 1973, pp. 74-84.

Seidler, Lee J., "The Accounting Principles Board in 1971: Private Men in a Public World," The Accountant's Magazine, April, 1972, p. 170.

Sterling, Robert R., "Accounting Power," Distinguished Lecture Series, Stillwater, Oklahoma: Oklahoma State University. Excerpts reprinted in Journal of Accountancy, January, 1973, pp. 61-67.

Trueblood, Robert M., "Ten Years of the APB: One Practitioner's Appraisal," privately printed, 1969.

APPENDIX A TO SECTION II

APB OPINIONS AND STATEMENTS

During the period 1962-1973, the APB issued thirty-one Opinions and four Statements.

Opinions

No.	*Title*	*Publication Date*
1	*New Depreciation Guidelines and Rules*	*1962*
2	*Accounting for the "Investment Credit"*	*1962*
3	*The Statement of Source and Application of Funds (Superseded by No. 19)*	*1963*
4	*Accounting for the "Investment Credit" (Amending No. 2)*	*1964*
5	*Reporting of Leases in Financial Statements of Lessee*	*1964*
6	*Status of Accounting Research Bulletins*	*1965*
7	*Accounting for Leases in Financial Statements of Lessors*	*1966*
8	*Accounting for the Cost of Pension Plans*	*1966*
9	*Reporting the Results of Operations*	*1966*
10	*Omnibus Opinion - 1966*	*1966*
11	*Accounting for Income Taxes*	*1967*
12	*Omnibus Opinion - 1967*	*1967*
13	*Amending Paragraph 6 of APB Opinion No. 9, Application to Commercial Banks*	*1969*
14	*Accounting for Convertible Debt and Debt Issued with Stock Purchase Warrants*	*1969*
15	*Earnings Per Share*	*1969*
16	*Business Combinations*	*1970*
17	*Intangible Assets*	*1970*
18	*The Equity Method of Accounting for Investments in Common Stock*	*1971*
19	*Reporting Changes in Financial Position*	*1971*
20	*Accounting Changes*	*1971*
21	*Interest on Receivables and Payables*	*1971*
22	*Disclosure of Accounting Policy*	*1972*
23	*Accounting for Income Taxes - Special Areas*	*1972*
24	*Accounting for Income Taxes - Investments in Common Stock Accounted for by the Equity Method*	*1972*
25	*Accounting for Stock Issued to Employees*	*1972*
26	*Early Extinguishment of Debt*	*1972*

(Opinions continued)

No.	Title	Publication Date
27	Accounting for Lease Transactions by Manufacturer or Dealer Lessors	1972
28	Interim Financial Reporting	1973
29	Accounting for Non-monetary Transactions	1973
30	Reporting the Results of Operations--Reporting the Effect of Disposal of Segment of a Business, and Extraordinary, Unusual and Infrequently Occurring Events and Transactions	1973
31	Disclosure of Lease Commitments by Lessees	1973

Statements

No.	Title	Publication Date
1	Statement by The Accounting Principles Board	1962
2	Disclosure of Supplemental Financial Information by Diversified Companies	1967
3	Financial Statements Restated for General Price-Level Changes	1969
4	Basic Concepts and Accounting Principles Underlying Statements of Business Enterprises	1970

APPENDIX B TO SECTION II

SUMMARY OF APB MEMBERSHIP AND OPINION VOTING

Board Member	*Affiliation*	*Opinion Voted On*
Marshall S. Armstrong	*George S. Olive & Co.*	*3-15*
Kenneth S. Axelson	*J. C. Penney Co., Inc.*	*13-17*
Gordon S. Battelle	*Battelle & Battelle*	*1- 2*
Donald J. Bevis	*Touche Ross & Co.*	*6-31*
Herman W. Bevis	*Price Waterhouse & Co.*	*1- 7*
John C. Biegler	*Price Waterhouse & Co.*	*8-12*
William M. Black	*Peat, Marwick, Mitchell & Co.*	*1- 2*
Carman G. Blough	*AICPA*	*1- 5*
Albert J. Bows	*Arthur Andersen & Co.*	*22-31*
Milton M. Broeher	*Broeher Hendrickson & Co.*	*11-31*
Leo E. Burger	*McGladrey, Hansen, Dunn*	*16-31*
Joseph Campbell	*Comptroller General of the U.S.*	*1- 2*
Arthur M. Cannon	*Standard Insurance Co.*	*1- 3*
George R. Catlett	*Arthur Andersen & Co.*	*6-21*
W. A. Crichley	*Diamond Alkali Co.*	*1-12*
Joseph P. Cummings	*Peat, Marwick, Mitchell & Co.*	*8-31*
Sidney Davidson	*University of Chicago*	*6-17*
Philip L. Defliese	*Coopers & Lybrand*	*6-31*
Robert L. Ferst	*Laventhol, Krekstein, Horwath & Horwath*	*18-31*
Walter F. Frese	*Harvard University*	*1-12*
Ira N. Frisbee	*Ira N. Frisbee & Co.*	*1- 5*
Oscar Gellein	*Haskins & Sells*	*22-31*
Newman T. Halvorson	*Ernst & Ernst*	*8-31*
Robert Hampton, III	*S. D. Leidesdorf & Co.*	*16-31*
Emmett S. Harrington	*Haskins & Sells*	*13-21*
Donald J. Hayes	*Arthur Young & Co.*	*22-31*
Clifford V. Heimbucher	*Farquhar & Heimbucher*	*6-12*
Charles B. Hellerson	*Hurdman & Cranstoun, Penny & Co.*	*13-31*
Thomas G. Higgins	*Arthur Young & Co.*	*1- 5*
Charles T. Horngren	*Stanford University*	*13-31*
Alvin R. Jennings	*Coopers & Lybrand*	*1- 5*
Louis M. Kessler	*Alexander Grant & Co.*	*13-15, 18-31*
LeRoy Layton	*Main Lafrentz & Co.*	*3-17*
Oral T. Luper	*Humble Oil Refining Co.*	*5-21*
John K. McClare	*S. D. Leidesdorf & Co.*	*8-12*
John W. McEachren	*Touche Ross & Co.*	*1- 3*
Herbert E. Miller	*Michigan State University*	*1- 2*
Maurice Moonitz	*University of California Berkeley*	*3- 7*

Board Member	*Affiliation*	*Opinion Voted On*
C. A. Moyer	*University of Illinois*	*1- 5*
Robert J. Murphey	*Murphey, Jenne & Jones*	*6-12*
David Norr	*First Manhattan Corp.*	*18-31*
Louis H. Penney	*L. H. Penney & Co.*	*3-12*
John Peoples	*Peat, Marwick, Mitchell & Co.*	*3- 7*
Weldon Powell	*Haskins & Sells*	*1- 2*
John W. Queenan	*Haskins & Sells*	*3-12*
Ira A. Schur	*S. D. Leidesdorf & Co.*	*1- 7*
J. S. Seidman	*Seidman & Seidman*	*13-17*
Leonard Spacek	*Arthur Andersen & Co.*	*1- 5*
Hassel Tippit	*Ernst & Ernst*	*1- 7*
Robert M. Trueblood	*Touche Ross & Co.*	*4- 5*
Wilbert A. Walker	*United States Steel Corp.*	*1-12*
George C. Watt	*Price Waterhouse & Co.*	*13-31*
Allan Wear	*Ford Motor Co.*	*22-29*
Glenn A. Welsch	*University of Texas at Austin*	*18-31*
Frank T. Weston	*Arthur Young & Co.*	*6-21*
Robert T. Witschey	*Witschey, Harman & White*	*4-10*
John H. Zebley, Jr.	*Turner, Crook, Zebley & Parry*	*1- 2*

APPENDIX C TO SECTION II

LETTER TO THE STUDY GROUP ON ESTABLISHMENT OF ACCOUNTING PRINCIPLES*

by

Charles T. Horngren

November 4, 1971

This letter tries to summarize my perception of the present role of the APB, particularly with respect to its power and its relation to the SEC. After serving nearly four years on the Board, I think much of the criticism of the present APB is attributable to at least some misunderstanding of the Board's basic function. This misunderstanding is compounded by the Board's and the SEC's public relations stance; both seem reluctant to admit that they set principles in close concert.

From time to time, I have heard grumbling by various APB members that we do not have to consider the SEC--that we will decide what is right and that is that. But that is wishful thinking, a clinging to the false idea that a private body is determining accounting principles. The SEC has all the ultimate power, and the APB formulates principles subject to whatever constraints the SEC exerts. This point may be obvious to individuals who are well acquainted with APB activities, but it is not at all clear to many others. As a result, the APB has endured some undeserved flak.

In my view, the (informal) organizational relationship is similar to decentralized management in industry:

*Reprinted with permission, Proceedings: Public Hearing on the Study of Establishment of Accounting Principles: Section B-Position Papers. AICPA, 1971, pp. 883-886.

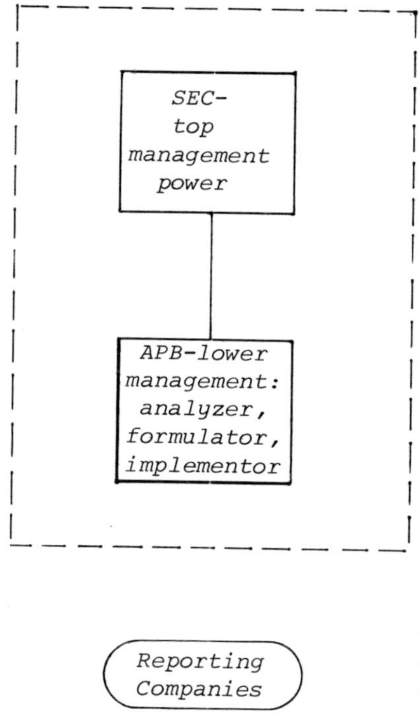

The product of this overall organization is a body of accounting principles or rules that govern financial reporting.

The products of these organizations are financial reports that measure performance and positions.

The dashed line indicates the overall organization. The objective of the organization in this context is (or should be) the "maximization of society's welfare" in the form of optimal financial reporting to investors. That is, principles (you may prefer rules, concepts, or some other amorphous words) must be devised in order to specify how measures of financial performance and position can best serve users.

Top management (the SEC) has all ultimate power to set principles for financial reporting. It has minimal resources and central staff to do the job, so it delegates the duty to front-line management (APB). As in all organizations, decentralization is adopted when top management believes that lower management has more information and capability to make decisions that achieve the overall goals of the organization (in this case, optimal financial reporting to investors). Lower management (APB) is given great freedom to make decisions because it is deemed sufficiently objective and more knowledgeable about the technical aspects of the job. Moreover, lower management works for zero salary and investigates nearly all of the topics chosen by top management. Obviously, lower management is also free to investigate many topics of its own choice.

Of course, as in all decentralized organizations, top management can set overall policies and constraints. It can exert veto power. On certain topics, it may heavily constrain the freedom to make decisions (e.g., the investment credit and, more recently, marketable securities). But top management cannot be too heavy-handed too often. Frequent interference with the freedom to make decisions means that decentralization with its many benefits (for example, the handy buffer against direct pressure by reporting companies on top management) is undermined. Often top management (the SEC) can take the convenient stance that lower management (APB) makes the decisions and that top management merely implements them!

As I see it, the SEC (top management) has used decentralization with a master's touch. Its lower-level management (APB) does an enormous amount of work for no salary and has just enough freedom to want to continue the arrangement. Moreover, it is dominated by practitioners, the individuals responsible for implementing the principles chosen. There is an evident efficiency here, because the work consists of both the formulation of principles and their implementation--an immensely complex task that will not be performed easily under <u>*any*</u> *institutional arrangement.*

The buffer role is clear:

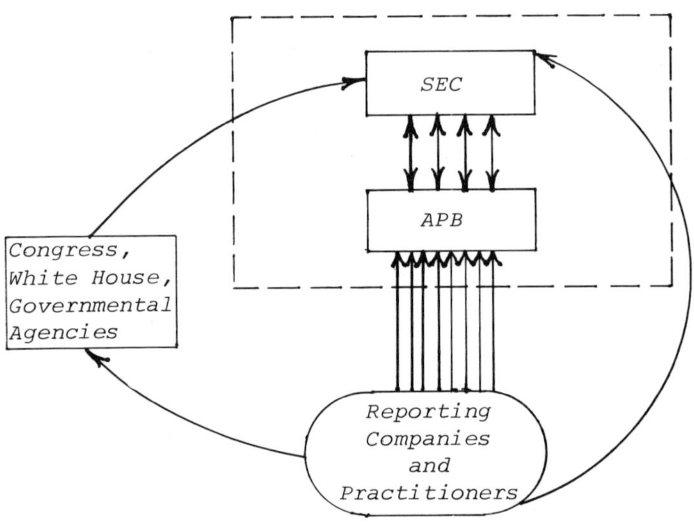

The lines represent the probable relative volume and direction of requests, views, suasion, pressure, etc., among some of the important parties regarding the formulation of accounting principles.

I do not claim that the APB insulates the SEC from all pressures or criticisms; however, the Board has been unjustifiably criticized for timidity or vacillation on several occasions when the basic explanation for the Board's behavior has been no assurance of support from the SEC. How many lower-level managers will proceed on critical issues without obtaining reliable assurance of top management support?

The above description is not flawless. Nevertheless, it is time to dispel the oft-heard myth that a private group is setting the accounting principles which are then enforced by the policing agency, the SEC. The job of devising accounting principles is a joint effort, a private-public institutional arrangement that should be explicitly admitted and publicized forthrightly by both parties along the top-lower management lines described above.

I leave it to others to suggest alternative institutional arrangements for the incredibly difficult task of formulating accounting principles. The focus of this letter is more narrow; it assumes that the SEC will continue to maintain the ultimate power. If so, a modified APB, or some similar successor thereof, necessarily must work as a lower-level management unit with only as much latitude as the SEC permits.

Whatever the form, I hope that business executives do not have any larger direct role in setting accounting principles than they now possess. Their views should be heard fully, but there is an inherent conflict between their role as managers and the task of measuring their own performance. An analogy might be having the baseball batter calling the balls and strikes.

Many business executives have vociferously stated that the APB does not pay sufficient attention to the views of industry. In my opinion, that is just not so. If anything, the Board is swamped by industry views. First, industry has direct representation on the Board. Second, the practitioners who dominate the Board listen carefully to the views of their clients. After all, in their everyday work practitioners talk mostly to business executives and to other practitioners, not to financial analysts and college professors. The opinions of financial executives come through loud and clear--and they are given painstaking consideration. For example, every recent APB Opinion has been changed considerably in response to industry reactions.

Let me stress that I am grateful for having been a member of the Board. Under the current setup, considering its many constraints, I think the APB has performed admirably. Admittedly, I am speculating, but more speed and objectivity might result if there were some full-time group that uses majority rule. This would be a deliberative body that would listen fully to all interested parties before reaching a decision.

I look forward to seeing your group's recommendations.

Sincerely,

Charles T. Horngren

cc: Accounting Principles Board

SECTION III

RESEARCH AND THE APB: THREE EXCERPTS

INTRODUCTION

In this section, the three researchers who did the studies on leases, pensions, and business combinations for the APB are the discussants. Although a formal research study was supposed to be completed before the Board issued an Opinion, this process was not always followed, particularly in the later years of the APB. This is discussed along with other institutional aspects of the Accounting Research Studies. As was typical of the backgrounds of those asked to undertake such research for the Board, the discussants' backgrounds are varied: one is an academician, Professor John H. Myers, now of Indiana University; one is a practitioner, Mr. Ernest L. Hicks, with Arthur Young & Company; and the third, Dr. Arthur R. Wyatt, joined Arthur Andersen & Company after completing his project, having previously been a professor at the University of Illinois. Although their views coincide on many issues, it should be remembered that Mr. Hicks had the most success in having his study recommendations on pensions incorporated into the APB Opinion on this subject, while Professor Myers' study recommendations on leases were only partially accepted in subsequent Board Opinions and Dr. Wyatt's study recommendations on business combinations were not incorporated into APB pronouncements. Supplementing the discussion is a list of the fifteen Accounting Research Studies published during the lifetime of the APB.

-- The Editor

SECTION III

RESEARCH AND THE APB: THREE EXCERPTS

1949	*CAP proposes to compile a comprehensive statement of "generally accepted accounting principles," but later abandons the effort as infeasible.*
1956	*AIA Executive Committee proposes that the CAP prepare a comprehensive statement of basic accounting principles.*
1957-58	*Alvin R. Jennings, incoming AICPA (formerly AIA) President, recommends creation of a research foundation and appoints a Special Committee on Research Program, of which Weldon Powell is Chairman, to formulate a specific recommendation. The Committee's principal concern is the lack of research, understanding, and agreement on the basic postulates and principles underlying accounting practice.*
1959	*Council accepts the comprehensive recommendations of the Special Committee on Research Program, replaces the research department by an accounting research division having an expanded role, and replaces the CAP and the Committee on Terminology by the Accounting Principles Board (APB) . . . .*
1959-60	*Perry Mason is named Acting Director of Accounting Research in November, 1959. On July 1, 1960, Maurice Moonitz becomes Director. (He is succeeded in 1963 by Paul Grady, as Acting Director, and in 1964, by Reed K. Storey, as Director.) During 1960, eight Accounting Research Studies are commissioned.*
1961-62	*AICPA publishes Accounting Research Studies 1 and 3, on postulates and principles, which are rejected by the APB as "too radically different. . .for acceptance at this time."*
1965	*Publication of Paul Grady's <u>Inventory of Generally Accepted Accounting Principles for Business Enterprises</u>, as Accounting Research Study No. 7.*
1966-67	*APB issues Opinions Nos. 8 (pensions), 9 (extraordinary items and earnings per share), and 10 (omnibus), which are endorsed by the NYSE. . . .SEC expresses pleasure with the Board's resolution of several difficult problems.*

1968-70 *Controversy over pooling-of-interests accounting becomes intense as the conglomerate merger movement reaches its zenith, then collapses.*

1969 *AICPA announces a new Unofficial Accounting Interpretations service to clarify the APB's intent on specific questions arising from APB opinions. Each interpretation requires the approval of the Executive Vice President and the APB Chairman.*

1969 *APB issues 60-page Opinion No. 15 on earnings per share, modifying Opinion No. 9. Extensive detail in the Opinion provokes criticism that the Board is trying to impose a "cookbook" on the profession. Institute issues a 189-page guidebook of unofficial interpretations of the Opinion.*

-- Excerpts are from Stephen A. Zeff's "Chronology of Significant Developments in the Establishment of Accounting Principles in the United States, 1926-1972," Journal of Accounting Research (Spring, 1972), pp. 220-227.

THE DISCUSSANTS

Ernest L. Hicks:

Mr. Hicks is a partner in the home office of Arthur Young & Company, at New York, and author of Accounting for the Cost of Pension Plans, Accounting Research Study No. 8. He is the firm's Director of Auditing Standards and is a member of its Accounting and Auditing Standards Committee. Mr. Hicks is Chairman of the Auditing Standards Executive Committee of the AICPA and has been a member of the Institute's Committee on Relations with the SEC. He has previously been Chairman of the Committee on Accounting and Auditing Procedure of the New York State Society of CPA's. He graduated from The Ohio State University in 1939.

John H. Myers:

Professor Myers is the author of Accounting Research Study No. 4, Reporting of Leases in Financial Statements, published in 1962. He is Professor of Accounting and a former chairman of the Accounting Department at Indiana University. From 1945-1968, he was on the Northwestern University faculty, becoming a professor and department chairman. All three of his degrees were earned at Northwestern University. A C.P.A., formerly with Arthur Andersen & Co., he has been a consultant. In 1973-1974, he was the Carman G. Blough Visiting Professor of Commerce at the University of Virginia.

Arthur R. Wyatt:

Dr. Wyatt is the author of Accounting Research Study No. 5, A Critical Study of Accounting for Business Combinations, published in 1963. A partner in Arthur Andersen & Co., he joined the firm in 1966 and currently is a member of the firm's Committee on Accounting Principles and Auditing Procedures. In that capacity, he was closely associated with the projects and deliberations of the Accounting Principles Board, and he is currently a member of the Accounting Standards Executive Committee of the AICPA. His three earned degrees are from the University of Illinois; for fifteen years, he was a member of that university's accounting faculty, becoming a professor in 1960.

THE MODERATORS

Faculty moderator is Associate Professor of Accounting Richard Northrup. A Phi Beta Kappa and graduate of Miami University of Ohio, he was formerly with Haskins and Sells. Student moderator is Delbert Haney, Vice President, Beta Alpha Psi, and President, Beta Gamma Sigma. A summa cum laude graduate in March, 1974, he is now with the Los Angeles office of Arthur Young & Company.

THE DISCUSSION

APB Research and ARS Nos. 4, 5, and 8:

HANEY, Moderator: We are focusing our attention on the Accounting Principles Board (APB) experience with accounting research. Under the APB, the fifteen accounting research studies were the most visual research output. (See the chapter appendix for a listing of these studies.)

In 1939, the AICPA developed a research group to work with its committee on accounting procedure. This group was to prepare background and technical material as a basis for the eventual preparation of accounting research bulletins. Soon the research department, as the group was called, also helped in the drafting of advisory statements on the interpretation of prior bulletins. In 1944, two changes occurred which had an important impact on accounting research. First, the research department began publishing interim research studies. Second, under a newly appointed Director of Research, Carman Blough, the exposure process and publication record for accounting research was much improved.

Despite the improvement in research output brought about by this research group, the AICPA's research effort continued to be criticized. In 1957, this criticism led to the establishment of a special committee charged with improving the Institute's research program and the method of establishing accounting principles. In the Fall of 1958, this committee presented its now historic report. One section of the report proposed that the proposed APB's Opinions be supported by accounting research studies. An additional research staff of approximately ten persons was to be assigned to the APB to conduct this research. It was to consist of a director, up to five senior members, three junior members, and even two secretaries.

Up until 1969 or during the first ten years of the APB, formal research studies were commissioned jointly by the APB chairman and the AICPA's director of accounting research. Although since 1969 only the full Board has authorized any accounting research studies, few were commissioned in the last years of the APB. But the Director of Accounting Research has always appointed the chief researcher and the advisory committee for any study authorized. These advisory committees, largely of professional accountants, were to serve as a means of keeping in touch with the business community and as a sounding board to critically discuss the study. Such an advisory committee also made the final determination as to whether the research study was to be published by the Institute. Dissents by members of the advisory committee from the conclusions of an accounting research study were not uncommon and were published along with the study.

Accounting Research Study No. 4, Reporting of Leases in Financial Statements, was conducted by Professor John H. Myers, then of Northwestern University (and currently of Indiana University). The study was authorized jointly in 1960 by the APB chairman and the interim Director of Accounting Research, Perry Mason. His study was published in May, 1962; the Director of Accounting Research then was Maurice Moonitz. Two opinions on reporting leases in financial statements were released subsequently by the APB. The Myers' study dealt mainly with the subject matter of leases covered in APB Opinion No. 5, which was issued in September, 1964. The APB adopted this opinion by a vote of 20 to 1. The later opinion on leases, No. 7, having been adopted by a unanimous vote, was issued in May, 1966. Two additional opinions on the subject of leases, Nos. 27 and 31, have been released subsequently by the APB. With respect to both the lessor and the lessee to the extent that leases give rise to property rights, Accounting Research Study (ARS) No. 4 recommended that these rights and related liabilities should be booked on the balance sheet. However, while recognizing that some leases were purchases in substance and as such should be recorded on the body of the balance sheet, the APB expressed the view in its Opinion No. 5 executory contracts could be adequately treated in footnotes to the statements.

ARS No. 5, A Critical Study for Business Combinations, was authored by Arthur R. Wyatt, then Professor of Accountancy at the University of Illinois (and now with Arthur Andersen & Co.). The study was authorized in 1960 by the Board Chairman and the Director of Accounting Research, Maurice Moonitz, and was published in June, 1963, under the same Director of Research. Consideration of the subject of business combinations by the APB was delayed until after ARS No. 10 on Goodwill was completed in 1968. In August, 1970, APB Opinion No. 16, which dealt in essence with the subject matter of ARS No. 5, was released along with APB Opinion No. 17 on accounting for intangibles under the then Board Chairman, Leroy Layton. The APB adopted Opinion No. 16 by the minimum margin of 12 to 6 and the Opinion No. 17 by a narrow margin of 13 to 5. Although three methods of accounting for business combinations had been recognized in ARS No. 5, both pooling and fair value pooling were to be used only in specified situations. The principal conclusion of the research study was that virtually all business combinations were in substance purchases. However, while viewing both purchasing and pooling methods as acceptable methods of accounting for business combinations, the Board expressed the view in its Opinion No. 16 that they were not to be considered as alternative treatments for the same combinations. In the same opinion, the Board then went on to set up complex criteria for the use of the pooling method and specified that any combination that did not meet these criteria must be treated as a purchase.

ARS No. 8, Accounting for the Cost of Pension Plans, was authored by Ernest L. Hicks, then and presently a partner in Arthur Young & Company in New York. The study was authorized in 1960 by the Board Chairman and the Director of Accounting Research, Maurice Moonitz. The original work was conducted by the Institute's research staff and later the subject was reassigned to Mr. Hicks by the Acting Director of Research in 1963, Paul Grady. In May, 1965, this study was published under still another Director of Accounting Research, Reed Storey. In November, 1966, APB Opinion No. 8, unanimously adopted by the Board, on the subject matter of ARS No. 8, was issued. It recommended that accounting for pension costs be on an accrual basis, that the actuarial cost methods then in use be considered acceptable, that provision for the normal cost of pension plans be made annually, and that prior service cost with interest be taken into expense systematically over a reasonable period of time after the adoption of a pension plan. Finally, unfunded prior service cost was not ordinarily to be treated as a liability on the employer's balance sheet. Thus, this opinion agreed with certain of the conclusions reached in ARS No. 8; the Opinion narrowed the alternatives in accounting for pensions but still left critics at both ends of the spectrum unsatisfied.

The APB Research Climate:

NORTHRUP, Moderator: What was the general research climate in which your study was conducted?

HICKS: It is interesting to think about these things again after so many years. In order to focus on the question, we have to go back to the environment that existed in about 1963. We weren't that far removed then from 1959, when the APB had been created; it was still an article of faith that research was to underlie the work of the Board. Research was to be the great hope on which the Board's acceptance was to be predicated and on which its future was to be founded. This climate prevailed at least through the time when my study was published. (It may be that you can mark the decline of that philosophy as beginning at that point.) Research was very much the order of the day; and so the climate for doing research was very good. It was believed that such efforts were important and worthwhile. People were willing to spend the time to consider the problems and to contribute to research by being members of the advisory committees. The Board itself was interested in the research that was going on. This was a pleasant climate in which to be involved in that kind of activity. Whether that would be true today, I couldn't promise; but things were pretty good then.

MYERS: It was really very fine. I enjoyed working with the people. They seemed to want the kind of things that I thought were right to do. I would like to work in that kind of environment again.

WYATT: I don't have too much to add, but it is a different observation. My description of the research climate when I did my study was one word, namely--neutral. I would say that the climate was not as satisfying as academic research had been for me and that is the only research experience I had had prior to that time. On the other hand, I would say that the climate was better than it may be at the present time, so I come out with the word, neutral. It was a very satisfying experience, but I don't think that the climate was particularly favorable or unfavorable.

NORTHRUP, Moderator: As mentioned earlier, the AICPA research staff seemed to be a skeleton one. What about the research framework of the Institute or the research staff situation when you undertook your study?

HICKS: Perhaps we should clearly differentiate between the framework and the availability of staff. The framework was quite sound. I think of the framework as covering what studies to undertake and who would do the studies, and who would name the advisory group. The very fact that there was an advisory group was part of the framework. It was a pretty good framework.

Since the research staff was limited in number, the Institute had to go outside of its paid staff to pick people to conduct and prepare the studies. I found that to be quite a delightful condition because if that had not been the case, I wouldn't have been involved in doing the pension study.

WYATT: As far as I am concerned, regarding the framework, the top man at the time that I did my research, Maurice Moonitz, was outstanding. I don't know that I could have done a study under anyone who would have been both more understanding and more challenging. His righthand man, Perry Mason, also was outstanding. The rest of the Institute staff was routine and not particularly helpful. On the other hand, I wasn't burdened with any of them. I selected my own research assistant who did an excellent job for me in most of my research. I had the guidance of two very top people. I think any researcher would like those conditions since these are the best arrangements possible.

MYERS: I agree with Art Wyatt on what he said. I think Moonitz and Mason were very excellent people to work with. They would "beat" me once in a while but they would always listen to me "beef" back at them. Points of view were always respected on both sides.

The Institute staff was available for me to call on. I did call on them for a few things then. You will notice some annual report summaries in the back of my monograph. The staff bird-dogged some of this material for me. The staff members made a lot of contacts for me in New York City, particularly in financial centers. The Advisory Committee was very useful, too; some members, of course, were more useful than others. This committee provided contacts for me; they needled me, "Haven't you spent enough time gathering information?" "Isn't it about time to write?" They were right, too. I also appreciated the fact that they hired outside people such as myself. Later they used people directly from the Institute staff. I thought it was a good framework in which we worked.

May I say one other thing about the framework that hasn't been brought out before? The Advisory Committee sat in judgment over what I was writing. They could agree or disagree with what I suggested, but they had no power to accept or deny publication based upon what I had said; they could deny only if the research was thought to be inadequate. Although there were times when they were disagreeing very strongly with what I said, they still thought it was good research and should be published.

One of my friends who was doing a similar research job was not as fortunate as I; his research was thought to be not adequate for publication, it wasn't published. Of course, he could try to get that piece of research published by anybody else who cared to publish it. This is an example of how these advisory committees voted. They voted not on whether the research answers were acceptable answers, but whether or not the research was of acceptable quality. That, I liked.

Reasons Why ARS Not Completed:

NORTHRUP, Moderator: According to Charles Horngren, one of our previous panelists, some APB research studies were commissioned but not completed. Could you cite reasons for commissioned research studies not being completed?

MYERS: Well, some studies were rejected because of the quality of the research. In some others, the researchers never completed their studies.

WYATT: There was a research study commissioned on accounting for intercorporate investments which was to cover the whole consolidated statements area and the reason it didn't get done was because the individual who was to undertake the research became the Director of Research and got so involved in administrative duties that he didn't have any time to do research. That is why that study was never completed.

HICKS: There was to be one on materiality that hasn't been published. Maybe the reason that one didn't get published was because the problem comes close to being insoluble.

Director of Research and Advisory Groups:

NORTHRUP, Moderator: Did the Director of Research or the advisory committee slow up or speed up the pace of your research; or were you pretty much on your own as far as the pace at which you proceeded?

WYATT: I don't think that either the Director of Research or the advisory group had any significant influence on the speed with which we worked. Probably the advisory group because they didn't agree with my conclusions did slow down publication, possibly as much as six months, which I would consider to be fairly nominal in the framework we had. I thought that Moonitz had a very positive influence. He was an individual who understood both some of the practical ramifications of what the conclusion of my research might do to the business community and the basic concepts on which I thought my conclusions were based. After many hours of discussion over the basic point on which we disagreed, the fact that I viewed the business combination event to be an accounting transaction of substance, he agreed to regard that as a valid starting point even though he might have approached it from a different standpoint.

My experience with my advisory group was mixed. I do not believe they contributed a great deal. I got a lot of help from several accounting firms that were not represented on the advisory group and, in some instances, not very much help from those that were. This explains my mixed feeling in regard to the advisory group.

MYERS: I mentioned previously the goading that my advisory group did to get me on with my work. I appreciated that. Art Wyatt mentioned the tremendous logical ability of Maurice Moonitz and certainly he provided that in my case, too.

I want to mention something else about Mr. Moonitz. I like to pride myself on good writing. I don't know whether others think I write well enough, but I like to think I do. Maurice Moonitz was a good influence with me on that. He helped me a great deal in expressing myself well and I still remember many of those lessons.

As far as the research advisory committee, there were some who didn't even come to the few meetings that we had. At the opposite extreme, there was the chairman, then managing partner of Price Waterhouse. He just turned over everything to me that Price Waterhouse had on the subject. Later at a meeting, one of these members that hadn't been very cooperative said, "Well, I don't like it; John Myers didn't come up with the right answers." My Price Waterhouse friend said to him: "Did you turn over to him all the material you had in your shop? Since you didn't, be quiet."

I made, as far as I am concerned, a close personal friend of the man who was chairman of the advisory committee. He was generally helpful. He was trying to help me reach the conclusions he had, but even if he did not succeed, it didn't bother him. Some other members of the advisory group did not provide much help.

HICKS: I worked with Paul Grady and then with Reed Storey. Each contributed in a different way and at different levels, but the contribution of each was substantial and remarkable.

Paul Grady, first of all, was essentially a practical business man, and that quality of his influenced the study. Reed Storey, I thought, was also intensely practical. John Myers speaks of a person who already fancies himself as a writer, yet finds himself learning at the feet of a master; that is how I remember Reed Storey's participation. That was not his only participation but his contribution was substantial in that respect.

The advisory group as a group contributed significantly to the study. I didn't meet with them as a group very often, perhaps only three times or so. I met with individual members more often. I sought them out. They contributed freely of their knowledge and experience, in general and on specific points. Contributions, of course, came from individuals other than those on the advisory group. I received many insights into the nature of the complex problem from others. Even after the study was in galley proof, I changed it as a result of insight gained from people who were not on the advisory committee but did have an active interest in the problem.

Just one other thing about spurring people on. I didn't get any shoves from the Research Director, but I can remember that the progress of the study took a quantum leap shortly after the Vice Chairman of our management committee called me on the telephone and said, "There is a whole big world out there waiting to hear what you have to say on the subject of pensions."

Contact Between Board and Researcher:

HANEY, Moderator: Did you sit in with the Board when they met to discuss your research study with respect to the proposed opinion or were you actively involved with the board in any way?

MYERS: This was my biggest disappointment with the whole study. Except for one meeting of the advisory committee which Weldon Powell, then Chairman of the APB, attended and then only briefly, I had no contact whatsoever with the APB. I feel a bit proud, though. I was the first one ever to have his name in print in the official bulletins by the APB as being wrong. I didn't know, however, that was going to come out until I read it in the final printed copy. I thought at least they would tell me in advance they were going to say that.

WYATT: I had the opposite experience, and I might say that you really didn't miss a whole lot. I think I probably would have had the same experience as John Myers in not having any contact with the APB except for an historical accident. Between the time my study was published and the time the APB got around to deciding about business combinations, I had stopped being a professor and was attending APB meetings regularly as an advisor to the Arthur Andersen partner who was on the Board. As a result, the Board couldn't very well ignore me during the time they discussed business combinations. The Board held several sessions in which I had an opportunity to expand on my thoughts on my research study and to evaluate any subsequent changes in the environment. But I believe that this was only because I happened to be there physically; I don't think there would have been any command performance otherwise.

HICKS: My experience was different. I was deeply involved in the drafting of APB Opinion No. 8, not so much with the full Board, but with a drafting group, which was made up of 3 or 4 people who were partners of Board members. It may be that by that time the Board was coming to recognize the value of that kind of help, or else this subject was esoteric enough that the value of help was emphasized. These people had been deeply into purchase and pooling accounting, but most of them hadn't dug so deeply into the peculiar problems of pension cost accounting.

In any event, the Board did turn to a drafting group and beyond that to the author of the research study and to an actuary by the name of Fred Sloat, who was a partner of Coopers & Lybrand, which has an actuarial division. Fred helped me a great deal with the study, and he contributed greatly to the work of drafting the opinion. He attended most of the Board meetings when the proposed statement on pensions was on the agenda and the Board relied heavily on his guidance in actuarial matters.

Selection of Research Topics:

NORTHRUP, Moderator: Do you believe that assigned research topics from the Director is the best way to get meaningful research done?

WYATT: Nobody, to my knowledge, was assigned a topic. I was interviewed to see if I would be interested in undertaking one or two topics. If one had a research organization and assigned a topic to an individual, you would be very lucky if you got an output that was even as good as the APB did. A researcher has got to be very interested in the topic to do well. I don't think you very often get that by assigning subjects to researchers.

HICKS: I would agree with that. Of all of us, I came the closest to being assigned to my topic. My partner, Thomas Higgins, a member of the APB at the time, was the chairman of the subcommittee on the pension subject, and that probably had quite a bit to do with the choice. Nevertheless, I don't think that I would have been assigned if I hadn't already been interested in the topic. In doing a job of this kind, you have just got to be deeply interested. I was, and people knew that. A fellow has to be able to immerse himself in his subject and has got to be completely fascinated by it. At least for the time, it has to be the most important thing there is.

MYERS: I would rephrase the question. Should research subjects be selected and then try to find the right man to do it? Yes, I think research subjects should be selected. I think the way they found me was quite acceptable. I don't know how many others they looked at before they spoke to me. They asked me if I would be interested in doing a job for them on this topic. I had already done some study of it, so I was interested. I was happy to do the job. In that sense of selecting and assigning me a topic. I thought the APB approach was great.

Reasons Why Study Recommendations Not Accepted:

NORTHRUP, Moderator: Why weren't all of your study recommendations adopted?

MYERS: I had a lot of recommendations, and when I look back at it, I find that the Board really adopted all but one of them. I recommended more disclosure. I recommended some leases should be capitalized. The Board adopted those things. Progress was made in reporting leases.

Now the recommendation that I made that they didn't accept was where to draw the line between those leases that should be capitalized and those that should not.

Why didn't they "see the light" and come up with my answer? There are reasons for their decision, I am sure, but since I had never been in on the Board discussions, I could only guess and you can guess as well as I can.

WYATT: It is hard to say. It is obvious that they didn't get enough votes in favor of my conclusions. But if one were to study the history of the Board deliberations on business combinations, many of the various proposals considered were similar to some of my recommendations. At one time, there was a 12-to-6 vote in favor of an opinion that would have concluded that all business combinations should be accounted for as purchases. That didn't hold up very long, particularly after it made The Wall Street Journal. So there is the problem of how far one can change a practice that is deeply embedded in the business community at any one time. The change to entirely purchase accounting would have been very drastic and very upsetting to the business community. Possibly by the next time it is considered, it won't be as upsetting.

Research recommendations are not accepted for various reasons. Sometimes the conclusions are unsound. That may well have been the fundamental reason why the conclusions of my Study No. 5 were not accepted. I don't believe that is true. But, as John Myers says, he advised on leases and I advised on business combinations, and neither one of us was told why certain advice was rejected. There is a whole business and political dimension to the accounting decision-making process. Accountants have to recognize that there are other things of significance in our society besides financial reports and measurement of income. Accounting, at any given time, can only change so much. Since accountants have gone so long with certain notions, it is very hard to remove such a notion over night. But I still have hope.

HICKS: In the opinion on pensions, the APB said that they had read the research study carefully and had thought a lot about it. The opinion agreed in most respects with the research study, but differed on one major conclusion. The one recommendation they discarded was probably as important as all of the others put together. This was the recommendation for amortizing the past service costs. Yet it comes down to what Arthur Wyatt said. It is extremely important to know what the business world is ready to accept at a particular point in time. The FASB is going to have to face the same question. In the pension case, the APB adopted a major position which was, and is, completely illogical. This is that the annual contribution must be at least large enough to accomplish an accrual of the vested cost over a period of twenty years. Now there wasn't much logic in that. But it was a compromise position, and it had this very practical consequence. In cases where there is substantial vesting, the difference between the provision thereby required and the provision that I would have required, based on full amortization, would almost always be minimal. You can express the range of the importance of matters by using expressions like material, not material, immaterial, inconsequential, forget-about-it, and minimal. The difference between these two provisions is usually minimal.

I have to give credit to those who supported that compromise. In view of what is happening in pension negotiations and also in legislation, which will impose substantial vesting as a condition of every pension plan, the difference becomes less and less.

Distinction Between Research and Rule-Making:

NORTHRUP, Moderator: If you undertook your study today rather than when you did, do you think you would get different results?

WYATT: I am positive I would not. The number of tables of analyzing the business combinations would differ, of course, because the patterns are a little different now.

The APB Opinion would have no effect on my research. All that the APB did in Opinion No. 16 was to waste resources of the accounting profession. It is almost impossible to deal with that Opinion on any rational or equitable basis. Eventually that fact will be recognized and something else will be done. Hopefully, on the next go-round, the FASB will not create another set of arbitrary criteria and try to force valid business transactions into an artificial framework so that a particular accounting result can be achieved. Eventually the FASB will have to understand this.

If I were to study the subject today, I would come to the same sort of conclusions as I did in my research study for the APB. The premises on which my conclusions were based are as sound today as they were in 1960. The experience of the intervening years merely adds further evidence in support of the conclusions reached.

MYERS: From the logical point of view, I came up with then the only answer that I can see today as to when leases should be capitalized and when they should not be capitalized. But if I were to do the study over again, I would probably approach it a little bit differently. I would probably do a lot of mathematical work and try to see what effects different treatments would have on the statements. I might be a little bit more politically oriented to achieve progress, but then I am not sure whether that would be the proper thing to do. As I look back at it, my role was to say what is right. It was for the Board to find out what compromises had to be made so the profession could make a step forward. I don't fault the Board for not having made an all-the-way step, but every step they take should be a step in the right direction so we can get the goal eventually. I come up now with the same conclusions that I did then.

HICKS: I would only add that I probably might be smart enough now to recognize the usefulness of the vested-benefits compromise.

NORTHRUP, Moderator: Since the APB opinion differed in several instances with the conclusions reached in the research studies, do you think it would have been feasible to have several official studies made of each of the most important topics instead of just one?

WYATT: The presumption of the question is that the researcher decides before he undertakes the study what the answer is going to be and then he comes out with that conclusion. If you had a series of researchers and they were truly researchers, it wouldn't make a great deal of difference how many studies you had; each one would reinforce the other.

The problem lies in the misconception that existed at the time the APB was formed and may still exist. We aren't going to solve all of our problems in accounting by research. That just isn't likely. Research, as John Myers points out, is aimed at coming up with the most appropriate answer. Research disregards politics and the other compromises necessary in making decisions. Decision-makers should acknowledge the political and other required compromises when deviating from the proper research answer, explain their decision on pragmatic grounds, and not try to justify the answer that they come up with as being the one that is most sound, the best conceptually.

That is one reason why the APB pension opinion has worked so well. The Board acknowledged in the opinion that they were compromising but they were going to cut off the extremes possible at both ends and move forward. In other opinions, they didn't acknowledge the compromise process even though they reached most conclusions through compromise. Instead they put out the conclusions for these opinions as if they were sound in theory. That was wrong.

HICKS: I am probably putting my foot into a hornet's nest besides mixing my metaphors, but I have trouble with this question of logic in accounting research and in accounting itself. One of our failures in accounting flows from the fact that we pretend that it's more logical than it is. I recognize that validity of what Art Wyatt was just saying about the arbitrary prescriptions, especially in regard to APB Opinion No. 16. Yet, I believe that we will not find an answer to the purchase-pooling problem in terms of pure logic, and I certainly don't think that we will find an answer to it by research, certainly not in the sense that research in other disciplines can find answers that lie there waiting to be discovered. Perhaps behavioral investigation offers some hope. If we put something on a piece of paper, something called "profit," how will a reader react? When he perceives those marks on the paper, will he buy, sell, or hold on? That is the kind of knowledge that I think is lacking in our accounting research and it may be that it's lacking because we just can't have it. But if we could have it, that could help us to find solutions to accounting questions. That is a speech I wrote three days ago, hoping that somebody might ask me the question. Even if you hadn't asked, I would have figured some way of saying it.

WYATT: He just stole all of what I was going to say.

I will agree that research in accounting is very different from research in the physical sciences. In the physical sciences, there is a fact which just must be discovered. Now accounting is a man-made device without facts for us to discover. Accounting only exists because it is useful.

Usefulness, of course, is going to change as society changes. Look at the changes in the interpretation of the Constitution that have come along in its nearly 200 years of existence. So it is very difficult to get at accounting truth. The Trueblood committee did us a great service when they said these are the objectives of financial statements at least for this year and maybe-next year. We can accept them as objectives for now, but society will probably create new objectives for us. One of the objectives the Trueblood Committee did not accept was to channel resources into socially desirable goals. I don't think accounting should be for that purpose but some might think so. Some lawmakers use the tax law for that purpose, but accounting objectives are going to change and whatever the purposes may be, accountants will have to serve those needs.

Safeguards of Studies:

NORTHRUP, Moderator: While personal biases obviously cannot be removed, what safeguards did you employ to assure that your study was an honest and objective effort?

MYERS: There was one man who was president of one of the leasing companies, Alvin Zises, who believed that I was coming up with the wrong answers. He admitted his biases to me, but he brought up arguments counter to what I was coming up with. He brought them up effectively, and he made me argue them with him. Now I didn't change his mind and he didn't change my mind, but because he argued with me, there has been nobody since my study was printed who has brought up an argument which I hadn't faced with Mr. Zises. I think he did do a great deal to keep me from going astray. If I hadn't been able to answer his arguments, I might have had to have changed my argument and been on the other side. Even as an antagonist, he was a real help.

WYATT: In my case, I didn't even know what a business combination was when I agreed to undertake the study. After it was completed, there were many who said I still didn't!

In my case, there were no preconceived ideas. I didn't begin to do any drafting until 350 or 400 different business combinations were reviewed; some of the reviews were superficial but many were most detailed. At one time, I had in fairly good draft form two sets of conclusions. One draft reached the conclusions that were published. The alternative draft reached the conclusion that most business combinations were poolings of interest. In review, one of them made sense and one of them didn't. That is how I concluded as to which one was going to be published. The alternative position had too many holes in it which you couldn't be comfortable in supporting. In undertaking research projects, I believe every effort should be made to get individuals to undertake a project who do not have a preconceived position about the topic. You need to know something about the subject, but you should not be committed to a particular position on the subject.

HICKS: My study was guided from the beginning by the statement of purpose which appears in the studies. This purpose is to provide an informative discussion of the accounting problems under review prior to the issuance of any APB pronouncements on the accounting problem. At the time that I undertook the work, there was discussion as to whether the research studies should reach conclusions or whether they should merely expose the issues. The FASB discussion memorandum is precisely that, an exposure paper. An exposure paper is a statement of issues and possible solutions. A document exposing the issues was precisely what I set out to prepare. Later, others thought it would be useful to express conclusions. Members of the Advisory Committee and the AICPA Research Director, Reed Storey, and others said, "You have been through all of this; you must know a lot about the problems. You'd better say what you think." I agreed, and that's what I did. The point is that I didn't start out with the idea that there was something to prove, but rather that there were issues to expose in the most balanced way possible. That ought to be one of the significant elements of any accounting research. Afterwards, if the researcher wants to use what he has developed to prove something, that may be useful.

The FASB Approach to Research:

HANEY, Moderator: Should current and future issues continue to be assigned to individuals as research projects?

WYATT: Yes, but that does not seem to be what the FASB contemplates. The FASB contemplates research in a neutral framework, namely that of a "discussion memorandum," which attempts to identify issues but does not reach any conclusions. That is one approach. Personally, I wouldn't want to undertake a research program of that kind. It's kind of like practicing doing nothing. Or in the game of golf, only putting on the putting green when the game is how well you can put the practice to use. However, apparently the FASB is going to go on with this routine of identifying issues and stopping there. It would be helpful, however, if they would also undertake some research projects like the APB studies.

HICKS: I understand that the foundations of the FASB statements are to be in the testimony taken following the exposure of one of the discussion memoranda. Is that generally your understanding?

WYATT: That is my understanding now. If that is what they do, they are doomed to failure more than the APB was. For example, in these discussion memoranda, people are asked to respond to issues but they are not told what the framework of the response ought to be. What are the objectives that the FASB is going to use to resolve these issues? If I knew what objectives they had in mind, I could respond in a helpful way. But, if I do not know their objectives, all I can do is respond in accord with my preconceived objectives. They can put my data in with everybody else's data even if our different objectives haven't been identified. They add up all the numbers and we have a vote, but the fact is that people vote for different reasons.

HICKS: That is a danger. One aspect of this is that corporations and to some extent practicing accountants, especially between December 15 and March 14, are not going to be able to respond meaningfully to something so general. I'm worried that they won't get the quality of input that they need. There is a danger in this.

NORTHRUP, Moderator: What is the FASB going to do with regard to research studies that the APB didn't do or wouldn't do?

HICKS: It remains to be seen what they will do in the course they are on now. Apparently, they are not going to do much about research studies except to publish "discussion memoranda" and use those to enlist reactions to be brought forth at a public hearing. On the basis of reactions at the hearings, the Board will wrap itself in a cocoon and come up with a standard, the new word for an APB Opinion.

I just don't see otherwise what they are going to do. I would go back to something that I concluded back in July, 1971, when somebody asked me to rehash the pension study experience to see if there was anything that could be useful to a reappraisal of the AICPA's research program. One thing became clear to me then and I put it into my answer. It is the same thing that made me decide in the end to put conclusions into the research study. It is the same point Art Wyatt made a few minutes ago. Until you put something down for somebody to latch on to, to object to, you may not arouse his interest, and you may not get a response. It just has to come out that way. Art Wyatt said he had several endings written for his research study and he picked one. I won't tell you how many I had or how many times I threw them up the stairs before they came out in the right order. But I do believe that if you are to get somebody's attention, you have to give him something to agree with or disagree with. That is the way of the world.

Rewards of Researchers:

HANEY, Moderator: What were your greatest satisfactions as a result of your study? Your biggest disappointment as a result of your study?

MYERS: That is a hard one to answer. My greatest satisfaction was to have a lot of people read what I had to say and think maybe I was right. My greatest disappointment was that the APB didn't agree.

HICKS: I have to answer that on a personal level, since that is the level where one finds what one's satisfaction and disappointments are. It's a pretty satisfying experience to produce something like a research study. There is a sort of personal pleasure that comes, I suppose, more for some than others. There are a lot of words in the study. Most of them are mine and so that is a great satisfaction.

As for disappointment, there was nothing major. I didn't cry very long when I learned the APB wouldn't amortize the past service cost, but I do remember being a little disappointed. And then I got a number of nice letters from people saying they liked the study, but I didn't get a single telegram.

WYATT: You are right, the question is one on a personal reaction level. I got two reactions, both the same kind really. In my case, I got the opportunity to work very closely with a person who has become a very close friend. The friendship has lasted and we still get together and talk about business combinations--for about 45 seconds before we talk about other matters. For one who had always been in an academic environment, there was satisfaction too in knowing that you could deal on a complex matter with non-academics, those in accounting firms and in the stock exchange and in the SEC, in a reasonably competent manner. At least, if all didn't agree with your conclusions, there were a number who did agree it was worthwhile to have it published. Probably this opportunity to participate in a research study triggered for me my subsequent decision to leave academia.

As for disappointments, I don't have any real disappointments other than a personal disappointment about my inability to be more persuasive for the ideas and the words that I had at my command. I have learned a lot more since then and have done a lot more writing. I may be more adept at it today, but I don't know. That was the disappointment.

BIBLIOGRAPHY

ERNEST L. HICKS:

Book:

Accounting for the Cost of Pension Plans, Accounting Research Study No. 8, AICPA: New York, 1965.

Articles:

"Materiality: A Useful Audit Tool," The Journal of Accountancy, July, 1962.

"Income Tax Allocation," Financial Executive, October, 1963.

"Materiality," Journal of Accounting Research, Vol. 2, No. 2 (Autumn, 1964).

"Comments on 'A Statement of Basic Accounting Theory,'" The Journal of Accountancy, September, 1966.

"Accounting Principles Board Issues New Rules on Allocating Income Taxes," The Journal of Taxation, June, 1968.

"APB: The First 3600 Days," The Journal of Accountancy, September, 1969.

"Pension Cost and the Auditor," Five Articles on Accounting for the Cost of Pension Plans, AICPA; New York: 1968. (Recommended by E. L. Hicks.)

JOHN H. MYERS:

Books and Other:

Statistical Presentation. Littlefield Adams & Co., 1950.

Audit Practice Case. Ronald Press Co., 1953 (Jointly with Ernest C. Davies).

Reporting of Leases in Financial Statements, Accounting Research Study No. 4, AICPA: New York, 1962.

Auditing Cases. Northwestern University Press, 1964.

Business Research: Test and Cases (jointly with E. E. Nemmers). McGraw-Hill, 1966.

"Leases," Handbook of Modern Accounting. McGraw-Hill Book Company, 1970.

Articles (selected):

"Tariffs and Prices--A Diagrammatic Representation," American Economic Review, September, 1941.

"Excess Profits Tax on Individuals," Taxes, December, 1941.

"Influence of Stock Split-ups on Market Price," Harvard Business Review, March, 1948 (jointly with Archie J. Bakay).

"Presentation of Long-Term Lease Liabilities in the Balance Sheet," The Accounting Review, July, 1948.

"The Meaning of Irregular Wording in Auditor's Certificates," Analysts' Journal, August, 1953.

"Special Inventory Problems of the Dealer in Collectors' Items," The Accounting Review, October, 1953.

"Some Examples of Useful Variations in the Modern Short-Form Audit Report," The Journal of Accountancy, November, 1953.

"Accelerated Amortization of Defense Facilities," The Journal of Accountancy, February, 1955.

"Inventory Disclosure in Annual Reports," Journal of Accountancy, July, 1955.

"Annual Reports to Employees," New York Certified Public Accountant, February, 1956.

"Useful Formulae for DDB and SYD Depreciation," The Accounting Review, January, 1958.

"The Periodic Stock Dividend--Boon or Sop," Commercial and Financial Chronicle, February 13, 1958 (jointly with Loyd C. Heath).

"The Critical Event and Recognition of Net Profit," The Accounting Review, October, 1959.

"Influence of Salvage Value Upon Choice of Depreciation Methods," The Accounting Review, October, 1960.

"Depreciation Disclosure," The Journal of Accountancy, November, 1965.

"Depreciation Manipulation for Fun and Profit," Financial Analysts Journal, November-December, 1967.

"Depreciation Manipulation for Fun and Profit," Financial Analysts Journal, September-October, 1969.

"A Set of New Financial Statements," The Journal of Accountancy, February, 1971.

ARTHUR R. WYATT:

Books:

Advanced Accounting, with N. M. Bedford and K. W. Perry. John Wiley & Sons: New York, 1960. Second edition, 1967; third edition, 1973.

Accounting: Basic Financial, Cost, and Control Concepts, with W. T. Anderson and C. A. Moyer, John Wiley & Sons, 1965.

A Critical Examination of Accounting for Business Combinations, Accounting Research Study No. 5. AICPA: New York, 1963.

A Statement of Basic Accounting Postulates and Principles, with others. Center for International Education and Research in Accounting: Urbana, Illinois, 1964.

Article (selected):

"Inequities in Accounting for Business Combinations," Financial Executive, December, 1972.

APPENDIX TO SECTION III

ACCOUNTING RESEARCH STUDIES SERIES

These fifteen studies during the lifetime of the APB are individual research projects to resolve specific areas of difference and inconsistency in the preparation and presentation of financial information.

No.	Title	Author	Publication Date
1	The Basic Postulates of Accounting	Maurice Moonitz	1961
2	"Cash Flow" Analysis and the Funds Statement	Perry Mason	1961
3	A Tentative Set of Broad Accounting Principles for Business Enterprises	Robert Sprouse and Maurice Moonitz	1962
4	Reporting of Leases in Financial Statements	John H. Myers	1962
5	A Critical Study of Accounting for Business Combinations	Arthur R. Wyatt	1963
6	Reporting Financial Effects of Price-Level Changes	Staff	1963
7	Inventory of Generally Accepted Accounting Principles for Business Enterprises	Paul Grady	1965
8	Accounting for the Cost of Pension Plans	Ernest L. Hicks	1965
9	Interperiod Allocation of Corporate Income Taxes	Homer Black	1966

No.	Title	Author	Publication Date
10	*Accounting for Goodwill*	*George R. Catlett and Norman O. Olson*	*1968*
11	*Financial Reporting in the Extractive Industries*	*Robert E. Field*	*1969*
12	*Reporting Foreign Operations of U.S. Companies in U.S. Dollars*	*Leonard Lorensen*	*1972*
13	*The Accounting Basis of Inventories*	*Horace G. Barden*	*1973*
14	*Accounting for Research and Development Expenditures*	*Oscar S. Gellein and Maurice S. Newman*	*1973*
15	*Stockholders' Equity*	*Beatrice Melcher*	*1973*

SECTION IV

TWO COMMITTEES FOR CHANGE: WHEAT AND TRUEBLOOD

INTRODUCTION

In this section, the discussants were members of the two recent AICPA Committees that suggested major changes in U.S. standards, the Study Group on Establishment of Accounting Principles (the Wheat Committee), and the Study Group on the Objectives of Financial Statements (the Trueblood Committee). Both discussants are Arthur Young Professors of Accounting; Professor David Solomons, The Wharton School, served on the former committee and Dean Sidney Davidson, University of Chicago, was on the latter committee. As might be expected, the institutional changes recommended by the Wheat Committee were easier to agree upon and implement than were the philosophical changes recommended by the Trueblood Committee. Supplementing the discussion are five appendices: two deal with the Wheat Committee report, the first (A) detailing how its recommendations have been implemented, and the second (B), a Price Waterhouse lecture given by Professor Solomons on this subject. Two other appendices are documents related to the Trueblood Committee Report, the first (C) being the chapter from the Report itself which summarizes the objectives and two, the FASB Discussion Memorandum which considers the Trueblood Report objectives. The last appendix is an article by two young Canadians drawing heavily upon the reports of the two committees in proposing Canadian institutional models for standards.

-- The Editor.

SECTION IV

TWO COMMITTEES FOR CHANGE: WHEAT AND TRUEBLOOD

1971 *Responding to criticism both inside and outside the accounting profession, the AICPA commissions two major studies. One deals with the process by which accounting principles should be established, and the second concerns the objectives of financial statements. The first is chaired by former SEC Commissioner, Francis M. Wheat, the second by former Institute President, Robert M. Trueblood. The AAA, in an action by its Executive Committee, also calls for a blue-ribbon commission to make a comprehensive study of the way in which accounting principles should be established. In view of the Institute's study on the subject, the AAA decides to hold its proposal in abeyance.*

1972 *The Wheat Study recommends that a seven-man, full-time Financial Standards Board be established under the auspices of a Financial Accounting Foundation, which is to be composed of representatives of the AICPA, FEI, NAA, FAF, and AAA. The Board's budget is between $2 1/2 and $3 million. A Financial Accounting Standards Advisory Council, made up of "persons conversant with and involved in the problems of communicating financial information," is suggested to keep the Board in touch with current thinking in the business and professional world. The entire recommendation receives the support of an overwhelming majority of the AICPA's Board of Directors and Council, and several Big Eight firms promise donations of $1 million to the Foundation. The APB continues its activities during 1972, but is to be replaced in early 1973 by the program recommended by the Wheat Study.*

-- From Stephen A. Zeff's "Chronology of Significant Developments in the Establishment of Accounting Principles in the United States, 1926-1972," <u>Journal of Accounting Research</u>, Spring, 1972, pp. 226-227.

THE DISCUSSANTS

Sidney Davidson:

Dean Davidson, Graduate School of Business, and the Arthur Young Professor of Accounting at the University of Chicago, was a member of the AICPA Study Group on the Objectives of Financial Standards, the Trueblood Committee, from 1971-1973. He is currently a member of the Financial Accounting Standards Board Advisory Council (FASBAC), Chairman of the AAA's Financial Accounting Standards Committee, and a member of the FASB force on accounting for leases.

He was a member of the APB from 1965-1970 and President, AAA, 1968-1969, and Director of Research, AAA, 1955-1956. He earned his three degrees from the University of Michigan where he was elected to Phi Beta Kappa, Beta Alpha Psi, and other honoraries. He is a CPA and received the Elijah Watts Sells Award for his examination performance in 1951. At the University of Chicago since 1958, he was previously at The Johns Hopkins University from 1949. Co-author or co-editor of six books, he has published twenty some articles in various leading periodicals, many of which have been reprinted, and he has been a contributor of a chapter or section of several books. His co-authored textbook, Fundamentals of Accounting, is now forthcoming in its fifth edition. He will resign as Dean and will be a Fellow, Center for Advanced Study in the Behavioral Sciences, Stanford University, 1974-1975.

David Solomons:

Professor Solomons, Chairman of the Accounting Department and the Arthur Young Professor of Accounting at the Wharton School, University of Pennsylvania, was a member of the AICPA Study Group on the Establishment of Accounting Principles, the Wheat Committee, from 1971-1972. He is currently heading the British Long Range Enquiry into Education and Training for the Accountancy Profession; his report on this enquiry (with T. M. Berridge), Prospectus for a Profession, was published in May, 1974.

He was Director of Research for the AAA, 1968-1970. He is a fellow of the Institute of Chartered Accountants in England and Wales. He earned his two degrees at the London School of Economics (B. Commerce and D.Sc. in Economics). At the University of Pennsylvania since 1959, he was at the University of Bristol (England) from 1955, and at the University of London from 1949, and at the London School of Economics from 1946. During World

War II, he was a Captain in the Royal Service Corps. He has been a lecturer and a visiting professor at universities throughout the world. Author of several books, he has published articles in various leading periodicals; in 1969, he received the AICPA Notable Contribution to Literature Award for his Divisional Performance: Measurement and Control.

THE MODERATORS

Faculty moderator is Associate Professor Orace E. Johnson, Ph.D. On the FASB's Task Force on Research and Development, he has published frequently in leading periodicals. Student moderator is Mr. David Bond, Beta Alpha Psi President-elect and a junior honors student. After graduation, he plans to go to graduate school.

THE DISCUSSION

The Two Committees:

BOND, Moderator: The AICPA held on January 7 and 8, 1971, a special two-day conference of 35 prominent CPA's representing 21 accounting firms. The AICPA President, then Marshall Armstrong, presided. The conference objectives were to reexamine how accounting principles should be established, and to explore the various alternative approaches to rule-making. After extended discussion, a resolution was adopted urging the AICPA President to appoint two study groups acting independently of each other to explore means of improving standard-setting for financial reporting. One group was to review APB operations and the other was to define financial statement objectives. The former group, authorized in March, 1971, became known as the Wheat Committee and the latter group, authorized a month later, became known as the Trueblood Committee.

In March, 1972, the Wheat Committee published its report; it proposed the Financial Accounting Standards Board (FASB), which started functioning in 1973. In October, 1973, the Trueblood Committee published its report; it has been an input to the FASB project on the conceptual framework for financial accounting and reporting. The objectives of financial statements, as identified by the Trueblood Committee, were to provide information useful for making economic decisions; to serve primarily those users who have limited authority, ability, or resources to obtain information and who rely on financial statements as their principal source of information about an enterprise's economic activities; to provide information useful to investors and creditors for predicting, comparing, and evaluating potential cash flows to them in terms of amount, timing, and related uncertainty; to provide users with information for predicting, comparing, and evaluating enterprise earning power; to supply information useful in judging management's ability to utilize enterprise resources effectively in achieving the primary enterprise goal; to provide factual and interpretive information about transactions and other events which is useful for predicting, comparing, and evaluating enterprise earning power; to provide a statement of financial activities; to provide information useful for the predictive process (including financial forecasts when they will enhance the reliability of users' predictions); to provide information useful for evaluating the effectiveness of the management of resources in achieving governmental and not-for-profit organizations; and to report on those activities of the enterprise affecting society which can be measured and are important to the role of the enterprise in its social environment. On January 20th of this year, the Trueblood Study Group met with the FASB on this subject.

Perhaps to demonstrate the complex task of the second study, some detail of the Trueblood Committee operations may be given. The Trueblood Study involved an inter-disciplinary commission of nine members, with a staff and special consultants of academics and practitioners. Solicited were the views of over 5,000 corporations, professional firms, unions, public interest groups, national and international accounting organizations, and financial publications. More than 50 interviews were conducted with executives from professional organizations, government, and all sectors of business. Thirty-five meetings were held with professional and institutional groups, culminating with three days of public hearings in New York.

JOHNSON, Moderator: What seemed to you the high points of the Wheat Committee deliberations?

SOLOMONS, Wheat: One was the day in the AICPA offices at 666 Fifth Avenue when seven men, asked to serve on the Wheat Committee, met with each other for the first time in March of 1971.

In one's reminiscences, it would be more interesting to talk about acrimonious differences of opinion and frictions that developed within the committee and the development of minority views and majority views. But, in fact, it wasn't that kind of committee since our proceedings were not like that. We proceeded with the utmost harmony. We did a workmanlike job. We came out with a report whose reception went beyond anything that we had even hoped for. It got immediate and almost universal acceptance and, more than that, it got almost immediate and almost complete implementation. The present financial accounting structure--the FAF, the FASB, and the Advisory Council--corresponds about 99% with what we recommended in our report.

JOHNSON, Moderator: Dean Davidson, were your experiences in the Trueblood Committee similar to those of Professor Solomons in the Wheat Committee?

DAVIDSON, Trueblood: Coming as I do from the University of Chicago where we are much inclined to emphasize the significance of market tests of effectiveness, I am a little uneasy when David Solomons is able to report that the Wheat Committee recommendations have been adopted and implemented through the operation of market forces, and I can't say the same for the Trueblood Committee report yet. That is a little troublesome to me.

Committee Controversy:

JOHNSON, Moderator: Was there controversy in the Trueblood Committee?

DAVIDSON, Trueblood: Yes, but then the Wheat Committee was considering institutional arrangements whereas the Trueblood Committee was concerned with philosophic approaches to accounting. It is an enormous tribute to the late Robert Trueblood and Oscar Gellein that we were able to get together on a unanimous report. At the outset, the group of nine people had what seemed to be irreconcilable differences. Somehow though, we were able to agree on a report that I am proud of, as are all the other members of the Study Group, I'm sure.

In my recollection of the committee's deliberations for a year and a half, the one thing that stands out was a willingness to listen to the other man's view. Our report results from that, despite some rather acrimonious discussion that occasionally crept into our deliberations. Because we listened, we were able to agree on almost all points and to incorporate the dissents within the body of the report. During the deliberations, we not only changed our minds, but some of us changed our positions.

JOHNSON, Moderator: Professor Solomons, was there any similar shift of opinion in the Wheat Committee members? You indicated earlier that they were pretty close together.

SOLOMONS, Wheat: I didn't mean to imply that we did not change our ideas in the course of a year. We certainly did change our ideas. I changed my ideas. If I had been asked half-way through our proceedings as to what our probable conclusions would be, I would have said that we would have voted for the continuation of a large part-time Board, not too dissimilar from the old APB. It was extremely interesting to see how, during the second half of the committee meetings, as we got more and more opinions presented to us from various sources, we did change our views. Certainly Frank Wheat and I in particular changed our views. Incidentally, without particularizing, this also must be true of the Trueblood group.

Not all members of a committee make the same kind of contribution to the discussion and not all members of a group contribute to the same extent. Some of our committee members made a larger contribution than others. Frank Wheat and I for a long time clung to the idea that we could recommend the continuation of a part-time Board. Frank was one of the last to give up that position and accept the inevitability of a small full-time Board.

My change in position on this issue was based more than anything else on our own experience on the Wheat Committee, meeting as it did relatively infrequently. We only met on eight separate occasions, as I can recall, for a total of about 14 days. But between one meeting and the next we were constantly losing momentum and taking the same thing up again. Even though we were in touch with each other between meetings, there was an enormous loss of momentum between meetings, and it was borne in on me inescapably that any group of men tackling difficult problems on a part-time basis was probably going to be less effective than if it did so on a full-time basis. We had a well-defined problem and our agenda was altogether less complex than the much less well-defined and more complex problems that had been the agenda of the APB. It more and more appeared that a full-time Board would have to be more effective, unless it was chosen in an irresponsible manner. There are other reasons for preferring a full-time board over a part-time Board such as the conflicts of interest issue, but the question of effectiveness was the deciding factor in changing my position.

DAVIDSON, Trueblood: I can certainly testify to that. The APB used to meet in three-day sessions every month and a half or every two months; we would usually be very pleased if after the end of the first day, we had brought ourselves up to the point at which we had ended the previous meeting. I can also testify to the shift in David Solomons' position because I could remember our having some fairly lengthy discussions in which I was urging a small full-time Board and he indicated that he was not yet convinced.

Institutional Changes Before Philosophical Changes:

JOHNSON, Moderator: Since the Wheat Committee recommendations have been implemented as institutional changes before the philosophical changes to be recommended in the Trueblood Committee had been even agreed upon by the Committee, does this put the cart before the horse?

SOLOMONS, Wheat: We were uneasy about being put into a position of having to make recommendations on procedure before the Trueblood Committee came up with its recommendations on principles. But we were given no choice in the matter. We were given more restricted time constraints within which we had to work than the Trueblood group was. We didn't think it was up to us to argue with them. It was unfortunate that the AICPA thought there was an institutional crisis for which some prescription had to be put forward while the more conceptual matters were being considered by the other group. Whether putting the cart before the horse in the long run will prove to have been a serious mistake, I don't know, since it is too early to say.

DAVIDSON, Trueblood: I would certainly agree that, in the best of worlds, we would have first have had a report on what the objectives of accounting should be and then a report on what is the best means of securing and implementing those objectives. The way things worked out proves once more we do not live in the best of all possible worlds.

But I did agree with the crisis feeling of the AICPA. After the Battle of Opinions Nos. 16 and 17, the effectiveness of the APB appeared so limited that something had to be done soon.

JOHNSON, Moderator: What was the nature of this crisis?

DAVIDSON, Trueblood: It certainly wasn't personal. As the Board during 1969 and 1970 retreated from a series of positions with regard to pooling, there came to be a feeling that it could not be relied upon for an even-handed public protection view with regard to accounting principles. By its actions with regard to business combinations, the Board insured that it could not long survive. This is not merely a reflection of my personal reaction to the disappointing conclusions of APB Opinion No. 16. The public response to the treatment of business combinations meant that some other device had to be found. At least that is my feeling.

SOLOMONS, Wheat: There was clearly some deep dissatisfaction on the part of certain "Big Eight" firms with the APB institutional arrangement. But, incidentally, assuming that the sense of crisis was justified, if the Institute had proceeded the other way around and put the Trueblood Committee to work and held up on the Wheat Committee until their report had come out, the Trueblood Committee probably would have had to work under great pressure and may well have done a less effective job.

JOHNSON, Moderator: Has there now been sufficient change in the institutional structure so that a comparable crisis is not likely to occur with any one of the topics that are now on the FASB agenda?

SOLOMONS, Wheat: I wouldn't like to say that a similar crisis could not develop. But I am prepared to say that the existing FASB is likely to be a more effective instrument than the APB was for standing up to pressure and surviving the crisis. Whether that judgment is true, of course, only time will tell.

The New Structure:

JOHNSON, Moderator: What is in the new structure that makes it more capable of standing up to pressure?

SOLOMONS, Wheat: The old structure was a large committee. Sid Davidson was a member for several years and consequently was much closer to its proceedings than I have even been. It functioned discontinuously. The APB structure was one in which there must have been either real or imagined conflicts of interest between large practitioners and small practitioners. The Board members, since they were part time, must always have felt a conflict of loyalty between their positions as members of the Board and their positions as members of their firm or company (or in the case of academics, their universities, although that conflict of interest would not be serious).

The new Board is small, working together continuously, and has no other affiliations or allegiances except to the Board itself. These characteristics of the FASB are the ones that suggest that it can stand up to pressure better than the old one.

DAVIDSON, Trueblood: I certainly agree that there were charges of conflict of interest with regard to certain Board members. I found no evidence of this during the deliberations of the Board. But it isn't enough for me to be convinced that there were not these conflicts of interest. The plain fact was there were widespread feelings throughout the financial community that you could not rely on the Board. I don't think those were necessarily justified but the fact that they existed tended to make the Board ineffective.

SOLOMONS, Wheat: There is another important consideration which causes one to have confidence that the new Board could stand up to pressure better than the old. The old Board consisted exclusively of CPA's. Since it was a creature of the AICPA, all of its members had to be members of the Institute. Although its base of support was nominally broader than the present Board because the old Board had eighteen members, its basis of real support was narrower in that it only represented the accounting profession. The new Board, in contrast, does represent a variety of outside interests. It is made up of persons with a variety of backgrounds, and, therefore, they should be able to draw on this fact as a basis of support.

The Philosophical Framework:

JOHNSON, Moderator: If I understand you correctly, this resistance to external pressure has come about without a consensus about the philosophical foundation that might have been developed by the Trueblood Committee?

SOLOMONS, Wheat: We can't judge yet whether the new Board will stand up to pressure. However, I am expressing confidence about the way they will proceed. But the absence of a philosophic foundation does have much to do with the way the Board will comport itself.

DAVIDSON, Trueblood: We don't know that there is the absence of a philosophic foundation. As David Solomons pointed out, there is an FASB committee on the conceptual framework that is being chaired by Marshall Armstrong, FASB Chairman, and with Bob Sprouse, another Board member, as Vice Chairman, that is trying to develop this philosophic framework. I have not given up hope that such a framework embracing many of the attributes of the Trueblood objective study report will yet emerge.

JOHNSON, Moderator: In spite of the fact that there may be some compromises of a very crucial nature in the Trueblood report which could be interpreted ambiguously?

DAVIDSON, Trueblood: True, you can't get out a document to which nine people subscribe without some compromises. I am willing to confess if they had just been willing for me to write the report that there would have been fewer compromises. Nevertheless, I am satisfied that even with the compromises the report does represent a distinct forward step in terms of a conceptual framework.

BOND, Moderator: Was there any particular objective on which there was the least amount of agreement?

DAVIDSON, Trueblood: Yes. It was clear that the one part on which there was the greatest and most significant disagreement was over the question of the extent to which value changes should be introduced into reported income numbers. The report, in one of its objectives relating to the balance sheets, says the current values should also be reported (reported is a carefully-chosen word) when they differ significantly from historical cost. In the next objective when we talk about the income statement or the statement of earnings, we say changes in the values reflected in successive statements of financial position should also be reported again but separately since they differ in terms of their certainty of realization. Reporting value changes, that is, informing readers of them is important, but to me the basic question is, "Does the value change become an integral part of the articulated statements or is it merely reported in some subsidiary fashion?"

The sharpest paragraph of disagreement in the entire report is on this objective. It is as follows:

> Members of the study group disagree on whether value changes that meet the qualitative criteria discussed in this report should be included in earnings. Some believe the objective should be to reflect certain value changes in earnings. Others believe that the inclusion of unrealized value changes in earnings may be desirable but is not practicable. Still others believe that their inclusion is neither desirable or practicable.

So here you have these three separate views; yes, we ought to do it and now is the time; yes, we ought to do it but later; and, then the third group that says never.

All of them agree that it should be reported but the question is whether in the basic statements.

I'm willing to tell you how I think it ought to turn out. It seems to me that we must include value changes in the statements of earnings in the integral statements and sooner rather than later.

Appeals from FASB Decisions:

JOHNSON, Moderator: Regarding the Wheat Committee's recommendations for the FASB structure of operations, what formal avenue of appeal does Sidney Davidson have if he were disappointed?

SOLOMONS, Wheat: Well, he is in a better position than most of us to bring his views to the Board because he is a member of the Financial Accounting Standards Advisory Committee (FASAC), which incidentally was not the least important part of the Wheat Committee's recommendations. The purpose of that committee was to give the FASB a set of antennae which would bring in diverse views. We stipulated that the membership of the advisory council should be made up of diverse sections of the financial community. Sidney is a member of that advisory council so he is in a particularly good position to bring his views to the attention of the Board.

But if you are talking about ordinary humans who are not members of the advisory council, they are going to have plenty of opportunities to make their views known on matters on the Board's agenda through the machinery of public hearings and so on.

If your question really is concerned with putting something on the agenda that the Board doesn't want to put there, there is no machinery for that except perhaps writing to The Wall Street Jounal.

DAVIDSON, Trueblood: I can testify to that in part. As you know, the Board recently released a discussion memorandum on general price level adjusted statements, and will be holding public hearings on that subject. The question of whether they ought to be properly moving in that direction arose in the December meeting of the FASAC. One member of that council urged such action vigorously and Marshall Armstrong, FASB Chairman, promised that the Board would give that issue some consideration and, sure enough, it did emerge in the discussion memorandum.

I do think that the Board is also receptive to receiving suggestions and comments from various individuals. You may recall a few months ago, they solicited comments as to the items that ought to go onto the agenda. I suspect they probably should and perhaps will do that again.

SOLOMONS, Wheat: I think the Board is bending over backwards to be responsive to the needs of the financial community. I hope it doesn't go too far.

In regard to appeals, an appeal procedure was considered time and time again in the evidence that was given the Wheat Committee. Our recommendation on this was a negative one in spite of the arguments from some of the Big Eight firms and from others proposing that there should be an appeal tribunal for those who didn't like the conclusions reached by the Board, short of going to the SEC.

We looked at this quite carefully. It seemed to rest on a misapprehension as to the nature of a standards board's proceedings. A standards board is really in the position of a legislature and is not a judicial body. Appeals are made from a judicial body but it wouldn't make much sense to have an appeal from Congress. The only way to appeal from Congress is to get Congress to change its mind and to lobby its members and so on, to make your views known to the press and otherwise. Or elect a new Congress. Of course, you can't exactly elect a new standards board, but if enough people expressed dissatisfaction with the board's proceedings, its composition would be changed.

DAVIDSON, Trueblood: The real danger is that there remain groups within the business and financial community who do feel that an appeals procedure exists. These appeals will be made to the SEC and to Congress. The real test for the FASB is going to come when they issue a statement of truly controversial nature and some groups, who feel that they have been dealt with if not unfairly at least not to their liking, will then try to see how much pressure they can apply to the SEC or to the Congress.

SOLOMONS, Wheat: We had a dramatic instance of that while the Wheat Committee was coming to the end of its work in December, 1971. When the APB was considering legislating in favor of the deferment method of dealing with the investment credit, Congress pulled the rug from under its feet: So we were quite aware of this danger. There didn't seem to be any way of building into our institutions protection against Congressional interference.

DAVIDSON, Trueblood: The board is likely to face its first crisis when it issues a statement as they are preparing to do with regard to the appropriate accounting for leases. The discussion memorandum on leases will be forthcoming shortly; there will be public hearings, an exposure draft, and the Board hopes to get a statement out on the accounting for leases before this year is over or early in 1975.

I suspect that the Board is going to call for increased capitalization of leases by lessees. That is not a popular view with many groups. What those groups who feel that their interests are challenged by such an opinion will do and how effective they will be with whatever they do is going to be the first major test for the Board. As long as they are going to face a major test, it is good that they are going to face it on an issue where all the logic is on one side, in my opinion.

JOHNSON, Moderator: Do you agree that one purpose of the Board is to dispel controversy?

SOLOMONS, Wheat: If there is one right way to account for a particular situation, the Board should be in a position to determine it.

DAVIDSON, Trueblood: If there is just one right way to account for it, it is not likely to come to the FASB.

SOLOMONS, Wheat: But I thought that you were always quite sure that you saw only one right way to solve issues when you were on the APB.

BOND, Moderator: Do you feel the FASB with its variety of backgrounds on its Board may be encouraged to seek out the widest acceptance of the lowest common denominator solution rather than the most desirable one?

SOLOMONS, Wheat: I don't have any particular concern in that direction. If you are referring to the variety of backgrounds for the FASB members, it was one of the objectives of our recommendation to bring more variety of background than the old Board had. It seems quite conceivable that one day the FASB may have an economist member on it. In fact, the backgrounds of its members are not as varied as they might have been.

I really place great reliance on the fact that these men will get into the habit of working together. Of course, you might say that that is not a very cogent reason for confidence; after all, the Supreme Court has had a habit of working together and has not too often come up with a unanimous opinion. I hope that the FASB doesn't go that way.

DAVIDSON, Trueblood: Maybe the Supreme Court doesn't get unanimous opinions because they are all lawyers.

Research: Trueblood Group, Wheat Group, and FASB:

BOND, Moderator: If the formation of accounting principles is a compromise among conflicting political or economic or social forces, what good is the statement of objectives?

DAVIDSON, Trueblood: The Trueblood Study Group did not accept that accounting principles should represent compromise between political, social, and economic forces.

The Trueblood Study Group felt that there should be an economic rationale for the underlying principles of accounting. The time is long since past when the courts or Congress will simply accept accounting principles because some group says that these are correct principles; instead, they must be grounded in some basic economic rationale. The Trueblood Study Group thought it was at least making a start to providing this rationale for accounting principles. This may be an immodest view but we did feel that such a rationale is absolutely essential.

JOHNSON, Moderator: Was it the Wheat Committee's recommendation that the FASB research be directed towards such fundamental considerations?

SOLOMONS, Wheat: As a matter of fact, it wasn't. This frankly was one part of our report that I am least confident about. In the report, the research work of the Board is to be addressed to specific problems which are on the Board's agenda, leaving fundamental research more to the accounting departments of the universities. I'm a little bit dubious about that dichotomy of research between fundamental research and applied research, though I suppose it is not entirely untenable. In any case, the research task which the Board has now set itself to doing is following up on the Trueblood report. This is fundamental research; it has to be.

To what extent the FASB research staff is involved in that, I don't know.

DAVIDSON, Trueblood: It is my understanding that the discussion memorandum dealing with the conceptual framework will merely say we will have read the Trueblood Report. The FASB Research Staff will not make much, if any, specific input into this memorandum.

SOLOMONS, Wheat: I don't know whether the analogy of the Supreme Court is helpful or not. I expect the Supreme Court and the clerks to the justices must be constantly doing legal research but I wouldn't expect it to be fundamental research. It would be legal research directed to the decision of cases. That is what eventually must be the character of the research of the FASB.

DAVIDSON, Trueblood: The Trueblood Committee held public hearings as did the Wheat Committee. At those public hearings, George Catlett of Arthur Andersen suggested an apt way of putting it. As in navigation, he suggested that the role of our group should be to hang the North Star up there in the sky for the FASB to steer toward. The Trueblood Committee should not spell out what the actions should be in any specific area but merely suggest a navigational fix for reaching decisions.

Now that is easier to say, I am afraid, than it is to implement.

FASB "Accounting Power" and the SEC:

BOND, Moderator: Suppose after a fair trial, the FASB fails? What then?

SOLOMONS, Wheat: My answer is fairly clear cut. The most likely alternative that would follow would be that the SEC would take over. Another alternative I suppose would be for Congress to set up a special regulatory agency to do the job that the FASB failed to do. But the most likely alternative is that the SEC would take the job over.

DAVIDSON, Trueblood: Maybe another way of putting that is that I think the FASB represents the last good chance to keep the establishment of accounting principles within the private sector rather than within the public sector.

JOHNSON, Moderator: Recognizing this, Bob Sterling of Rice University said that the problem is a lack of power. Since the accounting profession can't reduce their responsibility, the conclusion is inescapable that the power of the accountant should be increased. Do you agree with this analysis of the situation that the FASB must increase its power to enforce its standards?

SOLOMONS, Wheat: The FASB doesn't have any power to enforce its standards, but we were conscious of the futility of having a body which was capable of making these standards but without power to enforce them. This is why we set up the machinery the way we did. The appointment of the trustees of the FAF, the body that appoints the members of the board, is entirely in the hands of the Board of Directors of the AICPA, with the President of the AICPA an ex-officio member of the trustees of the foundation; and the foundation appoints the FASB. The last word, therefore, as to the composition of the Board is in the hands of the AICPA.

It had to be that way since the implementation or the enforcement of the standards set by the FASB has to be by those who are signing the audit reports, or the CPA's, with the backing of the SEC, of course. It would be very difficult to get the AICPA to agree to any kind of machinery that called upon its members to police the standards if it did not substantially have control. This is why we set it up with a considerable degree of control still residing with the Institute although not all members of the Board have to be members of the Institute.

There is also the position of the SEC behind the Board. I don't think the SEC in relation to the new Board is in a different position from what it was in relation to the old Board. We tried to get the SEC before we reported to show their hand as to what kind of board they wanted. They wouldn't necessarily go along with that but it seemed to us important to know what their thinking was. They were very careful not to show their hand, but kept on saying, "You make some recommendations and then we will react to them." That is the way it was. Their response was speedy and favorable when our report came out. I don't think anybody has complained that the SEC has failed to give the new Board all the support it could in the short time it has been in existence.

DAVIDSON, Trueblood: That is true but as Chuck Horngren said earlier, the ultimate power is in the hands of the SEC and only an act of Congress can alter that. Only judicial review limits the power of the SEC.

I should support my statement about the ultimate power being in the hands of the SEC by noting the proven unwillingness of the courts to overrule independent agencies that are presumed to have expert knowledge. But if the Congress were to grant authority to the FASB on accounting matters, I don't know that they would be any longer in the private sector. We have to say that at the moment power is in the hands of the FASB as long as the SEC agrees with the rulings of the FASB.

Disclosure - Measurement Controversy:

BOND, Moderator: What position should the FASB take on the SEC insistence in recent months in drawing a distinction between accounting disclosure and accounting measurement?

DAVIDSON, Trueblood: Sandy Burton, the SEC Chief Accountant, in accounting series releases has tended to draw on this distinction. Namely that the SEC feels that it should act promptly on disclosure matters even before the FASB has had a chance to consider the questions. But sometimes it is hard to draw a line between these two. For example, insistance by the SEC that there be footnote disclosure of the financial disclosure effects of a broader capitalization of leases is a disclosure question but before you can disclose you must first measure what these results are.

Marshall Armstrong has publicly questioned this distinction that the SEC is drawing. "The Financial Accounting Standards Board believes that the SEC has drawn distinction between accounting disclosure and accounting measurement which is (in the words of the Board) artificial and (again in the words of the Board) if imposed, could generate continuing problems."

JOHNSON, Moderator: Do you agree that the distinction is artificial and not viable and that it could not be feasibly implemented?

DAVIDSON, Trueblood: The SEC feels that there are important disclosure questions primarily with reporting for income taxes and for reporting of leases which cannot await the slow moving machinery of the FASB. It was appalling to me to discover that the first of the statements of the FASB of any substance was likely to be effective only beginning with 1976 financial statements if all of the safeguards laid down in the procedures are complied with. One of the strong bits of advice the FASAC offered was the unanimous feeling that this was just not quick enough and that the FASB was going to have to shorten some of the procedures that were spelled out in the procedures or else the Board would fail. Sandy Burton feels motivated to insist on disclosure of information that is essential to investors. If that won't come about quickly enough through the FASB, the SEC is going to have to require it.

SOLOMONS, Wheat: You haven't told us yet whether you think one can validly distinguish between disclosure and measurement. I think there is a valid distinction.

DAVIDSON, Trueblood: It is the same kind of valid distinction that is introduced by this word "report" in the disagreement that I was talking about within the Trueblood committee. Namely, that you can "report" value changes but you do not integrate them within the financial statements. Now, this is in essence what the SEC is saying. You can disclose the facts but you do not necessarily integrate them within the statement. As I hinted in my earlier comment, I did not view that as anything but a relatively unsatisfactory compromise.

I similarly think that the distinction that the SEC is raising is not a valid one because I am inclined as part of the Chicago school to believe to a very substantial degree in an efficient market hypothesis that says it really doesn't matter too much where the disclosure occurs. Yet as an accountant, I continue to be impressed by the controls over reporting that are introduced by subjecting reported data to the rigor of articulated statements.

FASB, AICPA Rule 203, and Judicial Action:

JOHNSON, Moderator: What about a conflict between the FASB and the AICPA, particularly with AICPA Rule 203?

SOLOMONS, Wheat: In the Wheat report, we printed a proposed new rule for the code of ethics for CPA's. Our form is not precisely the form in which it was subsequently passed by the AICPA Council. But the amendment substantially runs like this: a member shall not say that the statements are presented in accordance with GAAP if they depart from FASB standards or APB opinions unless he can demonstrate that, due to unusual circumstances, the report would otherwise be misleading. In such cases, the report must explain the departure, the approximate effects thereof, and the reason why compliance with the standard or the opinion would not result in a fair statement.

We thought that was an important change in the code of ethics since it opens a better "escape hatch" at its absolute minimum. It opens up a much better "escape hatch" for the auditor and the accountant employed by a company who thinks that slavishly to follow APB opinions or FASB standards would be misleading because his company was in a special situation where a departure is necessary in order to make the statements not misleading.

My statement is expressed negatively. But the AICPA President, Wally Olson, has put this in a positive manner by saying that CPA's now have the duty to see to it that the statements depart from FASB standards if they would otherwise be misleading. It is a very important step forward.

DAVIDSON, Trueblood: How often do you anticipate auditors in their opinions will avail themselves of this positive approach in Rule No. 203?

SOLOMONS, Wheat: Not too often. But it shouldn't have to happen too often if these standards are formulated decently so that it would not be misleading to follow them.

JOHNSON, Moderator: But the question is not how often will they, as an empirical matter, but should they?

DAVIDSON, Trueblood: Regarding Rule No. 203, I am glad that it exists but I would suggest that any exceptions to standards are more likely to be brought about by judicial action than by changes in the code of ethics of the AICPA.

Recent judicial action may be the impelling force for an important change in accounting, perhaps the most important in the last quarter of a century. Judge Friendly in his Continental Vending appeals court decision added one important word, a conjunction, to the traditional accountant's opinion. He said financial statements should present fairly <u>and</u> in conformity with generally accepted accounting principles rather than saying they should present fairly in conformity with generally accepted accounting principles. Implementation of the judge's decision is likely to result in significant changes in financial statements if they are to present fairly.

Owens Illinois and Sears-Allstate Examples:

One area of likely change is the accounting for marketable securities. For example, Owens Illinois showed their investment in securities of Owens Corning at a historical cost of $2 million in their balance sheet recently and in a footnote to the statement reported the current market value of these securities to be $175 million. The financial statement that shows the $2 million does present fairly in adherence to historic cost concepts, but the auditor may be in legal jeopardy, although he relies on the objectivity of such a measurement rule. Back in antiquity, Owens Illinois did indeed spend $2 million to acquire these shares of Owens Corning. But this may have no relevance in the real world, and if we rely on that objective, irrelevant number, we may be in legal jeopardy. An appropriate watchword for the accountant ought to be that I would rather be vaguely right than precisely wrong. Two million dollars is precisely the valuation of the wrong concept. Yet in the marketable securities case, we have the great situation where we can be precisely right because we all can get the same and correct valuation by reading the financial pages of the newspaper.

SOLOMONS, Wheat: I am on the side of the angels, too, in regard to the relevance of market values as distinct from the objectivity of historical cost. I suppose one could say that a statement which describes the investments as costing $2 million could not be said to be misleading, if in the light of the footnote they were said to be worth currently apparently $200 million. I don't think it is the best way to produce financial statements, but I wouldn't think it was necessarily misleading.

DAVIDSON, Trueblood: Let me give you another example. I give this example not in criticism of the companies involved since I am able to give the example only because of their full disclosure. Sears is a 100% owner of Allstate. Allstate, as do most insurance companies, has a very substantial portfolio of marketable securities. Again, don't quote me on specific numbers. But in one year, 1970, the value of the excess of market value over cost of Allstate's portfolio fell by well over $100 million. Yet they showed about $17 million of realized capital gains in that year. Even though they had suffered this enormous unrealized loss, they had realized capital gains because they were cashing in on some of the gains of an earlier period. The next year, 1971, the value of their portfolio increased and the excess of market value over cost went right back up by more than $100 million, and yet in that year, they had realized capital gains of a smaller amount, only about $6 million. Since Sears reports Allstate on the equity basis, they picked up in their financial statements the income as reported by Allstate in conformity with generally accepted accounting principles which included their realized capital gains as income, but excluded unrealized value changes. If you look not at the Sears' statements (in the front of the report) but at the Allstate statements (in the back of the report), you would discover there were big swings in market value. If you looked only at the Sears financial statements, you would read only about the realized capital gains which would have suggested that the year in which we took a terrible beating was the year in which we had the larger securities income, whereas the year when we did wonderfully well we didn't show as much income.

This does suggest why a conglomerate is anxious to acquire an insurance company through a pooling arrangement, when the insurance company has a substantial excess of market value over cost in their portfolio. It makes predicting income a lot easier because it just so happens you sell off those securities that produce the amount of reported income that you would like to report.

It's a little hard to believe that this may not be a little less than fully informative reporting.

JOHNSON, Moderator: Does this mean that the FASB will not really be concerned with the usefulness of information but rather with the uniformity of procedures to avoid management manipulation?

DAVIDSON, Trueblood: We have yet to see what the FASB is going to do on these important questions. If you say the APB Opinion No. 16 permitted this, I would agree.

AICPA Accounting Standards Executive Committee and Industry Audit Guide Committees:

SOLOMONS, Wheat: There is another aspect to the potential for conflict between the FASB and the AICPA that is worth bringing out in our discussion. The Institute has set up a committee to work with the FASB, the Accounting Standards Executive Committee. But there is a subsidiary standard-setting activity which the Wheat Committee recognized, which was somewhat outside the field of the APB and outside the scope of the FASB. I refer to the work of various Institute committees in preparing industry audit guides and similar statements. I understand that the work of these committees of the Institute, in particular committees that might feel the need to police certain industries, are being inhibited by the FASB. The FASB feels that it has a preemptive right exclusively to make declarations on accounting standards and that no committee or other arm of the Institute should make any pronouncements in that field.

The feeling of the Wheat Committee was that once the FASB made a pronouncement then it would be quite inappropriate for a committee of the Institute or for the Institute as a whole or indeed for any other supporting organization such as the FEI to come out with a contradictory statement. But until the FASB has issued a standard in some area, it seems to me that anyone has a right to make recommendations as to how a financial statement should be prepared. Then it is up to the FASB, if they think this is dangerously misleading, to come out with an authoritative statement. The Institute should not be put into a position where it is totally inhibited from working in areas where the FASB doesn't have the time to act.

Social Function of Accounting:

BOND, Moderator: How much different would the Trueblood Committee objectives be if the social function of accounting were regarded as the chief rationale rather than the narrow economic viewpoint taken in the report? Was this alternative taken into consideration?

DAVIDSON, Trueblood: Our overriding view was that we were concerned with the efficient allocation of resources within society. So we felt that this was an economic question and that the major goal of accounting reporting was to facilitate an optimal allocation of resources. We adopted a view that the public interest, that is the social interest, is served in the conventional case by people pursuing their own private interest.

There is also an objective in the report pointing out the need to recognize the social cost and benefits within the accounting system to the extent that those can be measured. Of course, Paul Fertig of Ohio State is one of those considering schemes for measurement and he can respond as to the difficulties in that regard. But the report does spell out this objective. Our report does suggest that before social factors can be introduced they really have to be capable of measurement.

SOLOMONS, Wheat: But I suppose the crucial area here was to report on social performance.

Accounting as a Process of Mapping:

BOND, Moderator: Professor Solomons has used both the analogy of the legislative body and the analogy of a judicial body to describe the functioning of the FASB. Which analogy are we to assume is more descriptive, or should we assume that both analogies can be used in different contexts?

SOLOMONS, Wheat: That is a penetrating question. I suggest that the work of the FASB is more legislative than judicial.

In thinking about the fundamental accounting concept, I have found it helpful to think of accounting as a process of mapping. It is as if the accountant is drawing a financial map which bears no resemblance whatsoever to the figures on the page but yet the figures on the page represent the terrain which he is mapping. Now the FASB, as best it can, is going to lay down rules as to how mapping is to be carried out. Is that a legislative or a judicial function? Truly, it is either or else it is both.

Incidentally, the one area I did have a slight difference of opinion on with the result of the committee but which wasn't important enough to lead to a dissenting opinion was on the question of the FASAC. The majority opinion on the Wheat Committee was in favor of having the chairman of the FASB as chairman of the Advisory Council. I thought the Advisory Council would be a more effective watch dog in the public interest if it could have an independent chairman and would have its own separate agenda and so on. I was a bit unhappy when we decided to have the one chairman for both bodies. Subsequently, since the report was issued, the charter and by-laws of the new Board and the Financial Accounting Foundation (FAF) to oversee it expressly state that the Advisory Council is not empowered to issue statements of its own over the head of or without reference to the Board. That is a rather unfortunate restriction of the Council's powers if, as I hope never happens, there is a serious difference of opinion between the Board and the Council. Incidentally, the only respect in which the implementation explicitly differed from our recommendations was in the size of the Advisory Council. We said it should have about 20 members; it has 27 or 28 members. This is a distinction of no great significance. I am substantially satisfied with the way the report was implemented and the way the new board has come into operation and with the way, so far, it has functioned.

DAVIDSON, Trueblood: As a believer in the ultimate triumph of truth and light, I do feel that the Trueblood Committee Report points the way to reasonable objectives of financial statements, and that the proper way of implementing those objectives will gradually emerge. There will be false starts and frustrating delays, but as David Solomons said in another connection, the terrain has been mapped and we will gradually find our way.

BIBLIOGRAPHY

SIDNEY DAVIDSON:

Books: (selected)

The Plant Accounting Regulations of the Federal Power Commission, University of Michigan Press, 1952.

(Editor with W. T. Baxter), Studies in Accounting Theory, R. D. Irwin, 1962.

(Editor with D. Green, C. T. Horngren, G. H. Sorter), On Income Approach to Accounting Theory, Prentice-Hall, 1964.

(Editor), Handbook of Modern Accounting, McGraw-Hill Book Company, 1970.

(With J. S. Schindler and R. L. Weil), Accounting: The Language of Business, Thomas Horton and Daughters, 1974.

(With J. S. Schindler and R. L. Weil), Fundamentals of Accounting, fifth edition, The Dryden Press, forthcoming.

Articles (selected):

(With D. Drake), "Capital Budgeting and the 'Best' Tax Depreciation Method," Journal of Business, October, 1961.

"The Meaning of Depreciation," University of Chicago Graduate School of Business, Selected Papers No. 2, 1962, reprinted in The Accounting Sampler, T. J. Burns and H. S. Hendrichson, editors, second edition, McGraw-Hill Book Company, 1972.

"Old Wine into New Bottles," The Accounting Review, April, 1963. Also reprinted in The Accounting Sampler.

"The Day of Reckoning - Managerial Analysis and Accounting Theory," Journal of Accounting Research, Autumn, 1963.

(With G. Sorter and H. Kalle), "Measuring the Defensive Position of a Firm," Financial Analysis Journal, January - February, 1964.

"LIFO Cost or Market and Compulsory Tax Reporting Requirements," Journal of Accounting Research, Spring, 1965.

(With J. Kohlmeier), "A Measure of the Impact of Some Foreign Accounting Principles," Journal of Accounting Research, Autumn, 1966.

(With F. T. Weston) "Accounting Changes," Financial Analysts Journal, September - October, 1968.

(With H. Bierman, Jr.), "The Income Concept-Value Increment or Earnings Predictor," The Accounting Review, April, 1969.

"Accounting and Financial Reporting in the Seventies," Arthur Young Journal, Spring - Summer, 1969. Reprinted in The Journal of Accountancy, December, 1969.

"Should Companies be Required to Publish Their Earnings Forecasts?" Institutional Investor, April, 1972.

"Publication of Budgets: A Forward Step," Reporting in the Seventies, B. Zuidi, California State University, 1972.

"The Study Group or Objections on Financial Statements: A Progress Report," Stanford Lecture in Accounting 1973, (Stanford University Graduate School of Business).

(With R. L. Weil), "On Holding Gains and Losses and the Evaluation of Management," The Accounting Review, July, 1974.

DAVID SOLOMONS:

Book and Monograph (selected):

Accounting Concepts and Standards: The Certified Accountants Educational Trust, London, 1974.

"Financial Accounting Standards: Regulation or Self-regulation?", Stanford Lecture in Accounting 1972 (Stanford University Graduate School of Business).

Other (recommended by D. Solomons):

AICPA Study on Establishment of Accounting Principles: Cases in Public Accounting Practice, Volume II, being the proceedings of the public hearing, November 3-4, 1971 (Chicago, Ill., Arthur Andersen & Co., 1972).

Corporate Financial Reporting: The Issues, the Objectives, and Some New Proposals, editors Rappaport and Revsine (Chicago, Ill.: Commerce Clearing House, 1972).

Storey, Reed K. The Search for Accounting Principles (New York: AICPA, 1964).

Uniformity in Financial Accounting: the Autumn 1965 issue of Law and Contemporary Problems, Duke Station, Durham, North Carolina.

GENERAL BIBLIOGRAPHY (SELECTED)

American Institute of Certified Public Accountants, Study Group on the Establishment of Accounting Principles, Establishing Financial Accounting Standards (The Wheat Committee Report), New York: AICPA, 1972.

American Institute of Certified Public Accountants, Study Group on the Objectives of Financial Statements, Objectives of Financial Statements (The Trueblood Committee Report), New York: AICPA, October, 1973.

Beaver, William H., "What Should be the FASB's Objectives?", The Journal of Accountancy, August, 1973.

Carsberg, Bryan, Anthony Hope, and R. W. Scapens, "The Objectives of Published Accounting Reports," Accounting and Business Research, Number 15, Summer, 1974, pp. 162-173.

Chambers, Raymond J., "The Trueblood Report: Many Curiosities," CA Magazine, December, 1973, pp. 19-20.

Cooper, S. Kerry and Don M. Guy, "CPA Firms View Accounting Objectives," Financial Executive, June, 1973, pp. 42-44, 46, 48, 50.

"Establishing Accounting Standards," Netherlands Study Group Reports, The Accountant, May 10, 1973, pp. 640-641.

Feller, B., "Accounting Standards - Objectives, Problems, Achievements," The Australian Accountant, Vol. 44, No. 7, August, 1974, pp. 392-401.

Fitzgerald, A. A., "Accounting Standards," Proceedings of the Australian Congress on Accounting, Sydney, 1949.

Kenley, W. John and George J. Staubus, Objectives and Concepts of Financial Statements, Accounting Research Study No. 3, Melbourne: Accountancy Research Foundation, 1972.

Kripke, Homer, "The SEC, The Accountants, Some Myths and Some Realities," NYU Law Review 45, No. 6 (December, 1970), pp. 1151-1205.

Mautz, Robert K., "The Trueblood Report: A Significant Shift in Emphasis," CA Magazine, December, 1973, pp. 17-19.

Nichol, Robert E. G., "The Search for the Objectives of Financial Statements: 'The Trueblood Report,'" The Australian Accountant, June, 1974, pp. 264-271.

Seidler, Lee J., "The Financial Accounting Standards Board: Goldfish in a Pool of Sharks," The Accountant's Magazine, October, 1973, pp. 558-564.

Skinner, Ross M., "The Trueblood Report: Brave New Beginning or Dead Line?", CA Magazine, December, 1973, pp. 13-15.

Sorter, George H., "Objectives of Financial Statements - An Inside View," CA Magazine, November, 1973, pp. 30-39.

Stamp, Edward, "The Trueblood Report: Acurate's Egg?", CA Magazine, December, 1973, pp. 15-16.

____________, "The E.E.C. and European Accounting Standards: A Strait-Jacket or a Spur?", Accountancy, May, 1973, pp. 9-16.

____________, "Establishing Accounting Principles," Abacus, Vol. 6, No. 2, December, 1970, pp. 96-104.

APPENDIX A TO SECTION IV

The Implementation of The Wheat Committee Recommendations STUDY ON ESTABLISHMENT OF ACCOUNTING PRINCIPLES*

The Study on Establishment of Accounting Principles was conducted under the sponsorship of the AICPA. The seven-man study group was chaired by Francis M. Wheat. The report of the study group, dated March 29, 1972, is frequently referred to as the Wheat Report.

The study group reported that notable improvements in financial reporting had been achieved through the work of the APB. The group noted, however, that difficulties had arisen under the APB arrangement, and that the time had come for a change.

The Wheat Report recommended the establishment of three new, affiliated organizations:

> *The Financial Accounting Foundation (FAF), a new foundation to be established separate from all existing professional bodies. The FAF would be governed by a Board of Trustees composed of nine members whose principal duties would be to appoint the members of the FASB and to raise the funds for its operation.*
>
> *The Financial Accounting Standards Board (FASB), whose function would be to establish standards of financial accounting and reporting. The FASB would have seven members, all fully remunerated and serving full-time, and with no other affiliations.*
>
> *The Financial Accounting Standards Advisory Council (FASAC), with approximately twenty members, whose assignment would be to work closely with the Standards Board in an advisory capacity.*

The recommendation for the establishment of the three new organizations was accepted by the AICPA in May, 1972. In the selection of trustees for the Foundation, the Wheat Report urged that appointments be made from lists submitted by the AICPA and from other organizations having a continuing interest in financial reporting:

*Adapted from Financial Accounting Foundation Report, July 1, 1972-December 31, 1973.

American Accounting Association (AAA)
Financial Analysts Federation (FAF)
Financial Executives Institute (FEI)
National Association of Accountants (NAA)

Each of these organizations is represented on the FAF and has pledged its support in the implementation of the Wheat Report recommendations.

On July 1, 1973, the FASB succeeded the APB as the designated standards-setting body in the private sector for purposes of Rule 203 of the AICPA's Rules of Content pursuant to action by the AICPA's Council at its May, 1973 meeting. On December 20, 1973, in a significant and unprecedented step, the SEC in ARS No. 150 formally endorsed the FASB as the organization in the private sector to provide leadership in establishing accounting principles. In so doing, the Commission stated that it "intends to continue its policy of looking to the private sector for leadership in establishing and in improving accounting principles and standards through the body's conclusions will promote the interests of investors." The Commission then announced that principles, standards, and practices promulgated by the FASB in its statements and interpretations will be considered by the commission as having substantial authoritative support, and that those contrary to FASB promulgations will be considered to have no such support.

APPENDIX B TO SECTION IV

FINANCIAL ACCOUNTING STANDARDS: REGULATION OR SELF-REGULATION?*

by

David Solomons

The Study Group's Proposals

I take it that it is not necessary for me to say much about the nature of the Study Group's work or about its recommendations, and I shall assume some familiarity with these matters. It will perhaps be enough to remind you that, after studying for almost a year the way in which accounting principles (or standards, as we hope they will now be called) are formulated, we recommend certain fairly radical changes in these arrangements. The principal changes are these:

1. *Replacement of the relatively large 18-man part-time Accounting Principles Board by a much smaller 7-man full-time Financial Accounting Standards Board.*

2. *The present Board is unpaid; the new Board, serving full-time will be adequately remunerated.*

3. *We propose to remove the requirement that all members of the Board must be members of the AICPA, a requirement which implies that they must all hold CPA certificates. While we recommend that at least four members of the new Board be drawn from CPA's in public practice, they need not be members of the Institute. On the other hand, all seven members could be members of the Institute; and I personally shall be surprised if we ever see a Board on which Institute members do not constitute a majority.*

4. *The new Board will not, like the old, be an organ of a single professional organization. The APB is a senior committee of the AICPA. The new Board will not be a committee of anything. It will be answerable, in some sense, to the trustees of a new Financial Accounting Foundation, who will appoint the members of the Standards Board.*

*Reprinted with permission from Stanford Lectures in Accounting, Price Waterhouse Foundation, privately printed, May 31, 1972.

5. We propose a voting rule for the new Board different from the APB's--five out of seven votes will be needed to pass a standard instead of the present 12 out of 18. This is not a drastic change. We wanted something more than a bare majority of the seven members and something less than near unanimity. Moreover, if the new Board does have its minimum complement of four CPA's, they will need at least one ally among the other members to get a standard approved. As to the size of the Board, I shall have something to say about that later.

6. The new Board is provided with a custom-built receiver for tuning in to signals from the financial and business community, the government sector, and users of financial information, in the form of the financial Accounting Standards Advisory Council. But this metaphor is seriously deficient, for a receiver is a passive instrument, a mere conduit for bringing in sounds from outside. It cannot take the initiative. It is our hope that the Advisory Council will be much more than a mere receiver, for in helping the Board to draw up its agenda and in reacting to its findings, it cannot help being an active participant in its work.

It is of course the change from an unpaid part-time Board to a paid full-time Board that represents the most radical departure from the past. The other changes do not. There are several important elements of continuity that are provided in our proposals. Most important of these is the position of primacy of the AICPA, which we have gone far to retain. All of the trustees of the Foundation are to be appointed by the Board of Directors of the Institute, even though four of the nine will normally be chosen from names submitted by other bodies. Four of the seven members of the Standards Board are to be CPA's, and it is more than likely that they will be Institute members, as may other members of the Board. Institute members are certain to be found on the Advisory Council as well. It seems to me that only those who can be satisfied with nothing less than a monopoly of authority for the Institute in the standard-setting function have cause to complain about these proposed arrangements.

It is of course the change from an unpaid part-time Board to a paid full-time Board that represents the most radical departure from the past. The other changes do not. There are several important elements of continuity that are provided in our proposals. Most important of these is the position of primacy of the AICPA, which we have gone far to retain. All of the trustees of the Foundation are to be appointed by the Board of Directors of the Institute, even though four of the nine will normally be chosen *from names submitted by other bodies. Four of the seven members of the Standards Board are to be CPA's, and it is more than likely that they will be Institute members, as may other members of the Board. Institute members are certain to be found on the Advisory Council as well. It seems to me that only those who can be satisfied with nothing less than a monopoly of authority for the Institute in the standard-setting function have cause to complain about these proposed arrangements.*

If there is anything to be said that can comfort those who regard as intolerable any diminution, however slight, of the Institute's role, I would say that it is better to give up a little than to lose a lot, and that shared authority is better than none at all. I am implying, of course, that only by broadening the base of support for whatever body is entrusted with the task of setting financial accounting standards can we hope to keep it in private hands, at least to the extent that it is in private hands at the present time.

Is Standard Setting Really a Private Function Now?

Charles Horngren in his recent forthright piece in the Journal of Accountancy[1] says that "it is time to dispel the oft-heard myth that a private group is setting the accounting principles which are then enforced by the policing agency, the SEC." The SEC, he says, is the top management, and the APB or any successor body must perform in a subordinate role, limited by constraints set by the SEC. Formally, there is no doubt that this is true. Under the Securities Exchange Act of 1934 the SEC was given the power to prescribe "the items or details to be shown in the balance sheet and the earnings statement, and the methods to be followed in the preparation of reports. . . ."[2] The Act says that the Commission "may prescribe" these things, not that it "shall prescribe" them. It is this wording, presumably, that has made it possible for the Commission to delegate the formulation of accounting standards to a private body to the extent that it has.

The extent of this delegation clearly looks different, according as it is viewed from the APB's vantage point or the Commission's. For members of the Board, if Horngren's point of view is a representative one, the overriding authority of the Commission is hard to live with, since it means that the Board must take criticism for actions or inactions which are in fact not fully within its control. On the other hand, the impression I got when the Wheat Study Group met with the SEC was that the Commission saw itself as exercising extreme restraint in its relation with the Board. For some of its lawyer critics it exercises too much restraint and leans too heavily on the APB. Professor Homer Kripke refers to "the SEC's almost perverse reluctance to take the responsibility for the substance of financial disclosure,"[3] and in the same article he says that "one must disagree with Dean Sidney A. Davidson of the University of Chicago, who has said that it is fortunate that the SEC has let its accounting powers lie dormant. In this writer's view, it is most unfortunate that the Commission has not asserted its powers more vigorously."[4] I note, incidentally, that Sidney Davidson's view, as quoted here, formed in part while he was a member of the APB, is strikingly at variance not only with Kripke's as to whether the SEC's passivity in accounting matters has been fortunate or not, but also with Horngren's as to whether passivity accurately describes the Commission's posture.

Formally, as I have said, we must agree with Horngren that setting financial standards is a joint private-public venture. Yet most of the activity has gone on in the private sector and it does not seem to me to be unrealistic to continue to talk about this function as still residing in the private sector. Almost everyone who gave evidence to the Study Group expressed a preference for keeping it there. This view stems partly from a rather widespread reluctance to see the already pervasive influence of government extend still further. But there are also more specific grounds for not yielding to a government agency, whether the SEC or some other body, an undisputed position of authority for dispensing financial accounting standards.

Why not a Public Board?

The Study Group's Report draws attention to the most important of these grounds. Government agencies are more directly susceptible to political pressures than private bodies, and when not subject to such pressures they are apt to let sleeping dogs lie. All in all, experience of government intervention in the accounting field does not inspire confidence that a governmental body can do a better job of setting financial accounting standards than a private body can. Experience last year when the APB came into conflict with Congress over the accounting treatment of the investment tax credit made it clear that a government standard-setting body would find it quite difficult to separate questions of accounting measurement from matters of public policy. Yet they can and should be kept separate. Congress and the Treasury Department have other means at their disposal for getting the results they want from tax legislation without dictating accounting rules. To take the accounting route to secure some desired policy objective is as if a traffic authority, wishing to enforce a speed limit, did so by tampering with speedometers. As a matter of fact, that analogy is not as far-fetched as it may seem. Legislatures do stop the clock when they run out of time at the end of a session. If it is that easy to distort the measurement of *time, might not accounting measurement fare as badly if entrusted entirely to a government agency?*

<u>How Best to Keep the Government Out?</u>

How best can the setting of financial accounting standards be preserved from further government intrusion? Three conditions, I suggest, need to be satisfied if there is to be much hope of success in this venture.

They are, in increasing order of importance:

1. *that the private body entrusted with the duty of standard-setting commands widespread support.*

2. *that there are no serious conflicts between the private interests of those setting the standards and the public interest, and no appearance of such conflicts.*

3. *that the job, in private hands, is being done effectively and expeditiously.*

All of these conditions are necessary--none of them alone is sufficient. I should like to comment on each of them, in order.

The private body entrusted with the duty of standard-setting must command widespread support.

The best way to provide that support is to bring in, as participants, elements in the financial community who now feel unjustifiably excluded. As I have already indicated, the Study Group proposes to broaden the base of support of the Board by giving bodies other than the AICPA a voice in the direction of the Financial Accounting Foundation and by opening up the Standards Board to non-CPA members. Thus there will be wider participation in the work of the new FASB than there has been in the work of the APB. The problem is to know where to stop. How widespread should this participation be? If financial executives, why not bankers? If bankers, why not the whole business community, the AFL-CIO, the League of Women Voters, the American Legion, and the NAACP?

Why not, indeed! This is not merely a rhetorical question, for all these groups are touched at many points in their lives by what accountants do. The Study Group's answer is to bring in as participants in the appointment and financing of the Standards Board a subset of the financial community that we have called the financial reporting community--CPA's, financial executives, financial analysts, and accounting educators. As for the Standards Board itself, there will be room on it now for three persons drawn from any group so long as they are "well versed in the problems of financial reporting," to use the language of the report. There is nothing in this language to exclude the president of the League of Women Voters, if she is otherwise well qualified.

This condition for keeping the standard-setting function in private hands--that the private arrangements should command widespread support--does not point to a small full-time board. Indeed, it points the other way. The larger the board, the more bases of support it has. This has been notably demonstrated by the present APB in one respect, in that it has been large enough to provide seats, continuously since its inception, for each of the "Big Eight." At the same time, the condition that members of the Board must be CPA's has had the opposite effect of tending to limit its support to a single segment of the community. Unfortunately, though a large board could meet my first test for nonnationalization, "widespread support," it is not likely to satisfy the other tests nearly so well, and it is because of that that the Study Group came out in favor of a small board. We hope we have resolved the dilemma by giving the small Board wide support through the composition of the trustees of the Foundation and through the large Advisory Council.

My second condition for successfully resisting the nationalization of financial accounting standard-setting is that there must be no serious conflicts between private and public interests within the group entrusted with the standard-setting function, and no appearance of such conflicts. *Probably enough has already been said on this subject to make further extended discussion unnecessary. The report of the Study Group makes it clear that we turned up no evidence of instances where members of the APB had clearly voted in accordance with client pressures, and contrary to their own best judgment. The argument that partners in large CPA firms have clients with interests on all sides of most important accounting questions, and that this alone will keep them honest, is a persuasive one, up to a point. But these interests, however diversified, will generally be united in favor of less control rather than more control, in favor of more freedom to pick and choose among available accounting methods as against more standardization. One need only cite the history of APB Opinion No. 16 on accounting for mergers and acquisitions as evidence that the diverse interests of numerous clients cannot be relied upon to insure that the public interest will emerge unscathed from the deliberations of a part-time board. I have heard the Chairman of the APB at the time that this debate was going on, Leroy Layton, describe graphically the way in which the Board buckled under pressure and retreated from the strong draft opin-*

ion with which it started to the compromise which eventually emerged. He blames the compromise on the Board's two-thirds voting rule; but I believe that the problem goes deeper than that.

If it is indeed a necessary condition for keeping accounting standard-setting in the private sector that serious conflicts between private and public interests be eliminated or at least minimized, it seems probable that a full-time board can satisfy this condition, and be seen to satisfy it, more effectively than any part-time board, however constituted. But some of the difficult questions which the trustees of the Financial Accounting Foundation will have to answer are already beginning to be asked. One question relates to leaves of absence. Is it enough for an accounting practitioner to take a five-year leave of absence from his firm to serve a term as a full-time member of the Standards Board? Is this what is meant by an "independent" Board?

It is difficult for an academic to say that this is not enough to assure independence. One of my colleagues at The Wharton School is at the present time exhibiting considerable independence as Insurance Commissioner for the State of Pennsylvania while on leave from the University of Pennsylvania. I might add that this leave will not be extended beyond two years. The former Attorney-General of the United States has just rejoined his old firm; and this practice is common throughout government. Yet I think the Standards Board should require members to make a declaration that there is no agreement, formal or informal, with their former firms or employers that they can rejoin them on leaving the Board. This would not preclude their rejoining, and I would expect that service on the Board would increase the attractiveness of a former partner or employee, so that he would normally be welcomed back if he wished to rejoin. But any kind of undertaking between the two sides at the time a member joins the Board as to what he will do when he leaves it in my view vitiates the concept of an independent Board. Let me make it clear that I am here speaking only for myself. So far as I can recall, the Study Group did not consider this question.

Another kind of question bearing on the independence of the new Board has also been put to me since our Report was published. This concerns the method by which the Foundation is to be financed. There have already been many promises of financial support from large public accounting firms covering the Foundation's first five years, and these already virtually assure its initial solvency. But outside the profession there are voices already asking whether a Board so financed can be truly independent. Could it afford to take an unpopular line and perhaps jeopardize its continued existence by endangering its financial support?

One can respond to these doubts in a number of different ways. If the private support is widespread enough, the loss of a few supporters need not endanger the Board's health. Alternatively, one can say that the accounting profession would be unwilling to tarnish its own image by pulling the rug from under the Board because the Board did not always vote the right way. I can think of other answers. But when all is said, I confess that I do not find voluntary financial support a satisfactory method of financing the Foundation except as a way of getting the new organization quickly off the ground. Some more systematic means of financing it should be found during the breathing space which the initial commitments by CPA firms and others will give the trustees. Some suggestions were made in our Report, and I hope the trustees will explore them once the new Board has been set up and is at work.

My third condition for keeping standard-setting in private hands is that those hands operate efficiently. *No stronger argument can be found to oppose government intervention in any sphere than to show that it is unnecessary because the activity in question is already being performed effectively. The United States is one of the few countries of the world that has left its telephone system in private hands. It is easy to make a strong case for the nationalization of such an important element in our communications network, especially since telephone service is a natural monopoly. Yet I have heard no clamor to have AT&T nationalized, and I believe that this is so because most people think that by and large the company has done a good job. Certainly the British Post Office doesn't do as well, with a much smaller system.*

If the level of efficiency with which accounting standards are set in the private sector is an important factor in protecting it from encroachment by government agencies, then it is essential to do everything possible to maximize that effectiveness. There are many different elements which go to make up effectiveness in this context. Timeliness is one element, both as regards the speed with which the Board recognizes and responds to the need for a standard, and as regards the speed with which the development and promulgation of the standard can be carried out. Another facet of what is meant by effectiveness is that the standards shall be responsive to the needs that prompted them. This will depend among other things on the technical skill of the members of the Standards Board, and on this score I have heard no criticism of the APB.

But responsiveness to need is not simply a matter of technical skill on the part of the members of the APB. Limitations on the time that they can devote to the Board's work are important.

The discontinuity in debate, which is inevitable with a part-time Board that can meet only for two or three days a month at the most, must result in much loss of momentum. It also leaves the research staff with less direction than I believe in the past it could have used.

Of course, it can be argued that time is needed for reflection during the development of a standard, and that the monthly meetings of the present Board provide such time. This is not a convincing argument against a full-time Board. Such a Board can also take time for reflection when that is necessary. It can do so by conscious decision, not because discontinuity is forced upon it by circumstances.

It may be worthwhile to record, as a footnote to history, how, as it seems to me, the Study Group came unanimously to favor a full-time Board. We certainly did not all start out from such a position, and in the early stages of our deliberations I believe there would have been a majority in favor of continuing with a part-time Board, though perhaps giving it a full-time chairman and even a full-time vice-chairman. But we gradually learned a lesson from our own part-time status as a Study Group. We learned that a heavy price in lost momentum is paid by any group that can meet only for one or two days a month, with all the supervening distractions of other activities in between, and that if this was true for us, who had a single, fairly well-defined task to accomplish, it was likely to be much more serious for a body like the APB, with its more complex agenda.

The connotation of the word "amateur" has sadly changed for the worse in our society in recent years. In many fields, it used to imply a superior status to that of the professional--superiority in dedication and often superiority in skill, as in the lawn tennis world. Those days are rapidly receding. Professionalism has conquered the world of sport. Lay magistrates, who still function in England, are regarded as an anachronism here. An amateur Standards Board is also an anachronism, I suggest, in the 1970's.

I have made it clear that I think a full-time Board will function more effectively than one which is part-time. Once that point has been conceded, it virtually follows that a full-time Board must be smaller than the present one, on grounds of cost alone, since a full-time Board must be remunerated. How much smaller? A review of government agencies and commissions provides models of all sizes--the Federal Home Loan Bank Board has only three members, many agencies (including the SEC and the Cost Accounting Standards Board) have five, the Supreme Court has nine, and the Interstate Commerce Commission has eleven. We thought that seven represented a reasonable compromise between compactness and diversity of composition. The size of the APB was changed once during its history. The size of the Standards Board can be changed if experience shows that we were wrong.

I conclude, then, that the proposed Financial Accounting Standards Board can substantially satisfy my three conditions for maximizing the likelihood that setting financial accounting standards can be retained in the private sector at least to the extent that they are now set there. And this is my answer to those who are opposed to a full-time Board because, they say, it will be easier to nationalize. What they mean, I think, is that it already looks more like a government agency, and that its very compactness would reduce the technical problems of nationalizing it. But these are surely superficial arguments. If the new Board works well, inspires confidence in its independence and enjoys widespread support, powerful arguments for nationalizing it will be lacking. That alone may not protect it; but if it does not, all that is left is to say, with Dr. Johnson, "though we cannot out-vote them, we will out-argue them."

The Nature of Self-Regulation

There is, however, a more philosophical kind of antipathy to a full-time Board which some people feel, based on the belief that it no longer represents self-regulation in as full a sense as the APB does. The APB is made up of working members of the accounting profession; the members of the Standards Board will stand apart because of its full-time character. I believe that this view is mistaken because it is based on an erroneous view of self-regulation.

Self-regulation clearly does not mean literally that each man regulates himself, any more than self-government means that each man in a democracy governs himself. Self-government doesn't even mean that all the agents of government are directly elected by those who are governed. Whether in a parliamentary democracy or a presidential system like that in the United States, it is accepted that most members of the executive and judicial branches of government are appointed, not elected. The hallmark of self-government is that the legislative branch is elected. In this country the senior members of the executive are also answerable to the electorate, not directly but because they are appointed by an elected President and they stand or fall with him.

If it is said that regulation of accounting standards by the new FASB will have none of the elective characteristics of a system of self-government, the answer must be that they will be no less a mark of the new organization than of the old. The APB is *not elected but is appointed by the Board of Directors of the AICPA; but the Directors are elected by Council which is in turn elected by the members of the Institute, so that in a rather indirect way, the APB can be said to rest on an electoral system. And so will the new Standards Board, except that an extra stage will have been introduced into the process in the shape of the trustees of the Financing Accounting Foundation, who will appoint the Board and will themselves be appointed by the same Board of Directors that now appoints the APB.*

As the Wheat Report indicates, the Study Group believes that by bringing in some representation of persons directly concerned with financial reporting other than the AICPA's members, there will be an enrichment of the self-regulatory process. The phrase we used, "the financial reporting community," is not an empty one. Some people will no doubt wish to give stronger representation to parts of that community than we have proposed; but we thought we had gone as far as was possible at this point in time, if enforcement was to continue to depend on the independent public accountant and not more heavily than it does at present on the SEC.

The Advisory Council

By no means the least important of the innovations proposed by the Study Group is the Financial Accounting Standards Advisory Council. It is to have about 20 members, appointed by the trustees of the Financial Accounting Foundation for one-year terms. Members of the Council can be reappointed indefinitely, though we suggest that normally a member should not serve for more than four years, for too little turnover on the Council will defeat our hope that it will be a source of new ideas and new contacts for the Standards Board.

Members of the Council will serve without pay, but it is not our intention that these positions should be sinecures. Formal meetings of the Council might not take up much time. Regular quarterly meetings, it seems to me, would suffice to keep the Council in close touch with the Board's activities without wasting time on unnecessary meetings, although in the first year of the new arrangements some different pattern might be called for. But there will be plenty for members of the Council to do between meetings, reading and reacting to draft standards, working directly perhaps on task forces concerned with particular standards, providing the Board and its staff with contacts, and gathering and conveying to the Board views on its work from the segments of the community to which the Advisory Council member is closest.

I see two rather different functions for the Advisory Council and at one time I favored having two separate bodies to per-

form them. There is the technical review of the work of the Standards Board. For this, considerable expertise in financial reporting will be necessary, and the skills and interests which will have to be harnessed to carry out this part of the Council's work are not too difficult to identify. But, distinct from this function, I see a need for the Council to act as a guardian of the public interest in the broadest sense. It would be naive to suppose that this function could be performed by persons altogether ignorant of the problems of financial reporting; but it does not call for the same degree of accounting expertise as the Council's technical function does. There is more room here for economists, lawyers, and representatives of consumer and labor interests, among others. Whether a single body can comprehend these diverse interests and perform these rather different functions remains to be seen. I shall not be surprised to find that our proposals for the Advisory Council call for more modification by the Trustees will not feel inhibited from improving on our proposals as soon as it becomes clear in what respects those proposals fall short of what is needed.

An Extension of the Advisory Council's Functions

In an article in a recent issue of the Harvard Business Review,[5] Walter Frese and Robert Mautz propose that "a voluntary, unaffiliated, and not-for-profit organization be established by and of general corporate management to review published annual reports and to comment on them." They suggest that the published financial reports of major United States companies be reviewed and graded according to their quality. The review panel "would issue an annual report in which these ratings were included, along with comments on the status of current financial reporting in general and suggestions for problems to study in order that reporting could be improved."

This article was published just before the Study Group's report appeared. I do not know what the authors would think about having their suggestion taken over and implemented by the new Advisory Council, but it seems to me a natural extension of the functions we assigned to it, and while I see little prospect of a special unaffiliated review panel being set up for this purpose, only shortage of money could prevent the Advisory Council from making a success of it. Moreover, while an unaffiliated panel could do nothing but give publicity to substandard reporting, the Advisory Council would be in an excellent position both to do that and also to alert the Standards Board to the need for a new standard or the revision of an old one, where its review pointed to it.

It is obvious that this kind of review of financial reporting practices is not unrelated to the work that has been done in recent years by the AICPA's Committee on Practice Review, although the committee has been more concerned with the duties of the auditor in relation to substandard financial reports, whereas Frese and Mautz were more concerned with the responsibilities of general management, and the Advisory Council would be concerned with both management and auditors. If the Advisory Council were to take on this review function, as I have suggested, it may be that part of the work of the Institute's Committee on Practice Review--the part concerned with accounting practices as distinct from auditing practices--would become redundant.

Conclusion

Since the Study Group's Report was published, I have been asked more than once what guarantee there is that the new organization can more successful than the APB has been. Of course, the answer has to be that there is no such guarantee. But let me first say that I do not believe that the APB has been unsuccessful. I believe that since 1959 we have seen a material advance in the standard of financial reporting, and the APB can take much of the credit for it. Perhaps progress should have been faster. But let no one look for guarantees. If we only made changes when we could guarantee success, we should probably still be lighting our homes by candles.

NOTES

[1]Charles T. Horngren, "Accounting Principles: Private or Public Sector?," Journal of Accountancy, May, 1972, pp. 37-41.

[2]Securities and Exchange Act of 1934, sec. 13(b).

[3]Homer Kripke, "The SEC, The Accountants, Some Myths and Some Realities," NYU Law Review 45, No. 6 (December, 1970), p. 1182.

[4]Loc. cit., p. 1177.

[5]Walter F. Frese and Robert K. Mautz, "Financial Reporting--By Whom?," Harvard Business Review, March-April, 1972.

APPENDIX C TO SECTION IV

A SUMMARY OF OBJECTIVES OF FINANCIAL STATEMENTS FROM THE TRUEBLOOD REPORT*

In the development of objectives of financial statements, the Study Group has attempted to identify and evaluate the desirable goals of the financial accounting process.

Accounting is not an end in itself. As an information system, the justification for accounting can be found only in how well accounting information serves those who use it. Thus, the Study Group agrees with the conclusion drawn by many others that

> The basic objective of financial statements is to provide information useful for making economic decisions.

In satisfying this objective, accounting should serve the goals of both the private and public sectors of the economy. By fulfilling the information needs of those in the private sector who make economic decisions, accounting assists in a more efficient allocation of resources, thus contributing to the attainment of broad social goals.

Users' needs for information are not known with any degree of certainty. The specific role financial statements play in the economic decision-making process has not been identified. This Study is therefore dependent upon certain assumptions which are supported by its research:

- *Users of financial statements seek to predict, compare, and evaluate the cash consequences of their economic decisions.*

- *Information about the cash consequences of decisions made by the enterprise is useful for predicting, comparing, and evaluating cash flows to users. (If the value of the unit of measure is unstable, that is, if inflation or deflation is so great that direct cash consequences are no longer comparable, such circumstances should be recognized in the financial statements.)*

*Reprinted by permission from Chapter 11, Objectives of Financial Statements, Report of the Study Group on the Objectives of Financial Statements, AICPA, October, 1973, pp. 61-66.

• *Financial statements are more useful if they include, but distinguish, information that is primarily factual, and therefore can be measured objectively, from information that is primarily interpretive.*

The objectives of financial statements developed in this Study are intended to follow logically from these assumptions.

Some users of financial information often have access to much more information than is available to users of general purpose financial statements. Therefore, users who ordinarily rely on financial statements alone may be served most by developing accounting objectives. Financial statements should meet the needs of those with the least ability to obtain information and the needs of others as well. Consequently,

An objective of financial statements is to serve primarily those users who have limited authority, ability, or resources to obtain information and who rely on financial statements as their principal source of information about an enterprise's economic activities.

Most economic decisions involve a sacrifice (something given or used up) and a benefit (something received). Creditors and investors are concerned with the ability of the enterprise to generate cash flows to them and with their ability to predict, compare, and evaluate the amount, timing, and related uncertainty of these future cash flows. Therefore,

An objective of financial statements is to provide information useful to investors and creditors for predicting, comparing, and evaluating potential cash flows to them in terms of amount, timing, and related uncertainty.

The primary goal of every commercial enterprise is to increase its monetary wealth so that over time it can return the maximum amount of cash to its owners. Economic decision-makers need information about the enterprise's degree of success periodically before dissolution, because they make decisions every day. A fundamental purpose of accounting is to provide interim measures of enterprise progress. Accounting earnings should measure such progress. They should recognize the notion of economic better-offness, but should be directed specifically to the enterprise's success in using cash to generate maximum cash.

Given appropriate financial information, the decision-maker uses his judgment to evaluate the enterprise's potential. This judgment aims at estimating the enterprise's ability to be better off, to generate more cash, and to have earnings convertible into cash at some future date. This ability is the enterprise's earning power. Therefore,

> An objective of financial statements is to provide users with information for predicting, comparing, and evaluating enterprise earning power.

An enterprise is accountable for its actions, or inactions, in discharging a wide range of responsibilities. Accountability involves the reporting of periodic measures of progress toward enterprise goals. Thus, measures useful for assessing earning power are also useful for accountability. Accordingly,

> An objective of financial statements is to supply information useful in judging management's ability to utilize enterprise resources effectively in achieving the primary enterprise goal.

The earning process consists of effort and performance directed at reaching the primary enterprise goal of returning over time the maximum amount of cash to its owners. The activities that are part of the earning process of the enterprise can be related to earnings cycles. An earnings cycle can be classified as completed, incomplete, or prospective. A completed earnings cycle involves a series of events whose entire impact on enterprise earnings and earning power is considered to have occurred. An incomplete earnings cycle involves a series of events underway whose full impact on enterprise earnings and earning power has not yet occurred. A prospective earnings cycle involves a series of planned events or unilateral actions. The earnings cycle concept is believed to be useful because the classifications assist users in evaluating uncertainties and the earning power of the enterprise.

Earnings as reported in financial statements have come to be, and in all probability will continue to be, the single most important criterion for assessing the enterprise's accomplishments and earning power. In the final analysis, ideal determination of earnings--the change during a period in the present values of future cash flows--can be approached no faster than the increase in user confidence in accounting measures permits. However, it seems reasonable to assume that, even in the long run, a distinction will have to be made between that portion of earnings resulting from completed cycles and estimates of recognizable progress toward the completion of incomplete cycles, and that portion of earnings arising from changes in value.

Economic decision-makers need both factual and interpretive information--identified separately to the extent possible--about transactions and other events in order to assess uncertainty. In all reporting, the assumptions, interpretations, predictions, and estimations that underlie the preparer's conclusions should be set forth. Thus,

> An objective of financial statements is to provide factual and interpretive information about transactions and other events which is useful for predicting, comparing, and evaluating enterprise earning power. Basic underlying assumptions with respect to matters subject to interpretation, evaluation, prediction, or estimation should be disclosed.

Based on an analysis of users' needs, it can be concluded that

- *Financial statements should emphasize information about transactions and other events that significantly affect enterprise earning power or changes in it. Such information should be stated in terms of action or prospective cash impact and should facilitate comparisons.*

- *Financial statements should report both facts and interpretations about transactions and other events.*

- *Financial statements should assist in the assessment of the uncertainties with respect to the amount and timing of prospective cash receipts and disbursements.*

- *Financial statements should report on series of transactions and other events, including value changes, in terms of earnings cycles.*

The Group concludes that these goals can be attained through financial statements consisting of a statement of financial position, a statement of earnings, and a statement of financial activities. Thus,

> An objective is to provide a statement of financial position useful for predicting, comparing, and evaluating enterprise earning power. This statement should provide information concerning enterprise transactions and other events that are part of incomplete earnings cycles. Current values should also be reported when they differ significantly from historical cost. Assets and liabilities should be grouped or segregated by the relative uncertainty of the amount and timing of prospective realization or liquidation.

An objective is to provide a statement of periodic earnings useful for predicting, comparing, and evaluating enterprise earning power. The net result of completed earnings cycles and enterprise activities resulting in recognizable progress toward completion of incomplete cycles should be reported. Changes in the values reflected in successive statements of financial position should also be reported, but separately, since they differ in terms of their certainty of realization.

(For some time there has been consistent demand for a single earnings figure. Members of the Study Group disagree on whether value changes that meet the qualitative criteria discussed in this report should be included in earnings. Some believe the objective should be to reflect current value changes in earnings. Others believe that inclusion of unrealized value changes in earnings may be desirable but is not now practicable. Still others believe inclusion is neither desirable nor practicable.)

An objective is to provide a statement of financial activities useful for predicting, comparing, and evaluating enterprise earning power. This statement should report mainly on factual aspects of enterprise transactions having or expected to have significant cash consequences. This statement should report data that require minimal judgment and interpretation by the preparer.

Each of the financial statements should be structured to enhance the user's ability to assess the following.

- *The extent to which sacrifices and benefits vary over time and among themselves, such as differentiation between fixed and variable expense.*

- *The extent to which sacrifices and benefits vary in relation to changes in the industry and the economy.*

- *The extent to which the occurrence of sacrifice and benefits, or their allocation to time periods, is discretionary or arbitrary. Examples are contributions, unusual research expenditures, or the recognition of gains or losses whose timing can be controlled.*

- *The extent to which sacrifices and benefits are unusual or infrequent and, therefore, require special consideration for predicting, comparing, and evaluating.*

- *The extent to which sacrifices and benefits pertain to various lines of activity of the enterprise.*

Financial statement objectives are based on the user's need for information useful for predicting, comparing, and evaluating earning power. The Study Group concludes that, to satisfy these information requirements, different valuation bases are preferable for different assets and liabilities. The objectives of financial statements cannot be best served by the exclusive use of a single valuation basis. Each of the valuation bases should be analyzed in terms of the stated objectives. Selection of the specific basis or combination of bases to be used is an implementation issue.

All economic decisions look to the future. Since economic decision-makers cannot know the future, they look to the past and the present. Financial statements that provide information about the past and the present are useful for making predictions on which to base economic decisions. In many instances, however, the past may not be a good indicator of the future. Publication of explicit forecasts of enterprise activities may well fit the objectives of financial statements. The important consideration is not the accuracy of management forecasts themselves, but rather the relative accuracy of users' predictions with and without forecasts in financial statements. Thus,

> An objective of financial statements is to provide information useful for the predictive process. Financial forecasts should be provided when they will enhance the reliability of users' predictions.

Many of the aspects of economic decisions concerned with governmental and not-for-profit organizations are similar to those of decisions concerning commercial enterprises. As with commercial enterprises, decision-makers are interested in predicting, comparing, and evaluating benefits and sacrifices in terms of amount, timing, and related uncertainty, even though they seek nonmonetary benefits. For governmental and not-for-profit organizations, assessments of performance should relate to the goals of the enterprise, even though these goals are essentially nonmonetary.

Managers of governmental and not-for-profit organizations are also accountable for their performance and goal attainment. Thus, reporting on such accountability is as important for not-for-profit organizations as it is for commercial enterprises. Consequently,

> An objective of financial statements for governmental and not-for-profit organizations is to provide information useful for evaluating the effectiveness of the management of resources in achieving the organization's goals. Per-

formance measures should be quantified in terms of identified goals.

The objectives structure of this report, while primarily directed toward private goals, applies at least indirectly to social goals as well. The accounting objectives in this report are intended to produce financial information that will facilitate decisions that advance the common good. Thus,

> An objective of financial statements is to report on those activities of the enterprise affecting society which can be determined and described or measured and which are important to the role of the enterprise in its social environment.

Information contained in financial statements to satisfy users' needs should possess the qualitative characteristics of relevance and materiality, reliability, freedom from bias, comparability, consistency, understandability, and the recognition of substance over form. Information is not useful unless it is relevant and material to the user's decision. In making decisions, users should be able not only to understand the information presented, but to assess differences in its reliability, to rely on its fairness, to compare it with information about alternative opportunities, and to assess its consistency with previous presentations.

. . . . . .

The Study Group concludes that the objectives developed in this report can be looked upon as attainable in stages within a reasonable time. Selecting the appropriate course of action for gaining acceptance of these objectives is not within the purview of the Study Group. However, the Study Group urges that its conclusions be considered as an initial step in developing objectives important for the ongoing refinement and improvement of accounting standards and practices.

APPENDIX D TO SECTION IV

CONCEPTUAL FRAMEWORK FOR ACCOUNTING AND REPORTING: CONSIDERATION OF THE REPORT OF THE STUDY GROUP ON THE OBJECTIVES OF FINANCIAL STATEMENTS*

Introduction:

In 1970, the Accounting Principles Board published its Statement 4, "Basic Concepts and Accounting Principles Underlying Financial Statements of Business Enterprise."[1] Statement 4 was primarily a description of acceptable accounting practices at that time.

In the Spring of 1971, the American Institute of Certified Public Accountants commissioned two study groups, each comprising members from industry, the financial community, the accounting and legal professions, and academe: (1) a seven-member group to study the establishment of accounting principles and to make recommendations for improving that process and (2) a nine-member group to study the objectives of financial statements in order to facilitate establishment of guidelines and criteria for improving accounting and financial reporting.

The 1972 report, Establishing Financial Accounting Standards, led to the formation of the Financial Accounting Standards Board (FASB) and the related Financial Accounting Foundation and Financial Accounting Standards Advisory Council.[2]

The concurrent deliberations of the second group extended into 1973, culminating with the publication of its report, Objectives of Financial Statements (hereinafter from time to time referred to as "Objectives Study" or the "Study") in October, 1973.[3] In recommending the establishment of the FASB and outlining its activities, the Study on Establishment of Accounting Principles contemplated that the Objectives Study would provide important guidance for the Board's activities.

The Report of the Study on Establishment of Accounting Principles states that financial accounting and reporting must rest on a set of conventions or standards "designed to achieve what are perceived to be the desired objectives of financial accounting and reporting."[4] This Report envisaged that the ongoing work

*Reprinted by permission, FASB Discussion Memorandum, Financial Accounting Standards Board, June 6, 1974.

of the FASB "should be to develop standards for preparing financial accounting information that will be consistent with these objectives."[5] *Such standards, the Report observes, will sometimes be fundamental and cut across all aspects of accounting; in other cases, the standards will be narrow in their application. What is of the greatest importance, the Report concludes, "is not whether the standards are fundamental or narrow but whether they contribute to progress in achieving the objectives of financial accounting and reporting."*[6]

Scope of the Project:

In choosing topics for its initial technical agenda in April, 1973, from among the many suggested by the Financial Accounting Standards Advisory Council and others, the FASB selected the project of "broad qualitative standards for financial reporting." The FASB expected that when the Report of the Study Group on the Objectives of Financial Statements *became available it would be of substantial help in this project. After extensive work on the project, the FASB concluded that the scope of the project should be broadened to encompass the entire conceptual framework of financial accounting and reporting, including objectives, qualitative characteristics, and the information needs of users of accounting information. A task force was subsequently selected for the project. As the initial step in what will be an ongoing project and in recognition of the primacy of the objectives of financial statements in its adoption of financial accounting standards, the FASB is now seeking views on the objectives of financial statements. In addition, views are sought on the qualitative characteristics of financial reporting.*

In view of the recent publication of the Report of the Study Group on the Objectives of Financial Statements, *and the earlier publication by the APB of Statement 4 as well as the other research noted in the selected bibliography (Appendix B), the Standards Board, with the advice and counsel of the task force, has concluded that further extensive research for the purpose of developing a discussion memorandum on the subject of objectives of financial statements and qualitative characteristics would be an unjustified duplication of effort. Accordingly, this Discussion Memorandum draws almost exclusively upon the Objectives Study. Views are sought on the objectives of financial statements and on the qualitative characteristics of reporting set forth in the Objectives Study. Although this Discussion Memorandum draws upon the Objectives Study, respondents are invited to present for consideration objectives and qualitative characteristics not specifically recognized by the Study.*

It seems eminently clear that an abrupt and immediate implementation of all the proposed objectives of financial statements as stated in the Objectives Study is not realistic and indeed was not contemplated by the Study Group. Rather, the Study Group states that objectives developed in the Study can be looked upon as "attainable in stages within a reasonable time" and urges that its conclusions be considered as "an initial step in developing objectives important for the ongoing refinement and improvement of accounting standards and practices."[7]

Consistent with the notion of moving forward one step at a time, deliberately progressing in stages toward the implementation of a set of stated objectives that are agreed upon, the general questions that follow are raised for consideration and public response. Subsequently, certain specific questions are raised with respect to each of the twelve objectives set forth in the Objectives Study. The reasoning, whether taken from the Objectives Study or other sources, underlying responses to all questions is important and is solicited.

General Questions

A. *Which, if any, of the objectives and qualitative characteristics set forth in the* Report of the Study Group on the Objectives of Financial Statements *should the FASB adopt at this time?*

B. *Which, if any, objectives and qualitative characteristics should the FASB subject to further study and consideration before deciding whether to adopt?*

C. *Should the FASB defer further consideration of any of the objectives and qualitative characteristics set forth in the* Report of the Study Group on the Objectives of Financial Statements? *If so, which?*

D. *Are there objectives or qualitative characteristics other than those set forth in the* Report of the Study on the Objectives of Financial Statements *that the FASB should consider?*

Objectives of Financial Statements:

The Objectives Study specified twelve "objectives" and identified seven "qualitative characteristics of reporting." To enhance communication at the public hearings, in this Discussion Memorandum the objectives have been numbered according to the sequence of their appearance in the Objectives Study; the page in the Objectives Study on which each objective is initially stated has also been indicated.

In presenting the objectives and qualitative characteristics set forth in the Objectives Study for consideration, it may be helpful to provide a context in which such objectives and characteristics might be expected to impact financial accounting in general, and the adoption of the standards by the FASB in particular. The Objectives Study makes reference to "an interrelated and compatible system of objectives, standards or principles, and practices or procedures." The Study states: "Objectives should identify the goals and purposes of accounting. Standards should follow logically from objectives, and should provide guidelines for the formulation of accounting practices compatible with the desired goals."[8] A hierarchical arrangement of such a system of objectives, standards, and practices is presented in Appendix A. That hierarchy attempts to portray the way in which the many facets of financial accounting and reporting might fit together to form a cohesive and operable whole.

In the remainder of this Discussion Memorandum each of the twelve objectives set forth in the Study is presented together with a brief discussion and certain questions about the objective. Most of the discussion is drawn directly from the Objectives Study. Response to the questions is solicited; however, respondents should not feel constrained to limit their comments only to those aspects of an objective that are addressed in the questions.

Objective One: The basic objective of financial statements is to provide information useful for making economic decisions.

This objective of financial statements is overriding and emphasizes the output of the accounting process rather than the accounting process itself. This objective affirms the supremacy of user needs which the Study recognizes are not precisely known, though the following assumptions about those needs and users' decision processes are noted in the Study:

> *Users of financial statements seek to predict, compare, and evaluate the cash consequences of their economic decisions.*
>
> *Information about the cash consequences of decisions made by the enterprise is useful for predicting, comparing, and evaluating cash flows to users. (If the value of the unit of measure is unstable, that is, if inflation or deflation is so great that direct cash consequences are no longer comparable, such circumstances should be recognized in the financial statements.)*
>
> *Financial statements are more useful if they include but distinguish information that is primarily factual, and*

therefore can be measured objectively, from information that is primarily interpretive.

The above assumptions about user needs which derive from the economic decision process underlie all of the objectives identified in the Study.

The Study suggests that "it may be that financial statements should not be limited solely to quantified information. Amplification, in narrative form, of data included in statements may be required." The expectation is that with an established set of explicit objectives, "the boundaries of accounting will be influenced primarily by users, their goals, and their needs for information."

Response to the following questions is solicited:

1.1 The Objectives Study acknowledges that "financial statements are not suited to the communication of all information that may have an impact on economic decisions." Are guidelines needed to circumscribe the "useful" information that should be provided by financial statements rather than by some other medium? If so, what guidelines might be appropriate?

1.2 What should be included in the term "financial statements"? Should this include supplementary statements and schedules or should the term be reserved for the basic balance sheet, income statement, and statement of changes in financial position, and the notes thereto?

Objective Two: An objective of financial statements is to serve primarily users who have limited authority, ability, or resources to obtain information and who rely on financial statements as their principal source of information about an enterprise's economic activities.

The second objective appearing in the Objectives Study identifies the users for whom financial statements are primarily intended. The Study states that "the identification of the primary users and of the financial information they need is fundamental to the operation of the basic objective."

Potential users of financial statements are a heterogeneous group with diverse interests. Specification of the audience for whom financial statements are primarily intended is therefore critical in providing guidance for improving accounting and financial reporting. According to the Objectives Study, financial statements are "especially important to those who have limited access to information and limited ability to interpret it." The

Objectives Study goes on to state that "financial statements should meet the needs of those with the least ability to obtain information and the needs of others as well."

Response to the following questions is solicited:

2.1 If the specification of the primary audience for financial statements is critical, on what basis should that primary audience be determined?

2.2 The Objective Study focuses on users with limited ability to obtain information. If, instead, the primary audience should be determined on the basis of ability to assimilate financial information, to what level of understanding should financial statements be addressed--for example, to the credit grantor or financial analyst, to the informed investor, or to the holder of securities who may be relatively unschooled in financial affairs?

2.3 Should there be more than one set of financial statements differing in degree of summarization, selectivity of data presented, classification of data, and other ways? For example, a set might be prepared for the credit grantor or financial analyst, and another set might be prepared for the holder of securities who may be relatively unschooled in financial affairs.

The next four objectives presented in the Objectives Study deal somewhat more specifically with the nature of information that is "useful for making economic decisions."

In this memorandum, Objectives Three and Four will be considered together.

Objective Three: An objective of financial statements is to provide information useful to investors and creditors for predicting, comparing, and evaluating potential cash flows to them in terms of amount, timing, and related uncertainty.

Objective Four: An objective of financial statements is to provide users with information for predicting, comparing, and evaluating enterprise earning power.

Objectives Three and Four are considered together in this memorandum because Objective Three is concerned with cash flow to the investor or creditor, and Objective Four is concerned with earning power which the Objectives Study notes in the long run is equivalent to "cash generating ability" of the enterprise. The Objectives Study states: "Users assess the earning power of pub-

licly held enterprises virtually every day. Market prices of their securities reflect composite assessments of earning power and the implicit ability to pay dividends."

Objective Three does not draw a distinction between an investment decision and a credit decision but views them as essentially the same. "Both groups are concerned with the enterprise's ability to generate cash flows to them and with their own ability to predict, compare, and evaluate the amount, timing, and related uncertainty of these future cash flows." The Study recognizes that cash flows to common stock investors include the proceeds from the ultimate sale of an investment as well as any cash dividends paid during the period the investment is held.

Objective Four contains a basic notion of the Study--earning power--which, in turn, has its essence in the ability of an enterprise to generate cash in the future. The Study asserts that cash generation and earnings approximate each other over long periods, which is to say "earnings can only come from cash generated by operations; cash generating ability and earning power are equivalent."

Questions raised by these two objectives to which response is solicited are:

3.1 *Is the emphasis in the Objectives Study on cash flow to investors and creditors and cash generating ability of the enterprise a proper one, or is the emphasis overstated or understated?*

3.2 *What are the implications of the emphasis on predicting, comparing, and evaluating potential cash flows to investors and creditors which, in turn, are dependent upon predicting, comparing, and evaluating enterprise earning power--for example, does this have implications for revenue recognition and asset valuation?*

Objective Five: An objective of financial statements is to supply information useful in judging management's ability to utilize enterprise resources effectively in achieving the primary enterprise goal.

This objective focuses upon management's accountability. "Since the principal goal of a commercial enterprise is to maximize cash return to owners, its management is accountable for progress toward this goal." Information which is useful for estimating earning power is also useful for judging management's accountability.

Response to the following questions on this objective is solicited:

5.1 *Is any potential conflict foreseeable between this objective and the preceding objective that emphasizes "predicting, comparing, and evaluating enterprise earning power"? If so, how should the conflicting objectives be acommodated?*

5.2 *Some have advocated that in order for financial statements to be useful reports on management's performance, management should be given little flexibility in determining the content and format of the financial statements. Others hold that because financial statements are management's reports in which management is expected to provide a financial description of its activities to stockholders, creditors, and other appropriately interested parties, management should be given considerable latitude in the selection of content and format. How should financial statements be viewed?*

Objective Six: An objective of financial statements is to provide factual and interpretive information about transactions and other events which is useful for predicting, comparing, and evaluating enterprise earning power. Basic underlying assumptions with respect to matters subject to interpretation, evaluation, prediction, or estimation should be disclosed.

This objective notes a distinction between factual and interpretive information. After the judgment is made to report certain information, the factual information requires "minimal additional judgments or interpretations for reporting" while interpretive information "requires significant judgments on the part of the preparer." Facts and results of interpretations should be distinguished; otherwise, users are unable to make their own judgments in terms of their own particular risk criteria.

Response to the following question on this objective is solicited:

6.1 *What are the implications of this objective for conventional financial statements? For example, does it suggest a different classification scheme is needed that distinguishes between factual and interpretive information, or does it require only that more explanatory material be provided with the financial statements?*

Four other objectives in the Objectives Study identify particular types of financial statements and describe some of the content necessary to provide the information needed to fulfill the more general objectives.

Objective Seven: An objective is to provide a statement of financial position useful for predicting, comparing, and evaluating enterprise earning power. This statement should provide information concerning enterprise transactions and other events that are part of incomplete earnings cycles. Current values should also be reported when they differ significantly from historical costs. Assets and liabilities should be grouped or segregated by the relative uncertainty of the amount and timing of prospective realization or liquidation.

The Objective Study states that "all business enterprises engage in related activities aimed at goals." The Study defines these related activities as cycles and further notes that earnings cycles can be classified as completed, incomplete, or prospective. Moreover, to assess the status of an enterprise at any point requires a statement of incomplete cycles (i.e., statement of financial position). In discussing the statement of financial position, the Study states: "Various current value measurements could be used as indicators of the prospective benefits of assets and sacrifices for liabilities, and of the current sacrifice or benefit aspects of holding them." Another dimension of this objective is the recognition that "the eventual realization of assets and satisfaction of liabilities involves varying degrees of uncertainty," and where realization is especially uncertain, the item in question "should be segregated and reported separately and in greater detail, perhaps in a separate statement."

The Study suggests that "the objectives of financial statements cannot be best served by the exclusive use of a single valuation basis." The valuation basis applied to an asset or a liability should be selected in relation to the stated objectives. For example, the Study states that: "The measurement bases of statements should be tested in terms of whether they produce information about the following:

> *Actual sacrifice for assets and actual benefit of liabilities.*
>
> *Potential benefit of assets and potential sacrifice for liabilities.*
>
> *Measurement of completed cycles and of recognizable progress toward completion of cycles.*
>
> *Measurement of value changes that provide the best current indication of the outcome of incomplete cycles."*

Questions to which response is solicited on this objective are:

7.1 *For which specific items in the statement of financial position is "current value" information most likely to be useful to investors and creditors? For those items selected, which form of "current value" should be reported? For those items selected should providing "current value" information be viewed as a short-term or long-term goal for financial reporting? For those items selected, should "current value" measurements be reported in the statement of financial position as supplemental information or in place of historical cost measurements?*

7.2 *What is the most effective way to convey information concerning the uncertainty of an item--for example, by special classifications in the conventional financial statements, by supplementary statements, by creating a new set of financial statements, by disclosing ranges of precision, or by some other means?*

Objective Eight: An objective is to provide a statement of periodic earnings useful for predicting, comparing, and evaluating enterprise earning power. The net result of completed earnings cycles and enterprise activities resulting in recognizable progress toward completion of incomplete cycles should be reported. Changes in the values reflected in successive statements of financial position should also be reported, but separately, since they differ in terms of their certainty of realization.

Using the notion of cycles, the Objectives Study observes that the essential question in developing a statement of earnings is whether earnings "should be measured only in terms of the results of completed cycles or in terms which also include estimates of progress toward cycle completion and recognition of value changes." While a completed cycle approach provides a measure of earnings with reasonable certainty of cash realization, it also excludes factors which are important in the process of making predictions. The Objectives Study states that an approach to earnings measurement that strikes a balance between completed cycles and progress toward completion of incomplete cycles "emerges as a more useful means for users to fulfill their own needs."

Questions raised by this objective are:

8.1 *This objective calls for changes in value to be reported separately. How should such separate reporting be accomplished--as a separate line item included in the measurement of periodic earnings, as separate information outside the statement of periodic earnings, or by some other method?*

8.2 *Objective Seven relates to the statement of financial position and Objective Eight relates to the statement of periodic earnings. Should these two financial statements be interrelated and use the same underlying data or might they be unrelated and use different data?*

Objective Nine: An objective is to provide a statement of financial activities useful for predicting, comparing, and evaluating enterprise earning power. This statement should report mainly on factual aspects of enterprise transactions having or expected to have significant cash consequences. This statement should report data that require minimal judgment and interpretation by the preparer.

To assess earning power, users need various types of information. The statement of periodic earnings shows progress and results, and the statement of financial position shows status. This objective calls for a statement of financial activities summarizing "those exchanges to which the enterprise was party during the period." The Study further states that such a statement should report activities having "highly probable" cash consequences.

This objective raises the following question:

9.1 *The Objectives Study specifically mentions certain kinds of items (e.g., sales backlog, purchase commitments) that should be disclosed in the statement of financial activities. What other information of a factual nature might be useful to the investor or creditor and included in the statement of financial activities? What are the implications of supplying such information?*

Objective Ten: An objective of financial statements is to provide information useful for the predictive process. Financial forecasts should be provided when they will enhance the reliability of users' predictions.

In this objective a fourth type of report is called for--the financial forecast. A great deal of oral and written discussion of the merits and demerits of providing to users financial forecasts of an enterprise's activities has taken place in recent years.

The question to which the FASB requests response is:

10.1 *At this time what action, if any, should the FASB take with regard to financial forecasts? (See the General Questions posed in paragraph 10 of this memorandum.)*

The previous four objectives of the Objectives Study identifying needed financial statements are followed by an objective of financial statements for governmental and not-for-profit organizations and an objective that calls for information about the role of the enterprise in its social environment.

Objective Eleven: An objective of financial statements for governmental and not-for-profit organizations is to provide information useful for evaluating the effectiveness of the management of resources in achieving the organization's goals. Performance measures should be quantified in terms of identified goals.

As in the case of commercial enterprises, users of financial statements of not-for-profit organizations "are interested in predicting, comparing, and evaluating the benefits and sacrifices in terms of amount, timing, and related uncertainty, even though they seek nonmonetary benefits." The goals of not-for-profit organizations, the Study recognized, are more difficult to measure and communicate in monetary terms. Nevertheless, the Study suggests that "the objectives of the financial statements of commercial enterprises can provide broad guidelines for the development of objectives in the not-for-profit sector."

This objective raises the following question:

11.1 Should "the development of objectives in the not-for-profit sector" be undertaken? If so, what degree of urgency exists for such a set of objectives? (See the General Questions in paragraph 10 of this memorandum.)

Objective Twelve: An objective of financial statements is to report on those activities of the enterprise affecting society which can be determined and described or measured and which are important to the role of the enterprise in its social environment.

This objective relates to a general area sometimes described as "social accounting." The Objectives Study noted that "our social and economic system assumes that the pursuit of private goals generally tends to fulfill the social ones." Nevertheless, it was felt that the objectives of financial statements applied indirectly to social goals as well.

In connection with the basic objective (Objective One) a question was raised about guidelines that might circumscribe the "useful" information that should be provided by financial statements rather than by some other medium. Response to the following question on Objective Twelve is solicited:

12.1 Are financial statements likely to be the most effective means for presenting information about the "activities of the enterprise affecting society"?

Finally, the Objectives Study sets forth in a separate chapter seven qualitative characteristics of reporting that information contained in financial statements should possess in order to satisfy users' needs. These qualitative characteristics are described in the Study under the following headings:

Relevance and Materiality
Form and Substance
Reliability
Freedom from Bias
Comparability
Consistency
Understandability

The essence of the seven qualitative characteristics is summarized succinctly in the following paragraph:

> *The qualitative characteristics of financial statements, like objectives, should be based largely upon the needs of users of the statements. Information is useless unless it is relevant and material to a user's decision. Information should be as free as possible from any biases of the preparer. In making decisions, users should not only understand the information presented, but also should be able to assess its reliability and compare it with information about alternative opportunities and previous experience. In all cases, information is more useful if it stresses economic substance rather than technical form.*

With respect to the qualitative characteristics, response to this question is solicited:

13.1 Would the set of qualitative characteristics given in the Objectives Study serve as the attributes of useful information that should be provided by financial statements? If not, what modifications should be made to these characteristics?

NOTES

[1]American Institute of Certified Public Accountants, Accounting Principles Board Statement No. 4, "Basic Concepts and Accounting Principles Underlying Financial Statements of Business Enterprises," (New York: AICPA, October, 1970).

[2]American Institute of Certified Public Accountants, Study on Establishment of Accounting Principles, *Establishing Financial Accounting Standards* (New York: AICPA, March, 1972).

[3]American Institute of Certified Public Accountants, Accounting Objectives Study Group, *Objectives of Financial Statements* (New York: AICPA, October, 1973).

[4]AICPA, *Establishing Financial Accounting Standards*, p. 19.

[5]*Ibid.*

[6]*Ibid.*, p. 20.

[7]AICPA, *Objectives of Financial Statements*, p. 11.

[8]*Ibid.*, p. 15.

APPENDIX E TO SECTION IV

ESTABLISHING FINANCIAL ACCOUNTING STANDARDS: ALTERNATIVES FOR CANADA*

by

W. Morley Lemon and David A. Wilson

Within the past few years, committees of both the American Institute of Certified Public Accountants (AICPA) and the Canadian Institute of Chartered Accountants (CICA) have conducted exhaustive examinations of alternative modes for the formulation of accounting principles and the conduct and funding of accounting research.

The purpose of this article is to examine four strategies for the formulation of these alternatives and from this develop and advocate an eclectic alternative. We first examine the status quo, *the organizational and institutional framework which we presently assess in the development of accounting principles.*[1]

The first of the alternative strategies considered is articulated in Skinner's recent book, Accounting Principles: A Canadian Viewpoint.[2] *From the Report of Task Force 2000 to the membership of the CICA we draw the second strategy,*[3] *and the third mode is that proposed by the AICPA Wheat Committee.*[4]

The content of each of these proposals will be reviewed briefly and discussed in terms of adaptability to the Canadian accounting environment. The authors will then propose yet another, fourth, alternative and advocate its adoption as the optimal strategy for the Canadian accounting profession to follow.

The Status Quo:

The development of Canadian accounting standards and research is presently conducted by the Accounting Research Committee of the CICA. This Committee normally comprises 22 members,

*Reprinted with permission from CA Magazine, June, 1974, pp. 21-24. The authors would like to express their thanks to Mr. J.R.M. Wilson for his valuable comments on an earlier draft of this paper.

selected to provide a broad diversification of occupational and geographical background. Although two-thirds of the members must be members of the CICA, the other members include representatives of The Financial Executives Institute of Canada, the Society of Industrial Accountants of Canada, the General Accountants Association of Canada, and the Financial Analysts Federation. This Committee's primary purpose is the issuance and revision of Research Recommendations in accounting problems.

The procedure of the Committee has been to commission a task force to analyze a particular problem. Upon completion of the task force's study, a summary of its findings is submitted to the Committee. The Committee reviews these findings and submits an exposure draft to the CICA membership and other interested parties for their review and comment. The draft, as amended by these suggestions, is then issued as a Recommendation which becomes an amendment to the CICA Handbook.[5]

Any supporting research, generally, is done on an ad hoc basis and is addressed only to present-day problems. Gertrude Mulcahy notes that there is little "pure" research undertaken, despite the need for it.[6] *Although attempts have been made to encourage academicians to undertake such research, academic reluctance and a shortage of funds have led to rather limited results. Therefore, a significant portion of accounting research in Canada is presently being undertaken by the larger accounting firms.*

Task Force 2000:

In March, 1969, Task Force 2000 was established by the CICA to determine "what the future role of the chartered accountant should be," and based "upon this assessment--(to) recommend what policies should be established by the organized profession to allow present and future members to fulfill those roles."[7]

One of the recommendations appearing in the Task Force's final report called for the Accounting and Auditing Research Committee to be renamed the Accounting Principles Committee, a suggestion which has recently seen implementation, at least in spirit if not in name. The primary goal of this committee would be the codification of accounting principles and the development of useful accounting statements. In order to achieve this goal the committee recommended the development of an Accounting Research and Development Foundation.

The Task Force Report raised a number of significant questions in connection with this Foundation. Specifically, it considered such issues as the funding and manpower required for in-depth accounting research. Similarly, the task force realized the importance of drawing from many disciplines in its research, as well as giving its work an international scope.

The Report of the Task Force echoes the thoughts of Gertrude Mulcahy in pointing out that, at present, little pure research is being done. Most of the research conducted by the CICA through its Accounting Research Committee is in response to a particular financial accounting problem; relatively little research takes place in the universities.

The Report states that "the present rate of development in accounting theory and the degree of success achieved in the application of new theories to practice are inadequate for a profession that aspires to develop accounting as a meaningful and useful tool in the future."[8] The proposed Accounting and Research Development Foundation is seen as a solution to these inadequacies.

Skinner: Accounting Principles:

In his recent book, Accounting Principles: A Canadian Viewpoint, Skinner suggests that management, external users, and public accountants all have an interest in and have attempted to play some role in the formulation of accounting principles. As a consequence, there has been no orderly development of a body of accounting principles. Rather, the emphasis has been on the haphazard development of principles that permit a variety of alternative practices, providing multiple answers to the same question. Skinner further notes that the accounting profession has generally acted to discourage the multiplicity of alternatives and to eliminate undesirable practices. The profession's approach, however, has not led to innovation, but has rather tended to be crisis-oriented. Fortunately, in the more recent past, the profession has taken a greater role and "evinced a greater interest in development of a coherent accounting theory."[9]

Insofar as research is concerned, Skinner also discusses the idea of a Foundation. He concludes that there would be merit in the Foundation establishing a broadly based membership by drawing from other nonaccounting bodies such as financial analysts and executives as well as members of the CICA.

Report of the Wheat Committee:

In early 1971, the Board of Directors of the AICPA organized a conference of the leading professional accountants. The purpose of the meeting was "to consider how the Institute might reappraise its standard-setting role and how that role could be made more responsive to the needs of those who rely upon financial statements."[10]

As a result of this conference, the Accounting Objectives Study (the Trueblood Committee) and the Study of Establishment of Accounting Principles (the Wheat Committee) were established by the Board of Directors of the AICPA. The former was to delineate "the objectives of corporate financial reporting;[11] the latter was instructed to "examine the organization and operation of the Accounting Principles Board and determine what changes are necessary to attain better results faster."[12]

Prior to the Wheat Committee's report, which was accepted by AICPA in April, 1972, the AICPA had charged the Committee on Accounting Procedure (1939-1959) and the Accounting Principles Board (1959-1972) with the joint tasks of promulgating acceptable accounting practices and overseeing accounting research.

While the APB did produce a number of "Opinions," the Wheat Committee felt the continuing association of Board members with their firms or companies led to criticism of their lack of independence. It also felt that since the APB was part-time and hence slow in reacting, that it did not use the research capabilities available to it effectively.

Its successor, the Financial Accounting Standards Board (FASB), is drawn from a broader area than the APB, including four CPA's from public practice and three additional members with financial expertise who need not be CPA's. These members are required to sever all business affiliations and are supplied with full-time administrative and research staffs. The period of office is five years, with one reappointment possible. Further, in order to attract the calibre of person felt to be most suited to the task of formulating accounting principles, the Committee's Report proposed an annual salary range of $75,000 to $100,000 for FASB members. The actual salary range is somewhat higher than that proposed.

A new body, the nine-member Financial Accounting Foundation, appoints the FASB which, in turn, reports to the AICPA through that body. Four of the members are CPA's in public practice; two others are financial executives (chosen from names submitted by the Financial Executive Institutes and the National Association of Accountants); one is a financial analyst (chosen from names submitted by the Financial Analysts Federation); and one is an academician (chosen from names submitted by the American Accounting Association).

The FAF also appoints, for renewable one-year terms, a twenty-

member Financial Accounting Standards Advisory Council to advise the FASB. Wheat, in order to ensure diversity of background, suggested that no more than a quarter of the Council be drawn from any one area.

The FASB has been launched with expectations that its size, the expertise of its members, and the fact that it is full-time will enable it to "attain better results faster."[13]

An Eclectic Alternative:

The report of Task Force 2000 recommends that "The accounting profession (in Canada) take the initiative to organize a separate and distinct Accounting Research and Development Foundation."

> *The objectives of this Foundation would be to conduct basic and applied research in accounting theory and techniques in response to changing needs. Although the Foundation would undertake to coordinate basic or pure research, it is vitally important that the results of this research be developed to a stage where they are suitable for application by practicing accountants.*[14]

At a purely conceptual level, the proposal advocated in the Task Force 2000 report is attractive. Yet any hope of instituting the recommendations of the proposal in their present form seems remote. A central theme to the recommendations of the Wheat Committee Report was the intensity of the capital and maintenance costs necessary to fund an adequate program of accounting research. It was the assessment of this committee that the salary and related payroll costs alone for the research activities to be conducted under their proposed Financial Accounting Foundation would range between a minimum of $500,000 and a maximum of $650,000 annually.[15]

While interim financing for the first few years of the FAF's existence has come from the contributions of a number of large accounting firms in the United States, it is apparent that this arrangement is only temporary and that a more permanent financing structure will inevitably come from an increase in member dues.[16]

It becomes starkly evident that if the funding of capable accounting research and the development of accounting principles is a significant problem for the AICPA, it may well be a myth to consider as feasible the funding of such work by the CICA. Given the inadequacies of the status quo *and its financial constraints under which any accounting research and development program must function in Canada, the authors propose an alternative strategy to those discussed in the preceding sections of the paper.*

The socioeconomic environment in Canada is similar in a great many respects to its counterpart in the United States. This similarity extends also to the corporate legal framework--the conduct of business through the corporate veil. Further, it is in this environment that accounting information is used in the making of those decisions which allocate the resources of society. In view of these similarities, we suggest that perhaps the CICA ought to subscribe to the same process for the establishment of accounting principles as exists in the United States.

In lieu of the establishment of a Canadian foundation for accounting research and development, the Canadian profession should arrange for a direct access to the pronouncements and other publications of the FASB and that a policy of "adoption by nonexception" be followed. Operationally, the CICA would establish an Accounting Standards Board, small in membership and of heterogeneous background,[17] to review the specific proposals of the FASB and to determine whether or not exception must be taken to a given opinion on the grounds of idiosyncracies in the socio-legal frameworks of the two countries (e.g., pronouncements relating to investment tax credits).

Members of this Board would serve on a part-time basis and would be selected solely for their abilities and capacities in the development and formulation of accounting principles. Coincidentally, an Advisory Council would be established to provide guidance and direction to the Standards Board. This Council would be considerably larger in number, say, twenty to twenty-two, and would represent the geographical and professional interest of the many subsets of the Institute's membership. Thus, while representation would be given to all interest groups through the Advisory Council, the responsibility for the establishment of accounting principles would lie with the smaller and more manageable Accounting Standards Board.

Pronouncements of the FASB could be classified into one of four groups in terms of their suitability to the accounting environment in Canada:

(a) those pronouncements which are applicable to Canadian accounting practice or are readily adaptable;

(b) those which are wholly inappropriate because of overruling corporate law or tax legislation;

(c) those with which the Canadian Board finds substantial

theoretical disagreement (such as the AICPA stance on R & D costs in extractive industries); or

(d) those which fail to cover areas where guidance is necessary in Canadian practice.

Clearly, the proposed committee structure offers little appeal for the establishment of accounting principles in those instances in which the pronouncements of the FASB fall into groupings (b), (c), or (d) above. However, it is that substantial proportion of accounting problems which are common to both societies and which are resolved satisfactorily by the AICPA pronouncements which offer potential economies to the CICA's bodies responsible for research into and the formulation of accounting principles.

Task Force 2000 addressed the problem of accounting research and development at a nonoperational level, substantially ignoring the dimension of any costs associated with their recommendation. Yet, even with this latitude, their report accurately recognized that "Canada is too small a country for a foundation to expect to perform all the research required. Where possible, the Foundation must ensure that it coordinates with accounting bodies in the U.S.A. and other parts of the world in its efforts to avoid duplication."[18]

The proposal in this paper simply extends upon the conclusions of Task Force 2000 and argues that only in those instances where the socio-legal constraints imposed by Canada dictate the development of accounting standards different to those developed by the FASB should the Canadian profession engage in the expensive and time-consuming task of developing its own standards.

Coincidentally, under the direction of the proposed Accounting Standards Committee, the CICA could engage in the more fundamental, pure, or basic research called for by both Gertrude Mulcahy and the Report of Task Force 2000. It would be anticipated that through the pursuit of a policy of "adoption by non-exception" the research staff and budget of the CICA would be released from a number of the constraints under which it presently functions. The slack thus introduced could most usefully be absorbed in the conduct and direction of pure research.

At the Frontiers of Our Profession:

In a global evaluation of the institutions presently conducting accounting research and developing accounting standards, one counts innumerable instances of duplication of effort and of inefficiencies in the organizational frameworks. The Canadian ac-

counting profession is presently at a decision point--a point from which many paths may be followed. The authors urge that our progress from this recognize the organizational issues which the Wheat Committee studied so carefully and note the solutions they generated to the problems inherent in a structure like that of the late Accounting Principles Board. We further urge that the CICA recognize the comparative advantages and disadvantages possessed by a relatively small but strong professional group and, accordingly, redirect the research efforts of the CICA to the more fundamental levels.

"It is essential that the Research Committee, to a much greater extent than it has in the past, should engage in initiating and overseeing basic research at the Frontiers of our profession rather than gathering together to record the best current practice."[19]

NOTES

[1]The status quo is most comprehensively and articulately set out in Stephen A. Zeff, Forging Accounting Principles in Five Countries: A History and an Analysis of Trends (Champaign, Illinois: Stipes Publishing Co., 1972), pp. 285-300. Last year the Board of Governors of the CICA split the Accounting and Auditing Research Committee into two new bodies, the Accounting Research Committee and the Auditing Standards Committee. While the committee functions have been separated and the membership increased, there is little a priori evidence to indicate that the functioning of this new group will be significantly different to that of its predecessor.

[2]R. M. Skinner, Accounting Principles: A Canadian Viewpoint (Toronto: CICA, 1972), Part II.

[3]Task Force 2000, Report to the Executive Committee and Council of the CICA by Task Force 2000 (Toronto: CICA, August 21, 1970), pp. 180-190.

[4]Study on Establishment of Accounting Principles, Establishing Financial Accounting Standards, Report on the Study on Establishment of Accounting Principles (New York: AICPA, 1972). This study is commonly referred to as The Wheat Committee Report.

[5]Zeff, Forging Accounting Principles, p. 293.

[6] Gertrude Mulcahy, "Pure Research--An Essential Ingredient of the Institute's Programme," Canadian Chartered Accountant, (September, 1968).

[7] The Report of Task Force 2000, p. 1.

[8] Ibid., p. 180.

[9] Skinner, Accounting Principles, p. 315.

[10] The Report of the Wheat Committee, p. 3.

[11] Kermit D. Larson and Gary L. Holstrum, "The Design of Financial Accounting Standards in the United States," (Unpublished Working Paper, Bureau of Business Research, The University of Texas at Austin, 1973), p. 1.

[12] The Report of the Wheat Committee, p. 93.

[13] Ibid.

[14] The Report of Task Force 2000, pp. 180-181.

[15] The Report of the Wheat Committee, p. 105.

[16] Ibid., pp. 78-80.

[17] While the precise structure of a Canadian Accounting Standards Board is not addressed in this paper, it is proposed that the membership of the Board include not only CPA's but also representatives of other subsets of the financial community such as financial analysts, investment dealers for example. It is also proposed that the total Board membership be limited in number to no more than seven or eight for the same reasons identified in The Wheat Committee Report.

[18] The Report of Task Force 2000, p. 183. A similar alternative was raised by Skinner (p. 318) but was neither discussed not pursued.

[19] Gertrude Mulcahy, "Pure Research--An essential ingredient of the Institute's programme," Canadian Chartered Accountant (September, 1968), pp. 184-6.

SECTION V

ACCOUNTING IN THE NEXT TEN YEARS

INTRODUCTION

In this final section three leaders of the profession, Richard T. Baker, Michael N. Chetkovich, and Ralph E. Kent, discuss with three representatives of the accounting rule-making agencies, Donald J. Kirk, Robert K. Mautz, and A. Clarence Sampson, the institutional outlook for accounting in the immediate future. Although the underlying issue is how and by whom will U.S. accounting standards be set, specific topics discussed range from general price-adjusted statements, business combinations, and segmented reporting to the disclosure-measurement controversy, information needs of investors, and if the SEC will supplant the FASB. Ten appendices are provided.

-- The Editor.

SECTION V

ACCOUNTING IN THE NEXT TEN YEARS

THE DISCUSSANTS

Representing the Accounting Profession

Richard T. Baker:

At the firm of Ernst & Ernst, Mr. Baker is the Managing Partner; he has been a partner in this firm since 1952, and with the firm since 1940. He is a member of the Board of Trustees of the Financial Accounting Foundation (FAF). He is a native Ohioan and received his Bachelor's Degree at The Ohio State University. At the university, he was an all-American basketball player and he was elected to Beta Alpha Psi. Author of several articles, he has been active in many organizations, including serving on the AICPA Council. He has received an honorary LLD degree. In 1972, the Omicron Chapter of Beta Alpha Psi elected him as its Outstanding Alumnus.

Michael N. Chetkovich:

At the firm of Haskins & Sells, Mr. Chetkovich is the Managing Partner; he has been a partner in this firm since 1952. Previously, he was with McLaren, Goode & Co., CPA's, San Francisco, from 1940. He is a native Californian and received his Bachelor's and Master's Degrees from the University of California at Berkeley. At the university, he was elected to Phi Beta Kappa, Beta Alpha Psi, and other honoraries. In World War II, he was a U.S. Navy Lieutenant. A former vice president of the California Society of CPA's and President of the California Alumni Club of New York, he is now active in the New York State Society of CPA's, the AICPA, the AAA, and many other organizations; on the AICPA Council, he is its Chairman of the Committee on International Relations and AICPA representative on the International Coordinating Committee for the Accounting Profession. In 1973, the Schools of Business Administration, University of California at Berkeley, elected him as its Outstanding Alumnus.

Ralph E. Kent:

Mr. Kent is Senior Partner, Arthur Young & Company, and President of the Board of Trustees of the Financial Accounting Foundation (FAF). AICPA President in 1969 and a lifetime member of the Institute's Governing Council, he was his firm's Managing Partner from 1959 to 1972. He is Chairman of the firm's Management Committee, and also of the Management Council of Arthur Young & Company (International). He has held many professional accounting organizational posts, particularly in the New York State Society of CPA's. Currently, he is a Commissioner of President Nixon's Commission on Personnel Interchange, a member of the Consultant's Panel of the Comptroller General of the United States, Vice Chairman of the Board of Trustees of Mills College, and President of the Ohio Society of New York. He is a native Ohioan and he earned his B.Sc. degree from The Ohio State University in 1937, where he was elected to Beta Alpha Psi. Active in alumni affairs, the honorary awarded him its Outstanding Alumnus Award in 1970. In 1973, he was awarded the AICPA's Gold Medal, its highest award.

Representing the Accounting Standard-Setting Bodies

Donald J. Kirk:

Mr. Kirk joined the Financial Accounting Standards Board early in 1973. Previously, he was a partner with Price Waterhouse & Company in its New York office; earlier he had been with the firm in its Washington, D. C. and London, England offices. He was raised in Ohio and he earned his Bachelor's Degree at Yale University (1959) and his MBA Degree at New York University (1961). He was a naval aviator from 1953 to 1957. He has served as an officer for various organizations concerned with local government, mental health, and conservation.

Robert K. Mautz:

Mr. Mautz is one of the five members of the CASB and a partner, since 1972, of Ernst & Ernst, Cleveland. Previously he was on the faculty at the University of Illinois for thirty years, where most recently he held an endowed chair in accounting. He also was with Haskins & Sells briefly before and after World War II, and with Alexander Grant & Co. for two years prior to going to the University of Illinois. His degrees were earned at the University of North Dakota (B.S.) and the University of Illinois (M.S. and Ph.D.). A former president of the AAA, he has been both a member and a director of the AICPA Council, and a member of the Comptroller General's Consultants Panel since 1966. A former editor of The Accounting Review, he has authored many articles and books; he is perhaps best known for his AAA monograph (with H.A. Sharaf), Philosophy of Auditing, 1961, Financial Reporting by Diversified Companies, 1968, and recently, Effect of Circumstances on the Application of Accounting Principles, 1972.

A. Clarence Sampson:

Mr. Sampson is Associate Chief Accountant, Securities and Exchange Commission. After ten years with the SEC, he achieved his present position in 1969. Previously he had been with Arthur Young & Company for two years, the Division of Litton Industries for two years, and with the Air Force for two years. He earned his B.S. Degree from the University of Maryland (1959) and he is a C.P.A. He has taught accounting and business finance for the University of Maryland in its office campus program. He has participated in programs for the FGAA, AICPA, NAA and others; he is also a member of these organizations.

THE MODERATORS

Faculty moderator is the Arthur Andersen Professor of Accounting and Chairman of the Accounting Department at Miami University of Ohio, Harry C. Lyle. A Ph.D. (Ohio State) and C.P.A., he is a former Ohio State faculty member. Student moderator is Mr. Terry Sternad, Beta Alpha Psi senior active and honors student. After graduation this fall, Mr. Sternad will join Haskins & Sells.

THE DISCUSSION

The Major Issue: How and by Whom Will U.S. Accounting Standards be Set?:

STERNAD, Moderator: We are currently entering a decade which could have long-lasting effects on the accounting profession. In this decade, the major issue likely to be largely settled is how and by whom accounting standards will be determined in the United States.

Currently the three bodies officially responsible for establishing accounting standards are: the Financial Accounting Standards Board (FASB), the Cost Accounting Standards Board (CASB), and the Securities and Exchange Commission (SEC). The FASB is regarded by many as the private sector's last chance to retain the standard setting function. The FASB's current agenda includes: research and development costs, start up and relocation costs, leases, price level changes, quality control, reporting by diversified companies, materiality, occurring future losses associated with things such as catastrophic events and even business combinations.

The CASB has statutory authority over cost accounting for government contractors. With such authority, it may or may not exert some influence on financial accounting. The CASB's current and lengthy agenda includes: accounting for unallowable costs, depreciation, standard costs, cost accounting period, costs of authorized employee absences, allocation of business unit general and administrative expenses to cost objectives, material cost, scrap termination accounting, special facilities, pension plans, allocation of burden, cost of capital, deferred incentive compensation, other labor related costs, direct and indirect charging, independent research and development bid and proposal costs, current value or price-level accounting, and terminology for cost accounting.

The third group we have is the SEC which has seen a substantial increase in its accounting standard-setting activity recently. Prior to 1973, the SEC Accounting Series Releases had been issued at an average of three or four per year. In 1973, 17 Accounting Series Releases were issued, a considerable increase. Currently the SEC is looking into the effects of inflation, forecasts, liquidity and the use of funds, leases, line of product reporting, and some other additional disclosure reports.

General Price-Level Adjusted Statements:

The first question is what about the implementation of price-level adjusted statements given the current high rates of inflation which may be even higher in the future?

KIRK, FASB: The FASB issued a discussion memorandum (DM) in January on the subject of general price-level adjusted financial statements. We had public hearings in April for two days. We received many views on the subject of general price-level adjusted financial statements. We heard orally from 23 people in those two days, but we also received approximately 130 position papers from industry, public accounting firms, and the academic world.

It would be an understatement to say that these views were varied. I can say with certainty that the Board still has the subject on its agenda, but we are considering what course of action to take.

There were many serious questions raised about the particular techniques involved. Most of us had assumed the techniques had been settled for 30 years. But for many individuals these techniques seem to require some additional experimentation. Also, very importantly, the user community raised questions about the usefulness of the data coming from general price-level adjusted financial statements. Even some preparers of the data indicated from their perspective there was some question about the usefulness of data, since in their minds there was more relevant information portrayed through the use of specific price changes rather than general price changes. The Board is faced with some desire on the part of the preparers to do something other than general price-level adjustments, and also with some questions raised by users as to the usefulness of the data that would come out of the exercise. We are still very much in the stage of assessing the comments we have received and trying to decide upon a course of action. So this is where the FASB stands currently on requiring general price-level adjusted statements.

STERNAD, Moderator: The SEC also has expressed some interest in this subject.

SAMPSON, SEC: I remind you that my remarks are only my responsibility and not that of the SEC Chief Accountant or the Commission. However, I must admit my remarks generally turn out to be a mixture of my own thoughts, Sandy Burton's thoughts, and the thoughts of other members of the staff.

With that introduction, you have to keep in mind that the SEC has two areas of interest here. These are: one, what statements are required and, two, what statements are permitted to be included in the filings of the Commission. The staff and the Commission have no present intention to develop any requirements in the area of general price-level adjusted statements or even fair value statements, which is one of the alternatives to general price-level adjusted statements.

But if we had had a company volunteer to prepare supplemental financial statements based on APB Statement No. 3, as it has existed for nearly ten years, we would have permitted it. If a company now came forward with such statements, we would permit it--even before the FASB were to act in this area. It is also true we have recently been requested to consider by a particular registrant to accept supplemental statements based on what is called fair value. There may be many differences of opinion as to how to get fair value statements. We have had a proposal made to us; the commission has reacted in a positive manner. When the proposal is made more specific, we may see a filing, which contains not only historical cost statements but some supplemental financial statements which are prepared on a fair value basis. Most of the staff and most of the commissioners with the rest of the financial community believe that more value disclosure is necessary. One of our concerns is how this present proposal before the FASB would impact on the consideration of putting alternative values into financial statements. The whole situation is fluid now, the staff and the Commission have no fixed ideas of which way we ought to go.

STERNAD, Moderator: Will those responsible for auditing and implementing the statements comment?

CHETKOVICH, Haskins & Sells: There isn't any question that, with inflation now being in double digits, we have to give early consideration to this problem. Some disclosure of its effects is necessary. But I am not sure what the techniques should be. Also anything we would come up with should not be a deterrent to the continued study of what other modifications might be necessary to historical cost, such as fair value, or whatever else proves to be the best answer along that line.

KENT, Arthur Young: We think there is a need for this information. There has been talk in the accounting profession for thirty years about general price-level adjusted statement information. Yet we know amazingly little about the mechanics. Further, we know amazingly little about the cost of preparing this information, even at this late date. It's true, as Mike Chetkovich says, with double digit inflation or with inflation such as has existed in Brazil and Argentina, we will have to do something.

But there is some need for more research here. There are many problems. Consider a large international company, for example, trying to prepare its general price-level adjusted statements. What kind of price-level are we going to adjust for the overseas operations? Are we going to adjust the German operations for German inflation? The French for the French? The South American for the South American? What kind of hodgepodge are we going to have when we get to the consolidated statements? With the many multi-national companies, it becomes an amazingly intricate question.

BAKER, Ernst & Ernst: Some of the problems with implementing price-level adjustments must be recognized despite the general helpfulness of some additional supplementary information of this sort. We need experimental time here to have some companies develop supplemental price-level adjusted statements. I would hate to see us move immediately for mandated statements which could lead to a rather chaotic situation. I am in accord with Mike

Chetkovich that we have to take a different approach with the extent of inflation we now have. We have got to work towards something. Yet I am glad to hear Don Kirk say that the FASB recognizes now that it isn't yet a solved problem. There is much more that needs to be done on it before we can say: "This is it," and everybody has to conform.

KENT, Arthur Young: I am intrigued with the comment made about fair value accounting and the fact that the SEC is apparently considering permitting a company to issue statements presumably in a registration statement reflecting fair value. What kind of a business was it?

SAMPSON, SEC: Let me make it clear, I said supplemental financial statements. This particular company involved land development, of all things; however, it's not what you might think of as a typical land development company. It is a seasoned company with a good track record with a record of past appraisals of the company's assets. They have a conservative basis of valuation. Also it isn't a settled matter yet either but I said I believe the commission is favorably considering it because of the desire and the need of users to have information about value.

BAKER, Ernst & Ernst: Is this in a registration statement under the 33 Act?

SAMPSON, SEC: The question is where would we permit them to be used, in an annual report to stockholders which isn't even filed, or in a 10-K which is in the 34 Act prospectus. There is some division of opinion among various members of the staff as to what ought to be done. It is possible that we could go part of the way but not all of the way. We won't know this until the company requests the commission to accept these statements. The commission will then decide whether or not to accept it.

BAKER, Ernst & Ernst: Is this the first request you have had?

SAMPSON, SEC: Yes, the first one I know of, and I'm sure I'd know of it.

KENT, Arthur Young: Will these be reported in some way independent of the statements covered by the auditor's report?

SAMPSON, SEC: Interestingly enough, the public accounting firm involved is willing to write a report which would basically say the methods and procedures followed appeared to be the right methods and procedures. Note I did not say an opinion. Another interesting aspect to this proposal is that the appraisal firm which is making appraisals for this company is independent in the sense that the accountants are independent. We have considered that element.

Business Combinations:

LYLE, Moderator: Many accountants expressed the view that the controversy over business combinations was a major factor in the demise of the APB. Yet the FASB recently announced that it has placed this subject on its agenda. Why?

KIRK, FASB: Explain why we did such a foolish thing? Is that it? We certainly have opened up old wounds based on the comments we have received, by putting it on the agenda. But let me explain how it did get there.

Actually a year ago, we knew we were going to take responsibility for the existing literature of the APB and the Committee on Accounting Procedures (CAP) as of July 1, 1973. During the summer, we issued a letter with wide dissemination, asking for suggestions as to which opinions might need modification, amendment, or interpretation. Some people have commented that we have received a surprisingly few number of responses--slightly in excess of 100. If you think about it, that is not many. But we heard from some very influential groups. There was also a fair concentration of criticism of APB Opinions No. 16 and No. 17. Those criticisms ranged from the need for complete reconsideration to what would be very substantial amendment of those particular opinions, primarily with regard to the criteria for pooling of interests.

The Board considered the possibility of an interpretation as a solution to the problem. It became obvious that that would not be possible. The only way we seemed to be able to deal with the subject was to put it on our technical agenda for total reconsideration. Although the subject is put on for total reconsideration, the Board has adopted what is a reasonable approach to a solution to a very thorny problem. We have chosen initially to try to deal with the many problems of differentiating pooling from a purchase. You are all aware of the treasury stock problems. Clarence Sampson can speak on these; he seems to have carved that area out for himself. But there are many others that are troublesome. It is the Board's intention to proceed with that aspect of the problem. Also at the same time, the Board will try to reexamine the conceptual basis, undertake some empirical research and find out if either or both of these methods are useful. We have the first task force meeting scheduled for June 7. So the subject will be getting more publicity in the near future. As to which direction we go on the problem in 1974 depends, in part, on the task force views.

LYLE, Moderator: Mr. Sampson, in responding to that, can you tuck into your response somewhere whether the Indiana Telephone Company, which includes price-level adjusted statements in its annual report, also includes them in their SEC filings?

SAMPSON, SEC: Indiana Telephone is not a case that I worked on myself; it was discussed in the SEC Chief Accountant's office at a time when I was in the Corporation Finance Division. Those statements are not included in commission filings. The reason they are not is that the commission's staff did not feel that the statements were prepared in accordance with APB Statement No. 3. If they had been prepared in accordance with APB Statement No. 3, it is likely that we would have permitted them to be included in a commission filing.

The area of business combinations explains to some extent why we have had so many more Accounting Series Releases in the last 18 months.

Even before Sandy Burton came to the Commission, there were many including those both inside and outside the Commission, who felt that the staff ought to take some steps to make its views on particular issues better known to accountants and the business community. In the past and today, we have conferences about problems, we listen to facts and agree with solutions, and we should give this to the public. Some of the Accounting Series Releases are of that nature. They are fully intended to let the public, the accounting and business community know how the SEC views a particular APB Opinion. This was true in the treasury stock issue. There were four Accounting Series Releases dealing with poolings of interest, stock purchases, and stock sales. Those four releases don't set accounting standards. They merely point out the way the Commission staff and the Commission believe the APB opinion reads. That is what we were intending to do. That is one reason why we have so many ASR's recently.

On the business combinations issue, Don Kirk has pointed out pretty well the basis for reexamining the problem. The Commission and the Commission staff did request that. We did say we thought that business combinations should be re-examined. There was a general dissatisfaction with some of the criteria. We all know that these resulted partially through a compromise at the time 16 and 17 came out. We feel that these should be revisited and that the FASB should do the revisiting. Believe me, I will be very happy if the FASB copes with it and we never have to say another word about it.

BAKER, Ernst & Ernst: But isn't it possible that you are going to have to say quite a bit more about it? This is one of the things that has plagued our whole profession for many, many years, ever since we faced it back in old ARB 48. ARB 48 was an expression of a sound philosophy which over the years has become eroded.

As an aside, I do applaud the idea that when the SEC does make a determination on some case, that determination should have widespread application. This is a great step forward for you to get something out on specific cases so that everybody at least knows the rules. I like everything you have done in this regard.

The business combinations issue is an extremely hot one. In the '60's, billions of dollars were lost in the stock market. Our profession, along with the SEC, played a very prominent role in the erosion of ARB No. 48 on a case-by-case basis. Regarding the pooling vs. purchase controversy, you need a genie to come up with an answer that would be acceptable to all the various feuding parties on such questions as whether we have poolings, whether we eliminate them, and whether we have further restrictions as to what is a pooling and what is not. This is going to be a very, very difficult thing to solve. I wish the FASB great luck.

KIRK, FASB: We will take any genie we can find.

KENT. Arthur Young: Nobody knows the answers to this terribly difficult subject. The FASB doesn't know the answers. The SEC doesn't know the answers. The profession doesn't know the answers. This is so because there are not clear-cut answers. The solution will have to be a compromise. The review of the criteria that Don Kirk referred to as the starting place for the FASB program will be helpful. But inevitably, there will be a bloody battle.

The fair value presentation that we referred to earlier has relevance. It certainly goes along an entirely different avenue than poolings where you carry over low values rather than put purchase values on financial statements. We appear to be going in divergent ways in that respect.

SAMPSON, SEC: I should emphasize that this fair value supplemental financial statement is only one financial statement on a permissive basis. Also, I don't know where financial statements are going in the future. They may go to fair value but it is certainly not going to be in 1975.

KIRK, FASB: I can second that.

Again Disclosure-Measurement Controversy with SEC:

STERNAD, Moderator: For the next area of discussion, I am going to read an item from a recent Journal of Accountancy "News Report."

> The Financial Accounting Standards Board believes that the Securities and Exchange Commission has drawn a distinction between accounting and accounting measurement which is artificial and is imposed to generate continuing problems.

SAMPSON, SEC: I suppose that one of the first things I should say is don't believe everything you read in the newspapers. There was a day when Sandy Burton and Al Levinson, Director of the Division of Corporation Finance, both got to work about 8 o'clock one day and each read the newspaper the first thing, and each grabbed the telephone and called the other one. They were really hopping mad.

The newspaper had reported that the SEC was about to get out a rule on disclosure of the effect of high interest cost. Sandy wanted to know why he didn't know anything about it and so did Al. It wasn't long before they heard from Marshall Armstrong who wanted to know the answer to the same question.

KIRK, FASB: That was a quote of Marshall Armstrong that was just read.

SAMPSON, SEC: There has been poor communication on this issue. It's not a question of whether a disclosure and accounting measurement are two entirely different things. There isn't anyone at the Commission that believes that a disclosure and accounting measurement are two entirely different things. The FASB has already gotten out its first standard dealing with disclosure which we heartily endorsed. We believe that the FASB does have to be concerned with disclosure.

For about 40 years, which is the life of the Commission, we have always had disclosure in SEC registration statements, or 10-K's which are not necessarily included in the certified financial statements which go into annual reports or which go into Part I of the Registration Statement. Part II does always contain schedules which are not required to be included in the certified statements. Ever since I have been with the SEC, supplemental note disclosures are required in 10-K financial statements and in registration statements which are not required in the annual reports. This recent criticism in this area is based mainly on a heightened awareness of disclosure, the fact that there are differences, and the fact that we have gotten out recently several new requirements for additional disclosure in 10-K Financial Statements.

We don't believe that this will have impact on the FASB in their determinations of what should go into financial statements. We believe they will have to make their best decision as to what goes into financial statements based on what additional information the public believes it should get in the SEC Registration Statement or outside financial statements.

There is much financial data which is not in the financial statements starting with the line of business data, which the FASB is now considering asking to be disclosed.

We don't see this the kind of problem that has been talked about in the newspapers. If I can paraphrase a commissioner at a meeting with representatives of the FASB present, he said, each should do our own thing. They should do what they think they should with respect to certified financial statements and if there are additional disclosures which we think are required under the securities act, we will ask for them in some fashion to be put into the disclosures made under the securities acts.

KIRK, FASB: We did have some exchanges with the SEC about the distinction between measurement and disclosure. It is not the conflict as it seemed to start out to be. But clearly we do not consider at the FASB that our area of concern is solely the measurement in the balance sheet and the income statement. As we get into some of the issues of today, we may not necessarily require only "measurement within the balance sheet or income statement" and by the same token, certain disclosures may also require measurements. Much of the debate on this subject started with Accounting Series Release No. 147 on leases, where clearly there was a form of measurement--impact on net income based on certain assumptions as to capitalization of leases--described as a disclosure matter. On that particular issue, we felt that the distinction really could not be made. There the measurement was an integral part of the disclosure, just as disclosure is an integral part of measurement. None of us can visualize balance sheets or profit and loss statements any more without additional disclosures of some sort. So disclosure and measurement are closely interrelated. This storm hopefully has blown over.

SAMPSON, SEC: Don't you think that No. 147 was a very special case, because of timing and various other things? I do.

KIRK, FASB: I hope it proves to be a special case. Time will tell. No. 147 was a very peculiar problem and let's hope that it does stay as "the special case."

KENT, Arthur Young: I would like to add just a word to that although I must say first that I admired the way that Clarence Sampson led the witness in his answer to that last question.

Dick Baker and I both happen to be trustees of the Financial Accounting Foundation (FAF) and Bob Mautz is a member of the Advisory Council. So we have a number here in addition to Don Kirk who are very much interested in the FASB. The trustees of the foundation have an overview function on the structure. If the structure that has been created for the FASB is not an adequate one, if a seven-man board has too many, or not enough, members and the rest of that program doesn't get the job done, the FAF trustees have, although I'm not suggesting that we are at this point now by any means, the responsibility to consider what changes should be made in the structure. This is by preface to saying the trustees have had a particular interest in observing the seeming differences of opinion that have arisen primarily between the SEC and the FASB. Obviously, the FASB does not want its territory undercut from it. The statutory authority for the establishment of principles rests with the SEC, but the SEC of record has not carried that out. This is by mutual agreement and it has worked well for the many years since it was initiated. The SEC has said time and time again that it is content to have standards set in the private sector.

The FASB is a brand new organization. Part of the problem has been that we had a gap between the winddown of the APB on June 30, 1973, and the windup of the FASB. The last of the seven full-time members of the standards board started work on the first of July, 1973. So it is an organization that has to get all of its pipeline filled before it can begin to be productive.

The SEC faces registrant problems et al. every day of the week. There isn't any organization that has more problems in financial reporting coming before it than the SEC does. In the days of the APB, it was possible for the SEC to take soundings with the APB as to their views on certain of these current questions that they had to deal with at the SEC. With the standards board getting started, and preoccupied and correctly so with its research function in an orderly start, they weren't really in a position to lend a great deal of assistance to the SEC on current problems. It is understandable that the SEC would find it necessary to have more ASR than the 3 1/2 that they have averaged in the years prior to 1972. At the same time I can understand the necessity for the SEC not to undermine the work of the FASB.

If it begins to undermine the work of the FASB, given its statutory authority, there will be no role for the FASB. We will then simply shut it down because there won't be any role for it.

However, these two organizations are going to be able to work together. They should. Both are serving the public interest. Both have integrity. Both are intelligently trying to deal with problems. I hope this just isn't wishful thinking that they will be able to work together. Of course, there are difficult areas in this relationship. When any organization has statutory authority and another organization is establishing the standards, there has to be a close relationship. There has to be input from the SEC to the standards board as there is from all other organizations. This is necessary so that the standards board can in fact do the best possible job in creating its standards. I am optimistic that the relationship will be a good one.

BAKER, Ernst & Ernst: You said it all. I really do think so.

CHETKOVICH, Haskins & Sells: I would like to add to Clarence Sampson's comments. The SEC approaches this from the standpoint of its own responsibilities, which we all recognize as very significant, for setting its rules the reports filed with the Commission. But in this day and age, all of us who are responsible for expressing opinions on financial statements would have to give careful thought to the possible consequences of not including the disclosures that the Commission pronounces to be important to the investor in all reports, and not just those filed with the SEC. There is a tendency, therefore, for any of these pronouncements to be considered as "generally accepted."

SAMPSON, SEC: I understand what you are saying. One of the ways this question can be answered would be when the FASB arrives at some kind of conclusion on the question of the conceptual framework on the financial statements and answers the question raised by the Trueblood Report as to who is the user. I hope the SEC waits until the FASB gets some answer in this area before we go off in some different way.

Quality Controls in the Practice of Accounting:

LYLE, Moderator: At the request of the SEC, the AICPA is looking into the question of quality control in the professional practice of accounting. Would you indicate what the SEC expects to accomplish in this area?

SAMPSON, SEC: This is one of the toughest parts of my job. We have an enforcement division of a couple of hundred people not counting the regional offices, and some of them have a couple of hundred of people themselves. They do a lot of work looking on to see what is going on in the markets and stock trading. From time to time, we find cases where the financial statements don't fairly present what has been going on in the company. In some cases, we find information which leads them to believe that the role of the auditor is not properly carried out in those situations. When this happens, our D. C. office is brought into it. We are required to look at what happened and make judgments about it.

As we look at these cases, we are convinced that suspensions of accounting firms, as they were known in the past, and there were very few of them, don't really work. It hurts the accounting firm's clients if you suspend the firm for 30 days or 60 days more than it hurts the accounting firm. So it is not the right answer.

What then is the right answer? After doing some thinking about this, we are trying to get some assurance that auditors are managing their practice in a way which is satisfactory for the public interest. This is really all we are trying to do. There are several ways to do this. We could go out and look at what is going on. But we don't have the staff or experience in auditing to start with. In a couple of cases so far, we have asked the AICPA, as the only logical body around who can provide members to write a report to the Commission. This report would say we have audited the auditors and we have found that they conduct their practice in a manner which is sufficient for you not to raise any question about their right and ability to conduct audits for the benefit of investors. This is the way that we are trying to accomplish it. We do believe that it might be useful to the entire profession, as well as to the Commission and investors to establish a general program so all auditing firms would be reviewed and thus not single out any one. If all auditing firms went through this periodically, with an independent third party taking a look at the way they conduct their practice, that would be a benefit. This is all we have said on that subject.

LYLE, Moderator: How do those in practice now expect to deal with this problem now and in the future?

CHETKOVICH, Haskins & Sells: It would take more than this program to tell you everything.

When we talk about quality control, we really are talking about the whole range of procedures and judgments that go into the expression of an opinion. This includes recruitment of quality people, training, audit procedures, supervision, concurring reviews, pretty much the whole concept of the operation and management of a practice. We have all been giving a good deal of thought to what we have done and are doing and what we might be doing in this area. In the final analysis, and without demeaning the importance of control procedures, our major reliance has to be on the competence and judgment of the particular individuals involved in that engagement and particularly the partner in charge of it.

KENT, Arthur Young: I can't let the subject go without commenting on it because otherwise it might be thought that I was in agreement with what the SEC is doing. A profession, if it is going to be a profession, has some responsibility to police the quality of the output of its members. Doctors have that obligation. Admittedly our national professional body has never really faced up to that. We have had a review program available but it has been used only by local practitioners, smaller firms, whereby representatives of other firms would come in and make an independent review to try to help that particular firm improve its quality. It is a foredrawn conclusion that every firm wants to do good work. I don't know any accounting firm of any size that wants to do poor work. We would be naive if we set out to do poor work. We would have been naive even before we reached the litigious climate that we are in today. We would be utterly out of our minds if we set out to do poor work when litigation is flowing as freely as it is now. So every firm wants to do good work.

The accounting profession has some responsibility to help its member firms to do good work and the profession does have a program being developed, which it will sponsor and which it will make available to member firms for independent reviews. This means reviews by trained and knowledgeable CPA's who are not associated with the firm that is being reviewed. Although the full scope of this has not been worked out, they will come in and they will reach conclusions as to the quality of the work being done, and where they believe improvement can be made and what that improvement will be. This is the way the profession will face up to this need for quality control.

But one thing troubles me very much about the SEC doing this since its scope isn't quite as limited as was described. If we get a cadre of people from the Institute to do the review, we can have a good review but that isn't the end of the SEC program. There are alternatives available to the SEC. They can ask higher education institutions to send professors in to make these reviews. Now professors are fine teachers and researchers, but those in accounting practice know more about auditing than anybody else. So we would like to have this work done by experienced auditors. The profession has the obligation and is facing up to this obligation. The SEC is sympathetic to having the profession do it even though the profession will never be perfect in the field. Consequently we can't be measured against the standards of perfection. But we are trying to do good work and nobody in practice has a different objective than that.

BAKER, Ernst & Ernst: I understand the problem that the SEC is facing. There have been a number of instances which would indicate that the accounting work was not what it should have been. We have a relatively new commission. I don't know what the length of service is, but the senior member has served about 2 1/2 years.

SAMPSON, SEC: A relatively new one except for Loomis.

BAKER, Ernst & Ernst: Anyway, the Commission is concerned about the quality of the work in the profession. As Ralph Kent says, the profession, too, is concerned about the quality of its work and the whole profession is continually being upgraded.

I feel that there is some tendency toward overkill about this professional review. The SEC is really leaving no stone unturned in trying to bring about a very fast and very abrupt change in the calibre of the audits that are being made. There are real problems, in my judgment, in doing this. You mentioned two cases in which there have been quality controls on public accounting firms. One is under a court order and that puts it under a completely different concept. That permits a group of people to come in and look at confidential information in the work papers of clients under the court order. This might be acceptable since you have no choice under a court order; but I am bothered somewhat how this would be done purely on a voluntary basis by a firm. Would they not be violating the confidence of their clients to turn over records tc people that conceivably could be doing work for competitors? I am for trying to get something to spur us to do better work but I'm not sure that this is the right vehicle for it.

SAMPSON, SEC: The only response I can make I guess is that this is the best vehicle we could think of at the time we worked with it and we would gladly embrace any ideas that we get from the profession or from any source which would further the common objective.

Segmented or Line of Business Reporting:

STERNAD, Moderator: There has been a great increase in the demand for line of business reporting with the rise of conglomerates lately and this subject is on the FASB agenda.

KIRK, FASB: I will respond but since Dr. Mautz is an expert on this subject even though it is not related to CASB, perhaps he should comment.

MAUTZ, CASB: Any time someone describes you as an expert, it's a good time to just nod your head wisely and maintain silence.

KIRK, FASB: I can again give sort of a status report as to where the FASB stands on this particular issue. As you know, it was one of the original seven on our initial agenda. We are now at the point where the DM which will proceed a public hearing has been approved by the task force. It has minor editing left to be done on it. The Board has to give it a final review. It should be available for public release, we would hope, within a month's time. A public hearing will be scheduled some time later this year on the subject. Its content will be rather mild compared to the FTC requirements. As you probably suspect, whatever we come out with that might conflict with the FTC requirements, might require another set of records to keep. But it's strictly at the DM stage now. The Board has done nothing more than try to be certain that as many issues as possible are included in the DM in order to solicit thoughtful responses from the public at the hearing.

MAUTZ, CASB: Let me speak as a CASB member. You know the CASB indirectly is very deep into line of business reporting because most government contractors are not only in government contracting, they are also in commercial work. Part of our task is to try to find ways to allocate costs properly between these two lines. The CASB has done more of this kind of allocation than the APB ever attempted to do or any one short of the FTC has attempted to do. Our Standard No. 403 had to do with the allocation of home office expenses to segments of the business. We worked out in considerable detail both a general principle and actual practical means of implementing the principle to make that kind of allocation. I would commend that particular standard to the FASB for two reasons. First, it gets into the subject very deeply, and second, it is the standard on which we have had the greatest amount of criticism. We may have learned something from a trying experience.

KIRK, FASB: We may get around to showing the differences in the two boards on this subject.

KENT, Arthur Young: Most people know that the accounting profession is struggling with the question of auditing company lines of business and there isn't much that is currently covered by an accountant's opinion. I don't know whether the SEC sees more. It is inevitable that auditors will be asked to express an opinion on line of business reporting. It simply involves getting into the allocations of common expenses et al., and means extending audit work in order to be able to do that. Ever since the first time we got into line of business results, I felt that the time would come and it isn't far away now when the auditors will be asked to audit line of business reporting. The auditing committee of the AICPA is now trying to establish some standards of auditing to be applied to this line of business work.

SAMPSON, SEC: We do not anticipate using the FTC breakdowns in SEC reports. In the line of business reporting, the SEC has made a conscious decision not to look at this till we see the results of the FASB DM, public hearing, and thoughts on the subject. This was despite some urging to take another look at our rules of disclosing line of business which are outside the financial statements.

The Overlap of Authority Between the CASB and the FASB:

LYLE, Moderator: What effect will the standards as promulgated by the CASB have on general or financial accounting?

MAUTZ, CASB: I once had the happy thought that we could draw a fairly clean line between the work of the CASB and the work of the FASB in developing financial accounting standards. I don't find that line nearly so clean any more for a number of reasons. Take some of the topics already discussed today, for example. You might think that business combinations would have very little to do with cost accounting standards. But if in the accounting for business combinations there are any implications for a change in recording the carrying amount of assets acquired, that has implications for depreciation and that has implications for contract cost accounting.

In the SEC's Accounting Series Release on inventory profits, there is an implication that such profits are not real. There is a further implication that somehow, therefore, true costs were understated, and that has implications for contract costs. If I were a contractor, I would be knocking on the CASB's door with ASR 151 and saying that we were entitled to something more than historical cost.

The CASB has price-level accounting on its agenda although that subject has had a very low order of priority so far. It could be boosted to a very much higher priority very shortly now due to the additional attention that price-level adjustments and fair value accounting are getting from other organizations.

The CASB will have an influence on general accounting in two ways. We must, by our assignment, get into certain questions which have strong implications for financial accounting. Depreciation is one of the subjects. When you start talking about cost and government contracts, you have to start thinking about depreciation. So we are under some pressure from various interests to give that subject attention and to develop standards which can be used by government auditors and others to determine whether contract accounting is satisfactory. Yet, when we announced our interest in that subject, we were immediately accused of infringing on financial accounting and the role of the FASB. I don't know how we can avoid the overlap entirely.

Hopefully, we can work out ways for cooperation between the two boards so that we have some joint research where we share our ideas. Our two boards have met together; our chairmen have met together; we have confessed our best intentions on both boards. So far, we have had no difficulties and hopefully we won't.

We can succeed only with a fair amount of tolerance on both sides, with less concern about "whose turf" specific standards may be and more concerned about each of us doing the best job we can.

There is little difference in the point of view. Financial accounting for years has been concerned about the possible understatement of cost and expenses, and it leans a little heavily on the side of conservatism to be sure that all costs are included. From the standpoint of government contracts, a major concern is whether there are costs maybe included which couldn't be included. So, the CASB perhaps leans a little heavily on that side.

We are going to have to work out such philosophical differences on a number of specific issues.

The extent to which our standards will have any impact depends on a number of factors. One of them is whether we ever do what the Internal Revenue Service is doing. That is establishing some sort of a conformity test. The IRS says you can apply certain accounting methods for tax purposes only if you also apply them in your general accounting. If we were to say that we will accept certain accounting practices for government contract purposes only if they are used also for general income determination, this might put some pressure on the contractor to use for financial reporting purposes those methods which give him the greatest amount of cost. Such an approach would be most unfortunate. Thus far, we have not developed any standards of that kind. Those proposed, we have been able to resist. I hope we will be able to continue to resist them so as not to put that kind of pressure on the FASB or on financial reporting in general.

I have another hope. That is that the method of developing standards that our board has worked out perhaps more by good luck than by skill, might provide a pattern for other groups. We take research very seriously, much of it applied research. We have a tremendous exchange of views and information between contractors and our staff and board before we begin to draft a standard; we have a very carefully worked out exposure process which gives everybody at interest a chance to have a say, and we publish our response to all the criticism of an exposed standard before we finally promulgate it. We have learned a great deal from this process. Some of the others, if I might say so, who dash off standards pretty rapidly might do so, too.

KIRK, FASB: Nobody has accused us of that yet.

KENT, Arthur Young: Mr. Moderator, from this end we have a technical question. We couldn't see who Bob Mautz looked at.

MAUTZ, CASB: It was straight ahead.

KIRK, FASB: The support of the CASB for the FASB has been tremendous. Their willingness to open their doors to us and their expression of support has been unqualified. It is appreciated. We are also appreciative of the fact that there is not what is referred to as a booking requirement in CASB's accounting standards. But we do recognize that we have clearly different objectives. This is my perspective and the Board's perspective and I think Bob Mautz has just expressed his views on it.

At the CASB the concern is about cost justification and pricing considerations. It is very clearly stated in the objectives of the CASB that "the allocation of all period costs to the products and services of the period is not a common practice for public reporting or internal management purposes. Yet this has long been the established cost principle for costing defense contracts procurement. The Board (CASB) will adhere to the concept of full costing wherever appropriate."

So it is quite clear that at least if our standards follow the traditional ones of past reporting referred to in the CASB objective that there could well be, and undoubtedly already is, a difference of view as to the objective of accounting. I think all parties must understand that and appreciate that difference in order for us to work well together.

Secondly, there can be pressures brought on financial reporting and it is a question of both sides understanding the different perspectives. In a recent proposed CASB standard, there is an indication that when the commercial accounting of a company is different than its government accounting, there is a tendency to say that the government accounting is incorrect. In other words, there is evidence that if for government contract purposes, cost is added on to an inventory item but not for commercial purposes, that cost would not be acceptable for contract purposes.

Why should that be when the purposes of the two costing systems might be entirely different? On the other side, if I change my accounting for commercial purposes, should that make it acceptable for government contract purposes? So there are pressures and there is a need to recognize, again on both parties' part, their basic difference in objectives.

KENT, Arthur Young: When the CASB was proposed, the Comptroller General testified against establishing it before a congressional committee. Do you believe that the CASB has now moved to the point where it is imbedded in an ongoing governmental activity, into the indefinite future? As it has carved out its role now, will that be a continuing role?

MAUTZ, CASB: I have to answer that in the affirmative. I think it does have a role. It is well established. If you look at the way the staff is set up, they expect it to be there a long, long time.

It's just possible, however, and even likely, that in time the Board will have pretty much performed its function. Then its work will slow down a good deal and the large staff wil no longer be necessary. In that happy event, the major problem will be merely keeping abreast of developments and getting out interpretations as necessary. Ours could be a one-shot assignment which eventually we ought to accomplish.

Investors: Average and Well-Informed:

STERNAD, Moderator: In some of the recent accounting series releases, notably the ones on disclosure, compensating balances, and income tax expense, the SEC has directed its attention to well-informed as opposed to average investors. Wouldn't a breakdown of this type between user groups have numerous effects on the way financial information is reported?

SAMPSON, SEC: We did touch on this earlier. The answers are still pretty much the same in terms of the SEC taking appropriate action to require information that it thinks is necessary either inside or outside the financial statements. The last question referred to Accounting Series Release No. 147 was a special case. In that release, we did say that that information should be included not only in 10-K's, but in financial statements and annual reports to stockholders. This was a reflection of the Commission's feeling that this information should be available to everybody now. So we really couldn't wait two or three years to give the FASB the proper time to consider the matter and take care of it.

We also said that when the FASB deals with this subject we will reconsider this and we would probably rescind it or amend it or do whatever is necessary. We mean those words but nobody listens.

BAKER, Ernst & Ernst: We heard!

KENT, Arthur Young: We listened!

KIRK, FASB: The FASB was quoted earlier as having said something about the dichotomy between measurement and disclosure. The FASB is not taking any position officially on the distinction between the average and the sophisticated investor. But clearly it is of concern to us. It is an area on which we hope we can focus in what is known as the conceptual framework project on our agenda. Initially this would involve a public hearing on the Trueblood Committee Report. The FASB is concerned as to whether such a distinction can be made. Certainly in our discussions with members of the Trueblood Committee, we were not persuaded to change or eliminate our concern over this. We feel that such a distinction is possibly impossible, if that's sayable? But also one which is fraught with problems. You can visualize what may happen. The SEC's attitude might be, well we'll deal with what the sophisticated investor needs in the 10-K. We will also dictate what else has to go into the annual report in front of the financial statements and we will leave the FASB to struggle with what the average investor needs.

Clearly, we can't have that sort of long-range relationship at all. There has to be a meeting of the minds on this particular subject. We hope that coming out of our conceptual framework subject that our positions will merge through public input.

KENT, Arthur Young: May I read briefly from two items here and then ask Clarence Sampson to comment?

SEC ASR No. 147 essentially affects airlines and retailers. Here is how J. C. Penney complied with the new requirement in its

1973 annual report. As I read it, please reflect as to whether this is a meaningful type of disclosure to a typical investor.

> The Company has revised its method of computing lease commitments to conform with guidelines recently published by the SEC. Based upon these guidelines, Penney's commitments under non-capitalized financing leases were $608 million at year end, 1973 and $521 million at year end 1972. These commitments are stated at the present value of all future minimum payments under these leases after excluding executory expenses, which are property taxes, maintenance, insurance and other amounts that do not constitute payments for property rights. Rent expense applicable to non-capitalized financing leases was $72 million in 1973 and $60 million in 1972. Minimum annual rents under non-capitalized financing leases at year end amounted to $66 million including executory expenses. If financing leases had been capitalized and the resultant property rights amortized on a straight-line basis over the primary terms of these leases, the basis net income would have been reduced $8 million in 1973 and $5 million in 1972.

I also want to refer to a formal comment to the FASB on one of their DM which referred to No. 147 in a couple of places.

> The increases on required disclosure now being imposed on issuers of financial statements threaten to drown the readers in a flood of information that is becoming extremely difficult to appraise as to relative importance.

The second comment:

> Disclosure must serve to complete accounting presentations, not to burden them. New disclosure standards should fill a clear need for necessary information and should never be based on possible utility to an unidentified or vaguely defined or specialized class abuser. This particular firm deplores the recent tendency of the SEC to impose on issuers of financial statements an increasing burden of disclosure acknowledged to be outside the interest of the ordinary user of financial statements. An inexorable law of diminishing returns governs disclosure. Readers of financial statements are soon overwhelmed by a spate of information that runs the gamut of relative importance and must be evaluated by the reader.

SAMPSON, SEC: This information needs to be made meaningful to the average investor. We think it can be. Whether or not it is,

I will leave for somebody else to answer. The question as to who is the user of the financial statement is one the commission is not settled on how we are to go. Their minds are open on this user issue.

Whether annual reports ought to be made more simple and send less to shareholders or something in between is something on which there is no complete agreement about by the commission staff and which will be dealt with from time to time as issues come up.

The recent proposal by putting things in the annual reports to stockholders was I think well conceived in that there is a lot of information in 10-K which is not in an annual report and should be. For example, line of business reporting. Many, many companies have not put that information in their annual reports. It should be in there. The only reason we acted is that many companies are not doing it. There are a lot of other things which are dealt with in that release. But I will admit publicly that we don't have all of the answers, and on this particular answer about users we are going to look for guidance and see what the FASB comes up with and go from there.

KENT, Arthur Young: I remember hearing Sandy Burton talk on this subject and at that time we were headed down the right avenue. There is a need for sophisticated information to be available to financial analysts and to institutional investors who have great influence on our markets. The thought at that time was that the basic financial statements which appeared in annual shareholder reports would continue to be essentially the type of disclosure that we have had heretofore. That will always be improved and it is under a state of change at all times but nothing as sophisticated, for example, as the footnote that I read from the J. C. Penney statement. The thought at that time was that anybody who wanted supplementary information could write the company for it, as where now many companies are suggesting they should write in for 10-K's. This new type of disclosure has set financial reporting back a good many years because very few people are going to understand that J. C. Penney footnote. They can read it, but then won't know how to do something with it. Under proper study by sophisticated financial analysts, it will be meaningful. But financial analysts are a very limited group. I am not underestimating their influence but I would suggest that it would be desirable to give them their information in supplementary fashion rather than to confuse 30 million shareholders.

SAMPSON, SEC: I appreciate your comments, but there is one thing we have to keep in mind, although it isn't said very often. There are a lot of investors in this country that don't read financial statements; that is said a lot. But there are other investors who consider themselves to be serious analysts and they want the information and what we are trying to do is work out the program which gives those people the information who want the information.

BAKER, Ernst & Ernst: It is a tough balancing act to try to carry water on both shoulders, in the 10-K and in the annual report. If information is in the 10-K and would be available to everybody, it should be in the annual report as well. But I sympathize with what Ralph Kent has said.

Trying to meet that requirement for data about leases gave us fits. Just getting the information was difficult enough, but then we also had to satisfy the clients that it was necessary. I can't really remember having anything brought to my attention indicating that clients thought this was going to be beneficial in any way. Of course, I also appreciate the problem of trying to work out a balance between not enough and too much disclosure. It certainly is not easy.

Will the SEC Supplant the FASB?

LYLE, Moderator: Do you expect that the SEC will substantially or partially supplant the FASB as the principal rule-making body for the accounting profession?

KIRK, FASB: I don't think so. I agree with what Ralph Kent said earlier that we would go out of business one way or the other if that occurred.

SAMPSON, SEC: And I said earlier that the SEC doesn't expect that to happen.

What's Ahead In the Next Ten Years:

CHETKOVICH, Haskins and Sells: Looking ahead to what might be expected in the field of accounting in the next decade, it is quite safe to begin with the prediction that there will be no slowdown in the pace of developments; if anything, we can look for acceleration. There is little likelihood, either, of any early end to controversy and criticism although one might hope, and possibly expect, that there will be some leveling off in volume and intensity.

With the creation of the FAF and the establishment of the FASB, there is a whole new approach to the development and/or delineation of accounting standards and concepts. While we have high hopes for the success of this new agency, it is unreasonable to assume that it can solve all the problems or satisfy all the critics. There is nothing like a state of perfection in the performance of this function and, even if there were, attainment of that state would not necessarily be so recognized and acknowledged on any widespread basis.

I believe strongly that the FASB can and will perform its task very creditably. Certainly, it would appear to present the best approach yet conceived for dealing with this most difficult responsibility, that of prescribing accounting standards. Because of the stature and quality of the members of the Board, the research capabilities supporting them, and the processes for achieving a high degree of input to and exposure of their proposed pronouncements, there is a good reason to expect that their statements will be sound. The true and difficult test will lie not so much in the quality of these statements, but in their general acceptance. We know, all too well, from all aspects of life, that the "right" answers are not necessarily the most popular ones, that the best medicine sometimes is the hardest to take.

There is considerable activity on the international scene, much more than ever before, and reason to expect some progress toward achieving a greater measure of uniformity in international accounting standards. Recognizing the great difficulty of achieving any high degree of uniformity within a single jurisdiction, we cannot anticipate rapid strides in this direction. The progress will be slow and painful. However, there is machinery in being, in the persons of the International Accounting Standards Committee (IASC) and the International Coordination Committee for the Accountancy Profession (ICCAC), whose commitment to and initial progress toward this objective are impressive and give promise of greater achievement. Certainly there is great incentive and need for attention to the international area, with the growth of multinational organizations, the increasing movement of capital across national boundaries, and the other developments shaping a global-economy.

The past decade has been a rather tumultuous one for accounting and for those who practice it. It is important to recognize that the attention focused on accounting, critical though much of it may be, is also a recognition of its great significance to the functioning of our system of free enterprise. In this context, of equal importance to the establishment of sound standards, and probably more difficult of attainment, is the need for a clearer understanding of the objectives and the limitations of accounting and, with such understanding, the achievement of a better balance between expectation and capability. This is a task we must address ourselves to energetically, even as we recognize that human nature being what it is, we can hope only to narrow the gap and not to eliminate it.

APPENDICES TO SECTION V

For a bibliography for this section, a great variety of background material is substituted. In the appendix (A), the current membership of the FAF, the FASAC, and the FASB is given and the administrative process of the FASB described. In the next two appendices (B and C), the current membership of the SEC is given and the SEC Chief Accountant identifies what he regards as the major issues currently. The following two appendices (D and E) deal with the CASB: in the first, its administration and membership is described and in the second, a critique of the CASB is reprinted. The remaining appendices reprint critiques by a leading banker, Walter B. Wriston; a leading critic in the media, Professor Abraham J. Briloff; and two journalists. The announcement (subsequent to this program) of a Public Review Board for Arthur Andersen & Co. also is included.

APPENDIX A TO SECTION FIVE

FAF, FASAC & FASB MEMBERS AND FASB OPERATIONS*

The FAF:

The FAF by-laws charge the Trustees with four responsibilities:

1. To appoint the members of the FASB. The FASB is to have and exercise all the authority of the Foundation relating to standards of financial accounting and reporting, including the conduct of all related activities.

2. To appoint the members of the Financial Accounting Standards Advisory Council (FASAC).

3. To raise and allocate the funds required to support the new structure.

4. To review periodically, and to change as necessary, the basic structure of the standard-setting organization, including the size, composition, and functions of the FASB and the FASAC.

The members of the FAF and their business affiliations are:

Name	*Business Title & Affiliation*
Ralph E. Kent, Chairman	*Senior Partner, Arthur Young & Company*
Richard T. Baker	*Managing Partner, Ernst & Ernst*
John C. Biegler	*Senior Partner, Price Waterhouse & Co.*
Ivan O. Bull	*Managing Partner, McGladrey, Hansen, Dunn & Co.*
Samuel A. Derieux	*Partner, Derieux, Baker, Thompson, & Whitt*
James Don Edwards	*Distinguished Professor of Accounting College of Business Administration, The University of Georgia*

*Adapted with permission from Financial Accounting Foundation Report, July 1, 1972 - December 31, 1973, p. 15.

Willian H. Franklin	*Chairman of the Board Caterpiller Tractor Co.*
Thomas A. Murphy	*Vice Chairman, General Motors Corporation*
Thomas C. Pryor	*Senior Vice President, White Weld & Co.*

The FASAC:

Twenty-seven men and one woman were appointed as charter members of the FASAC for terms expiring September 30, 1974. In their full-time positions they are corporate executives, partners in accounting firms, investment bankers, financial analysts, economists, lawyers, professors, and Government employees. No single sphere of background experience dominates the Advisory Council.

As unsalaried Council members, they meet in joint sessions with Board members, generally once each three months. The functions of the FASAC include providing advice to the FASB as to its agenda topics and priorities, helping it to set up task forces, reacting to proposed statements and interpretations, and otherwise assisting the FASB when called upon to do so.

The members of Council and their full-time positions are:

Name	*Position and Affiliation*
Marshall S. Armstrong	*Chairman, FASB*
Andrew Barr	*Consultant, AICPA*
George R. Catlett	*Partner, Arthur Andersen & Co.*
Donald C. Cook	*Chairman and Chief Executive Officer, American Electric Power Co., Inc.*
Sidney Davidson	*Dean, Graduate School of Business, University of Chicago*
Philip L. Defliese	*Managing Partner, Coopers & Lybrand*
Frank Forester, Jr.	*Executive Vice President, Morgan Guaranty Trust Company of New York*
Charles C. Hornbostel	*President, Financial Executives Institute*
Herman J. Kocour	*Partner, Elmer Fox & Co.*

Harold Q. Langenderfer	*Professor, School of Business Administration, University of North Carolina*
John J. Lordan	*Director, Office of Financial Management, Office of Financial Management Policy, U.S. General Services Administration*
Robert A. Malin	*Senior Vice President Reynolds Securities Inc.*
William McChesney Martin	
Robert K. Mautz	*Partner, Ernst & Ernst*
Charles T. McGarraugh	*Senior Vice President Northwest Bancorporation*
Robert A. Morgan	*Controller, Caterpiller Tractor Co.*
Ellsworth H. Morse, Jr.	*Assistant Comptroller General of the United States*
James J. Needham	*Chairman of the Board New York Stock Exchange, Inc.*
David Norr	*Partner, First Manhattan Company*
C. Reed Parker	*Executive Vice President, Duff Anderson & Clark, Inc.*
Felix G. Rohatyn	*General Partner, Lazard Freres & Co.*
Stanley J. Scott	*Managing Partner, Alford, Meroney & Co.*
Dr. Frances G. Stone	*Industry Specialist, Merrill Lynch, Pierce Fenner & Smith, Inc.*
E. Palmer Tang	*Partner, Touche Ross & Co.*
Allan Wear	*General Auditor, Ford Motor Company*
Francis M. Wheat	*Partner, Gibson, Dunn & Crutcher*
John A. Willis	*Controller, Union Carbide Corporation*

Charles T. Zlatkovich	*Professor, College of Business Administration, The University of Texas at Austin*

The FASB:

The seven full-time charter members of the FASB were appointed over a four-month period ending in February, 1973. Each of the seven appointees was engaged in other activities from which he had to resign in order to accept appointment to the Board. All Board members had started work by July 1, 1973.

Four of the Board members came from public accounting, one from corporate accounting, one from the federal government, and one from academe. In age they range from 41 to 68. Their terms of appointment are staggered to expire from 1974 to 1978. No Board member may serve more than two consecutive full five-year terms.

The members of the FASB, their former business affiliations, and the expiration date (September 30) of their terms, are:

Name	*Former Business Title and Affiliation*	*Term Expiration Year*
Marshall S. Armstrong *Chairman*	*Managing Partner* *Geo. S. Olive & Co.*	*1974*
John W. Queenan *Vice Chairman*	*Managing Partner (retired)* *Haskins & Sells*	*1975*
Donald J. Kirk	*Partner* *Price Waterhouse & Co.*	*1976*
Arthur L. Litke	*Chief, Office of Accounting & Finance* *Federal Power Commission*	*1977*
Robert E. Mays	*Controller* *Exxon Corporation*	*1977*
Walter Schultze	*Partner* *Peat, Marwick, Mitchell & Co.*	*1978*
Robert T. Sprouse	*Professor of Accounting,* *Graduate School of Business* *Stanford University*	*1975*

FASB Operations:

The importance of establishing to public satisfaction the independence and objectivity of FASB members has been recognized. Personnel policies have been formalized under which each Board member is charged with being mindful at all times of his public responsibilities, the sensitivity of his position, and the need for public confidence in the fairness of the deliberative process of the FASB.

Each FASB member is required to confirm periodically to the FAF Trustees that he is in compliance with rules of conduct relating to relationships with former employers, personal investments and obligations, outside activities, and speeches and publications.

The FASB operates under rules of procedure developed by the FAF and under operating policies established by the FASB itself. Briefly summarized, these rules and policies contemplate that the following steps will precede issuance of a statement of Financial Accounting Standards:

- *Preparation of a preliminary definition of the problem and bibliography of existing literature on the subject.*
- *Appointment of a task force to consult with the FASB in planning research and identifying alternative solutions for each item on the agenda. A task force normally will be comprised of persons with special expertise in the subject under consideration, including members of FASAC.*
- *Research, generally by the FASB research staff, including review of existing studies.*
- *Preparation of a discussion memorandum, with the counsel of the task force, outlining alternative solutions to the problem as the basis for a public hearing.*
- *Conducting a public hearing, generally with at least 60 days' notice, but not less than 30 days.*
- *Revision of the draft Statement, if indicated, as a result of comments received during exposure.*
- *Final deliberation by the Board and an affirmative vote of at least five of the seven members before*

a Statement of Financial Accounting Standards is issued.

The rules of procedure also permit issuance of a Statement following exposure for public comment but without one or more of the other steps if in the judgment of the FASB on the basis of existing data, an informed decision can be made in that manner.

Interpretations of FASB Statements or of pronouncements by predecessor bodies may be issued in clarification, exploration or elaboration without public hearing and without general public exposure, though all proposed interpretations must be submitted to the FASAC for comment for a period of at least 15 days. The FASB's voting requirement for issuance of interpretations is the same as that for Statements.

A task force generally is appointed for a project after the Board has approved the preliminary definition of the problem. The present task forces range in size from 11 to 16 members. A total of 98 authorities in industry, the accounting profession, the financial and academic communities, and government have been actively engaged on task forces assisting the FASB with its various projects.

The staff includes three major categories of personnel: technical advisors, research, and administration. Each member of the FASB has a technical adviser. In addition, there is a senior technical adviser to the Board. The technical advisers assist FASB members in planning projects, evaluating data, and drafting documents. In addition to the director of research, there are 11 members of the research staff with varied backgrounds in public accounting, industry, government, teaching, and financial analysis. The administrative staff, headed by the director of administration, includes both technical support and administrative support personnel. Technical support includes the library staff, task force administrative assistants, and a publications staff. Administrative support includes the internal operations administrator and staff, office services manager and staff (typing, filing, duplicating, shipping and receiving, switchboard, and reception), and a personnel manager and meetings coordinator. There also is a full-time relations counsel.

Research facilities include a reference library and microfilm files of annual reports to shareholders, Form 10-K reports to the SEC, and other types of financial reports. The library can accommodate 8,000 volumes and is equipped with microfiche viewers and computer terminals. The FASB is participating in the AICPA's computerized accounting information retrieval system, and has access, via remote terminal, to a time-sharing facility.

APPENDIX B TO SECTION V

THE SEC: LIFE BEGINS AT 40*

Created by Congress as an independent agency, the SEC began operations on July 1, 1934, with Joseph P. Kennedy as Chairman. Its assignment was to maintain fair, efficient, and orderly markets for securities and to regulate their distribution for the protection of investors.

A year earlier, Congress had passed the Securities Act of 1933, then known as the "truth in securities" law. Its primary objective was to require public disclosure of all material information, through a registration statement and a prospectus to potential buyers so securities could be evaluated by investors.

The Utility Holding Company Act was added to the Commission's responsibilities in 1935 with its mandated dissolution of holding companies and their geographic integration. Regulation of investment companies and investment advisers was added in 1940. Self-regulation of the over-the-counter market under SEC supervision came still later.

Today, with fewer than 2,000 employees, the Commission is charged with protecting the interests of 100 million Americans who as owners or beneficiaries have a stake in the values established in securities markets. But, regulating the capital markets means more than policing stock exchanges and third-market dealers.

It means supervising the activities of about 5,000 broker-dealers and 3,500 investment advisers, regulating 1,300 investment companies, bringing enforcement actions to assure financial responsibility and fair dealing, studying 1,000 corporate reorganizations each year, obtaining full and accurate information from 10,000 corporations, and watching the trading in another 10,000.

It also means overseeing the development and application of principles of accounting and financial reporting, developing a body of law on fair dealings in securities, and through the proxy process fostering corporate democracy and fiduciary obligations among directors, officers, and stockholders.

*Reprinted with permission from The Week in Review, Haskins & Sells, July 5, 1974, pp. 5-7.

For these purposes, it is questionable whether the Commission's budget of $34 million for the 1973-1974 fiscal year and its present payroll of 1,919, although at an all-time high, is sufficient. Of the 1,919, 1,227 are in the Washington headquarters and 692 are in the nine regional and seven branch offices. There are 1,219 professionals on the staff of whom 590 are lawyers and the balance are accountants, financial analysts, and economists. Of its budget appropriation, it usually returns about 70 percent to the general fund of the Treasury through its fees and other service charges. Its staff was deployed last year as follows:

Percent of Work Force	Duties
33	Fraud Prevention
27	Disclosure Programs
	Regulation of:
25	Market and Broker-Dealers
13	Investment Companies
2	Utility Holding Companies

It will hire 225 more persons for the 1974-1975 fiscal year, mostly in the fraud prevention area. During the last fiscal year, the SEC initiated 146 civil cases that resulted in 270 injunctions against 578 defendants and referred 67 criminal cases to the Department of Justice; the Justice Department, whose deputies alone have power to enpanel a grand jury, obtained 38 indictments involving 169 defendants from these cases of which less than half were convicted. In issuing a security, the issue requires an accountant, a lawyer and a broker; the accountant must be certified by the SEC, the lawyer admitted to practice before the SEC, and the broker registered. Of the 4,000 brokers registered, about 200 do 80 percent of the brokerage business and of the 2,000 accounting firms certified, a higher concentration applies. Under the SEC's concept of "institutional responsibility," a fraud is committed even if the issuer of the security committed fraud unwittingly. Five commissioners head the SEC staff.

Ray Garrett, Jr., was a nationally recognized authority on corporate disclosure and finance as well as utility company regulation before coming to Washington. He has the added advantage of having worked in the SEC at the staff level and he knows those now directing its various divisions.

Philip A. Loomis, Jr., long known as the SEC's "genius in residence," has a brilliant legal background. He was formerly General Counsel of the Commission and he is its leading expert on the Securities Exchange Act.

A. A. Sommer, Jr., who arrived in Washington just behind Mr. Garrett, had already achieved national stature as an authority on the responsibilities of corporate officers and as an expert on the Securities Act of 1933. He also is an expert on regulation of the over-the-counter market by the National Association of Securities Dealers, of which he was a Director.

John R. Evans is one of two professional economists ever to be made a member of the SEC. He also brought to the Commission 10 years of experience in commercial banking. His service as an administrative assistant to a member of the Senate has also proved valuable to the Agency in its relations with Congress.

Irving M. Pollack is an attorney who came up through the ranks to be a member of the Commission. His 20 years experience as a market regulator and "top cop" of the Enforcement Division qualifies him as the Agency's foremost consumer advocate.

Time will tell how capably the Commission proves itself in dealing with the second securities industry revolution. The second securities industry revolution is the SEC's attempt to develop a whole new system in order to bring back the individual investor into the marketplace. Effective registrations of common stock for cash sale for 1973-1974 were the lowest of any period since 1953. It projected central market calls for a thorough overhauling of the nation's capital markets and a new method of operations. The Commission has made it clear that nothing will be allowed to stand in the way of its reorganization plans despite the numerous criticisms it has received. But, even its embattled spokesmen would agree that as presently constituted it is the strongest Commission so far in its 40-year history.

APPENDIX C TO SECTION V

THE SEC AND THE WORLD OF ACCOUNTING IN 1974*

by

John C. Burton

As I look at 1974, it seems to me that if 1973 could be called the year of increased disclosure, 1974 might be called the year of the auditor. Perhaps it is not coincidental that in the Chinese calendar the year ahead is known as the year of the tiger! I believe that 1974 will see the beginnings, and perhaps to some extent the conclusions, of a number of major steps that will affect the accounting profession primarily in its role as auditor rather than in terms of measurement and disclosure. First, improved quality control and the problem of professional discipline which I have already touched upon will undoubtedly take a high priority this year both at the SEC and the AICPA.

Second, I think the question of the auditor and fraud is one that has to be attacked this year. The historical posture of the auditor, which seems to be that fraud is not what the CPA is responsible for finding, has to be reconsidered. This is not to say that the auditor should devote his attention to looking for thefts from the petty cash fund, which I think is what the auditor is primarily talking about when he says he is not responsible for fraud. We have seen too many cases of massive management fraud where management has obscured the reality of corporate activity from the auditor. This is something to which the accounting profession has to turn its attention. I believe that the AICPA committee headed by Marvin Stone, which is looking into the Equity Funding matter with the purpose of articulating the lessons to be learned, is one that will help in this direction.

A third area that I think will see some substantial development in 1974 is what has been called the "auditor of public record" concept. Increasingly it is being recognized that the auditor has some responsibility beyond an annual visit to the corporation in order to audit the financial statements of a particular year. I think that the auditor has to recognize that he has a public responsibility in the broad framework of public financial

*Reprinted by permission from "Statements in Quotes," The Journal of Accountancy, July, 1974, pp. 59-69. Excerpts from a speech by the Chief Accountant of the SEC, before the Dean's Forum in Los Angeles, California, on January 17, 1974.

reporting by corporations. This means that as long as he is the auditor of record, which in the case of a public company means that there has been no 8-K filed with the Commission that indicates he has resigned or been fired, he should feel some responsibility to review all public financial reporting of that company on a continuing basis. It is apparent that what has to be done in this respect is to develop meaningful standards for auditor responsibility. I do not contemplate, for example, a quarterly audit. But on the other hand, it seems to me that public orientation and reporting expertise should have greater impact on interim statements than has been the case traditionally. This is not an area into which the SEC or the accounting profession should rush blindly, but it is an area which must receive considerable attention. I think that 1974 will see that attention given.

This year should also see a better approach to the problem of how uncertainty should be dealt with in the auditor's opinion. The AICPA auditing standards executive committee is now hard at work on this subject.

In addition, we should see progress in dealing with a number of problems of independence. On one front, the ethics committee of the AICPA is working on the problems of family relationships. A paper should be forthcoming shortly. On another, the Commission is looking very seriously at the problem of independence as it relates to adversary relationships in lawsuits. The litigious world we live in has created a number of problems in this respect.

Even more fundamentally, I think some attention must be given to the most basic problem of independence: the lack of appearance of independence that arises because the auditor is paid by his client. By saying this I am not advocating in any sense that the auditor shoud not be paid by his client. I do not favor some of the proposals that have been made which suggest that there should be a sort of central pot out of which the auditor is paid. But I do think that a number of institutional steps may be taken to improve the basic appearance problem, and I think that these are consistent with the way in which outside directors are increasingly feeling. One step might be the increasing formalization and use of the audit committee of the board of directors. Another possibility is the extension of the period of time for which an auditor is appointed. While I would hesitate to suggest the academic concept of tenure, a three- or five-year term might be appropriate. This might tie in with the "auditor of public record" concept. Some additional legal rights such as those that exist in the United Kingdom, where auditors have an absolute right to attend stockholders' meetings and to communicate with shareholders in the event they are displaced, may be appropriate. In addition it may be that auditors should have the right to at-

tend meetings of the board of directors. Other legal rights may well be part of this package.

An additional auditing and accounting problem which has to be solved this year is that of related party transactions. On the accounting side, this requires attention to whether or not profits may be legitimately reflected in financial statements when they result from transactions with related parties. It may be, for example, that such "profits" under some circumstances should be treated as contributions to capital. From an auditing viewpoint, the question of what responsibility exists for the problems of auditing outside the particular entity that you are looking at must be faced. It may be that an auditor must have access to the books and records of all parties which are related to the entity he is auditing. Some of our most dramatic cases in the past year include the Westgate (SEC v. Westgate California Corporation et al.) case and the U.S. Financial (SEC v. U.S. Financial, Inc. et al.) case where the related party problem was the key. Somehow or other an auditor has to get some kind of handle on this.

While it seems to me that perhaps the most significant new steps that are going to be taken in 1974 will be taken by the profession and the Commission in regard to the audit function and audit responsibilities, this is not to say that I think the year will be inactive on the reporting front. Of course, the Financial Accounting Standards Board is going to be moving ahead in bringing items out of its pipeline, and these will be significant. The SEC has a number of outstanding proposals on which final action will no doubt be taken this year. Our analytical summarization proposal, the annual report proposal, the accounting alternatives proposal, and our statement of policy on forecasting need to be developed during the year. Beyond this, there are some general problems in interim reporting, price level and fair value, working capital, and uncertainty which will need some attention this year, although there are no specific plans for releases in the near future in these areas.

Basically, what I'd like to leave with you, however, is my view of the SEC's role in this changing world. I believe the Commission is going to be an active participant. I think it will be a catalyst. But I don't believe it can be a dominant force. The accounting profession and the business community must accept change in these areas. The Commission can encourage, but we can't do more. If we are able to work together, I think all of our interests will be served. I personally remain very optimistic that this will be the case in 1974 and in the years ahead.

NOTE: As a matter of policy the SEC takes no responsibility for the statements of individual members of its staff and accordingly what is said here is the author's own view and does not necessarily represent that of the commission.

APPENDIX D TO SECTION V

CASB--MEMBERS AND OTHER*

The CASB was created as an agent of the Congress in August, 1970 by an amendment (Public Law 91-379) to the Defense Production Act of 1950. The Comptroller General of the United States, Elmer B. Staats, is designated by Public Law 91-379 as chairman of the CASB. Pursuant to that law, he appointed four members to serve with him on the Board for a term of four years each. The Board members appointed in January,1971 are:

Member	*Business Title & Affiliation*
Herman W. Bevis	*Senior Partner, Price Waterhouse & Co. (retired)*
Robert K. Mautz	*Partner, Ernst & Ernst*
Charles A. Dana	*Director of Government Accounting Controls, Raythcon Company*
Robert C. Moot	*Vice President--Finance, AMTRAK*

On March 5, 1971, the Board selected Arthur Schoenhaut, then Deputy Controller of the Atomic Energy Commission, as Executive Secretary; and on April 25, 1971, Harry R. Von Cleve, who had served as General Counsel of the General Services Administration, became the Board's General Counsel. As of June 30, 1973, the Board had a full-time staff of 34 employees--22 professional and 12 administrative and clerical--including those with backgrounds in government, industry, the accounting and legal professions, and the academic community.

Before the promulgation of any Standard, the CASB makes an in-depth study of the subject area. It includes extension research and careful testing of alternative proposals. Although the precise nature of the research varies somewhat, depending upon the subject under consideration, certain basic elements of the research procedure are followed each time.

*Adapted with permission from Cost Accounting Standards Board, Progress Report to the Congress, 1973, U. S. Government Printing Office, 1973.

After a topic has been authorized by the Board for research, authoritative materials on the subject are reviewed, including sources such as books and theses, government procurement regulations, pronouncements of accounting and regulatory groups, Court and Board of Contract Appeals decisions, government agency reports of problems, and Disclosure Statements filed by Contractors with the Board. At the time of reviewing these materials, issues and sources of problems related to the topic under research are identified, e.g., recognition of underlying cost concepts, inadequacy of guidelines, misunderstanding in interpreting existing regulations.

Concurrently, the initial phase of liaison with various contractors and governmental agencies is begun through correspondence, telephone conversations, personal interviews, or plant visits to obtain empirical data and to discuss actual practices and the underlying accounting concepts.

With information gained from both library research and field visits, there is usually prepared an issues paper and a list of questions to be answered concerning those issues. At this stage, views of appropriate committees of various professional associations are sought.

Based on this research, a preliminary draft of a proposed Cost Accounting Standard is developed which is discussed with appropriate groups such as professional accounting associations, contractors, and government agencies. After considering suggestions made, a draft is mailed to many of the organizations and individuals who have volunteered to participate in the Board's research process. The draft Standard is usually accompanied by questions designed to elicit information concerning potential administrative problems and estimated costs of implementation. Also, certain statistical data may be obtained directly from contractors or may be obtained for the Board by the Defense Contract Audit Agency.

After comments on this preliminary draft are analyzed, the Board publishes a proposed Cost Accounting Standard in the Federal Register. This initial publication, which is viewed by the Board as an integral part of its research process, serves as a public solicitation by the Board for comments on the proposed Standard. After this initial publication, a number of contractors and government agencies are visited to discuss further all aspects of the proposed Standard, with additional special emphasis on the anticipated administrative costs of implementation and the probable benefits to be achieved through adoption of the Standard.

On the basis of careful consideration of all comments submitted by the public and the further discussions with outside organizations, the Board makes appropriate revision of the proposed Cost Accounting Standard and publishes it for the second time in the Federal Register. The Board's reasons for revising or not revising various sections of the proposed Standard in accordance with the comments received are also included in the second publication in the form of extensive prefatory remarks.

Standards promulgated by the Board are sent to the Congress at the time of the second publication in the Federal Register. The Standards become effective unless the Congress, within 60 days of continuous session, passes a concurrent resolution stating in substance that it does not favor the proposed Standard. The Board's promulgations have the full force and effect of law.

In an effort to facilitate its research process, the Board is exploring the practicality of developing one or more computerized cost models for purposes of simulation and testing of preliminary draft Standards. Because of the need for close staff coordination in developing cost models, the work is being performed by in-house staff. A preliminary version of a computerized cost model, currently operational, is capable of reclassification of costs between direct and indirect, creation of new cost pools, introduction of new allocation bases, and inclusion or exclusion of cost pools in allocation bases. Further development of simulation techniques should facilitate evaluation of changes in government contract costs caused by changes in cost accounting practices and considerations of estimated costs of implementation of changes in cost accounting practices required by proposed Standards.

APPENDIX E FOR SECTION V

THE COST ACCOUNTING STANDARDS BOARD (CASB)*

by

John J. McNally

What is The CASB and Why Was It Created?

As the cost of the defense effort and the number of negotiated defense contracts increased over the years, defense agencies became increasingly aware of the importance of adequate and uniform cost accounting procedures. During the late sixties this awareness developed into congressional concern when it was alleged that contractors were making excessive profits on government work through the manipulation of their costs. That concern led first to an 18-month study on the feasibility of applying uniform cost accounting standards to negotiated defense contracts and eventually to the creation of the five-man Cost Accounting Standards Board.

The Board is directed by statute to promulgate cost accounting standards designed to achieve uniformity and consistency in the cost accounting principles followed by defense contractors in estimating, accumulating, and reporting costs under federal contracts. In addition, the legislation directed the CASB to promulgate regulations requiring defense contractors to disclose in writing their cost accounting practices which the contractor must agree to follow consistently.

What Contracts or Contractors are Covered by CASB Regulations?

All national defense contractors and subcontractors proposing on negotiated contracts or subcontracts in excess of $100,000 are required by statute to complete the Board's Disclosure Statement which details the contractor's cost accounting procedures and practices. The CASB has temporarily exempted from its Disclosure Statement requirements those contractors or subcontractors whose negotiated national defense prime contracts subject to

*Reprinted by permission from "News & Views," The CPA Journal, July, 1974, Volume XLIV, No. 7, pp. 15-16.

CASB coverage totaled less than $10 million during each of the federal fiscal years 1972 and 1973. This exemption is transitional and will in the future be reduced or removed to achieve the statutory requirement. Nondefense agencies do not require the filing of the CASB's Disclosure Statement.

The Board's cost accounting standards must be applied to all negotiated national defense contracts or subcontracts in excess of $100,000, unless otherwise exempted. Although the legislation creating the Board limited its activity to defense contracts, all civilian agencies have adopted the CASB's standards for nondefense contracts in excess of $100,000.

How Are Standards Promulgated?

In the early stages of the development of a standard, the CASB circulates questionnaires and/or statements of issues to selected companies, government agencies, and business and professional groups to obtain information on current practice, and to determine if there is a need for a standard. Thereafter, a limited circulation is made of a preliminary draft of a standard followed by a "public exposure" through publication in the Federal Register. The final standard is then published in the Federal Register, accompanied by CASB responses to the comments received. Both houses of Congress have a period of 60 days of continuous session after final publication of a standard in which to reject any proposed standard.

What Has Been The Activity of the CASB to Date?

The CASB first made its influence felt when it promulgated the Disclosure Statement discussed above. The Board published recently a separate Disclosure Statement for the use of colleges and universities that are subject to the disclosure requirements of the CASB. Cost accounting standards published by the board to date include:

- *Standard 401 - Consistency in Estimating, Accumulating, and Reporting Costs. This standard became effective July 1, 1972, and requires that a company be consistent in presenting cost data in making price proposals on a contract, and in subsequently accumulating and reporting the actual cost of performance under the contract.*

- *Standard 402 - Consistency in Alleviating Costs for the Same Purpose. This standard also became effective July 1, 1972, and is designed to eliminate instances in which the same type of cost is charged in the same time period to a contract both as a direct cost and as a share of indirect cost, a practice termed "double accounting."*

• *Standard 403 - Allocation of Home Office Expense to Segments. This standard governs how a contractor may allocate expenses of its corporate headquarters to various divisions, subsidiaries, or plant. Contractors must follow this standard as of the beginning of their first fiscal year after September 30, 1973. Application of this standard is currently limited to contractors who are subject to the CASB's Disclosure Statement requirements.*

• *Standard 404 - Capitalization of Tangible Assets. This standard requires that contractors establish and adhere to formalized policies with respect to the capitalization of tangible assets, and provides minimum capitalization criteria of $500 in cost and a two-year life. This standard became effective for fiscal years beginning on or after October 1, 1973.*

• *Standard 405 - Accounting for Unallowable Costs. This standard sets forth guidelines for both identification in the contractors' records of specific costs that are unallowable by law or regulation and the cost accounting treatment to be afforded such costs. "Unallowable costs" shall include directly associated costs which must also be identified, and, if part of an allocation base, must remain as such and include as "unallowable costs" the indirect cost allowable thereto. This standard became effective April 1, 1974.*

• *Standard 406 - Cost Accounting Period. This standard sets forth criteria for the selection of time periods (usually the contractors fiscal year) to be used for contract cost accumulation and allocation. The effective date of this standard will be July 1, 1974.*

• *Standard 407 - Use of Standard Costs for Direct Material and Direct Labor. This standard provides criteria for the establishment of standard costs and the distribution of variances. It is expected that the effective date of this standard will be October 1, 1974.*

The Board has a number of subjects under consideration for future standards. The more prominent of these and their status in the promulgation process are:

1. *Compensated Personal Absence - proposed standard exposed in the Federal Register.*
2. *Cost of Material - draft standard exposed on a limited basis.*
3. *Depreciation - proposed standard exposed in the Federal Register.*

4. *Allocation of Segment General and Administrative Costs - draft standard exposed on a limited basis.*
5. *Pension Costs - statement of issues exposed on a limited basis.*
6. *Cost of Capital - statement of issues exposed on a limited basis.*

Impact of the CASB

With the adoption of CASB standards by civilian agencies, CASB rules apply to most all companies doing business with government. Some companies, especially smaller contractors, may be faced with the need to make major changes in their cost accounting and contract reporting of practices in order to comply with the standards. A major portion of the companies contracting with the federal government may be forced for the first time to formalize and reduce to uniting their cost accounting principles. Failure to comply with CASB standards can result in adjustment of costs and profits related to work performed under government contracts.

Concern and Commentary

In evaluating the activity of the CASB during its approximately three and one-half years of existence, contractors, industry groups, and professional organizations have voiced a number of concerns. The more significant of those concerns are:

- The Board's standards are too detailed and rigid. Little attention is given to alternatives, and the cost and difficulties of application for both large and small companies are not adequately considered.

- The CASB has, in the view of some, extended its role beyond the development of criteria for cost allocation into the development of techniques for cost determination, which is believed to be an element of generally accepted accounting principles. Advocates of this position believe that the Board's standards should not conflict with generally accepted accounting principles, and be addressed only to the allocation of costs between government and nongovernment business activity.

- The exposure given to statements of issues and early drafts of standards is too limited. A more widespread reaction to the issues could enhance the research process, and additional time should be provided for comment.

The CASB has had and will continue to have a significant impact upon companies contracting with the government. That impact will be less jarring if both the Board, its staff, and contractors commit themselves to constructive cooperation. Such cooperation will be effective only if all parties are objective in their approach and cast aside the natural desire to seek answers which provide specific benefits to the government or the contractor. If it can be agreed that the common goal is improved cost accounting principles, achievement of that goal can be accomplished only if the parties are less rigid in their individual approach. The Board must recognize the need for alternative methods, and its standards should set forth broad principles rather than detailed cost accounting procedures. Contractors must acknowledge that improvement is needed, and must trade their current resistance for constructive participation. Agreement upon these needs could result in transforming the current discord into harmony.

APPENDIX F TO SECTION V

A BANKER VIEWS: PROFESSIONAL SELF-REGULATION, LENDERS' INFORMATION NEEDS . . .

by

Walter B. Wriston*

Recently, Walter B. Wriston, chairman and chief executive officer of First National City Corporation and its major subsidiary, First National City Bank, presented his views on accounting's future as a self-regulated profession, the special information needs of lenders, . . .

- - -

"The history of the nation suggests that whenever any segment of society grows large and prominent, it produces a few characters who do something reprehensible or that is viewed as being against the value system of the time. The next step is that the profession or organization involved forms a self-regulating body. Since self-regulating bodies almost inevitably fail to self-regulate, the government takes over that responsibility. It's happened in the securities business, in banking, and now in the automobile industry."

"The last couple of self-regulating professions are accounting and law, and lawyers are in terrible trouble. Any self-regulating group that permits someone like, say, William Kunstler to disrupt the dignity of the American courtroom and doesn't kick him out of the Bar Association, is failing the citizenry. And it's not just Kunstler. Look around Washington. A lot of members of the bar, like Agnew and Dean and Ehrlichman, are also in big trouble. The idea that because you're a member of the bar your moral standards are higher has gone down the drain. It is almost inevitable that the legal profession will be regulated from outside before long."

"The accounting profession now stands at one minute to midnight in maintaining its claim to self-regulation. This didn't come about through fraud or through occasional lapses of quality

*Reprinted by permission from World, Peat, Marwick, Mitchell & Co., Spring, 1974, pp. 48-49.

control. The Achilles heel of the accounting profession is that its most influential members can't agree on most things. There is a sense of general frustration with accountants from the business community. It's not that we don't believe the numbers that you produce or that you have occasional lapses; it's simply that you don't agree among yourselves. One firm says, 'I'm going to book the investment tax credit this way,' and another says, 'no, you're not; this is the way.' You'd better agree soon or the government is going to do it for you."

"The Financial Accounting Standards Board should go a long way in bailing the accounting profession out of this dilemma. It had better because, if it doesn't, the SEC will. In the past two years, the SEC has issued 30 accounting press releases and prepared regulations; the AICPA has issued less than 15. I'm not talking about quantity. I'm a night school accountant. But that's a two-to-one ratio. Now, the FASB is a tremendous advance, but it's issued one exposure draft in four months. That's hardly the kind of productivity we need from a national commission."

"I'm willing to concede that the issues you bare in accounting are terribly complex and that honest men and women have honest differences. But as the proud employees of an organization that filed 3,700 reports last year with the Federal Reserve alone, I don't think I overstate the case to say that your survival depends on your ability to resolve your differences in a timely manner."

"The accounting profession still has time but if you don't want to see a future of bookkeepers filling out government forms, it is absolutely essential that the FASB move rapidly. I know how tough that is because you're all intelligent, you all have theories of how it can be done. The terrible truth is--it doesn't make any difference how you resolve these questions. It's going to help somebody and hurt somebody else. If you have any influence with the FASB, you'll tell them to get busy and issue 30 regulations, most of which you'll disagree with violently. That's fine. As long as you follow them, you'll have a profession. If you don't, you could wind up being an organization of bookkeepers."

"When I came into the banking business, we were asset-conscious and we loaned money on that basis. Well, assets give you a warm feeling, but they don't generate cash. The first question I would ask any borrower these days is, "What is your break-even cash flow? That's the one thing we can't find out from your audit reports and it's the single most important question we ask. It's important that you figure out a way to present the difference between real cash flow and accrual cash flow."

"Your certification and your work is the thin line that stands between most companies and disaster because nobody in senior management, or an outside director, has time to go out and find out the things you report. Now I can just see a group of attorneys and a group of partners sitting around together figuring out how to write a certificate that allows the lowest possible profile from a class action suit. That's the only way you can explain what your certificates say. I understand that because I got sued for $20 million once. I went home and told my wife. It was the best thing that ever happened because she knew it gave me a certain amount of class. So, I understand why these things are hedged. But if you're lending money and you read the thing, you won't lend the money. Put yourself on the other side."

APPENDIX G TO SECTION V

PRESCRIPTION FOR CHANGE*

by

Abraham J. Briloff

In speeches and a book Unaccountable Accounting *I have pointed up the manifestations of irresponsibility on the part of such vital sections of our society as: Lawyers, the Courts, Financial Analysts, the Banking Fraternity, Regulatory Agencies, the Academic Community, Corporate Managements (especially Financial Management) and, of course, the Independent Attesting Auditor, the CPA (who embraces all of the consequences of the corporate activity in the certified statements).*

In short, the principal theme of my previous statements was that we are all responsible in greater or lesser degree; to adapt Mr. Justice Blackmun's assertions before the American Bar Association last Summer, we are all responsible for the "glue of our corporate structure becoming unstuck."

There are no panaceas, no nostrums which will exorcise the evils which created this serious crisis in confidence, this gap in credibility. Consistent with the description of the pluralistic pattern of perversity, my proposals for critical change are addressed to the multiplicity of sectors in our total society.

The sequence of the following proposals is not intended to imply any order of priority. Of course, some of my proposals will be seen to affect our particular profession more directly than others, thereby giving us a greater challenge and opportunity for direct involvement than others. But direct or remote, it is my considered view that unless there is something of a major moral renaissance in the totality of our existence we are just not going to make it as a complex civilization.

A "Distant Early Warning System":

What then are my proposals for change?

*Reprinted by permission from Management Accounting, July, 1974, pp. 63-65 and 71.

First, I urge that the Securities and Exchange Commission, the New York Stock Exchange and other exchanges, the Financial Analysts Federation, and the Institute of Chartered Financial Analysts--whether separately or collectively--develop something of a "Distant Early Warning System." By this I mean that even before the implications or ramifications of a new accounting concept (or novel application of a traditional concept) are fully discerned; before the SEC, et al., have seen fit to condemn or limit that practice, that the DEWS point out that the development has been discerned and will be "monitored." The very existence of such a promulgation should serve to "cool" the intensity of creative accounting practices.

The groups I have named for the formulation of this roster of potential Cleverly Rigged Accounting Ploys (hence "CRAP") are at the very forefront of recipients of the output of the accountants' art; accordingly, they should be capable of the early recognition of any new phenomenon on the accounting horizon. It may well be that the analysts may believe themselves to be deprived of a competitive advantage by their being required to share their discoveries promptly. This is the price any one of us should be prepared to accept for the sake of the effectiveness of the free market system.

Then, I would look to these groups--the SEC, the exchanges, the analysts' federations and institutes--to identify the accounting and law firms which are inordinately identified with corporate fiascos and to move to censure such firms, just as we would censure a drug or food manufacturer which is found to be producing a deleterious product. The SEC censure might take the form of the constraints recently imposed on Touche Ross or Leventhal, Krekstein, Horwath and Horwath; the exchanges and analysts might reject (or at least find unacceptable) submissions carrying the imprimatur of the "accident prone" lawyers or accountants.

Turning to the judicial system, I would urge that judges continue with their present bent to broaden and intensify the third party responsibility of the professions vitally identified with the publicly-owned corporations, again, especially, the legal and accounting professions. While thus expressing approbation for the courts' present tendencies, I do have serious misgivings in two important respects.

Judges and the "Consent Decree":

First, is the rather arcane phenomenon of the "consent decree" whereby a defendant to a serious complaint agrees to accept the court's judgment but without conceding error. This absurd process, at least as I have observed it, means nothing more than a prohibition against the defendant to again commit adultery with the same consenting party, in the same place, at the same time, and in the same way. Change any of these variables and the decree is rendered "inoperative." Pointing up this absurdity is the ritual in which the press announcement of the decree is invariably followed by a statement from the defendant that he is not conceding anything--he just wants to avoid the additional litigation and expense.

Second, is the tendency on the part of the courts to treat Executive Suite Crime far less severely than Street Crime. The cynic has observed that the latter gets you into jail, the former into the Social Register.

Moving to the profession of the law, it would, of course, be presumptuous for someone who is not a lawyer to point out what the law requires of them--but which they seem to overlook or to ignore. In short, they would do better to stop thinking of themselves as the advocates of management, or that even the corporation is their client. Instead, they must recognize that when it comes to publicly-owned corporations, or corporations otherwise involved in the public sector, neither the corporation nor its management is the client--instead, to use Mr. Justice Brandeis' assertion, "the situation is the client."

Specifically, as a February, 1973, Notre Dame Lawyer *commentary put it, "when the attorney learns that management is about to perpetrate a fraud, he must make efforts to dissuade management. . . . Failing that, he has a duty to reveal the facts to the SEC to prevent fraud from occurring. The attorney-client privilege does not bar such disclosure. . . . Nor would the rules of ethics bar disclosure to shareholders where, upon a showing of cause. . .they believed that management is acting adversely to their interest."*

What all this tells me, a layman insofar as the law is concerned, is that the attorney for a publicly-owned corporation, at least, had better recognize the overriding responsibilities to the shareholders and all others to whom the corporation professes a responsibility. And an attorney who accepts a designation to the Board better recognize that he is potentially in double jeopardy. And if he doesn't like the intensified heat; then he should follow the Truman Doctrine and "get out of the kitchen."

Wrestling with the Term "Fair":

As to Corporate Management, those who are directly and intimately involved in the structuring and implementation of the corporations' transactions and then the writing of their historical narrative, I will rely heavily on the forthright counsel given by SEC Commissioner A. A. Sommer, Jr., when addressing the Cleveland Treasurers Club some months ago. The Commissioner urged the financial management of publicly-held companies to recognize that theirs is a professional responsibility. Accordingly, he insisted that:

1. The professional responsibility of corporate accountants is even broader than that of the independent auditor. Their responsibility, especially, is to produce statements which are fair, and not merely GAAP-fair.

2. While the term "fair" may be amorphous and abstract, yet we are constrained to live with it in so many contexts; we cannot abdicate the responsibility of wrestling with it in this particular area.

3. Financial executives have "an obligation" not only with respect to the integrity of the financial statements, but they also must make their responsibility the full program of corporate financial reporting. They must be alert lest the more meticulously prepared financial statements are not prostituted by misleading graphs, charts, or assertions in the textual portions of annual reports and other documents.

For My Academic Colleagues:

For my colleagues in the grooves of academe I also have some specific counsel. Briefly, remember that we are not merely the purveyors of the traditional wisdom, but also among the creators of discoverers of the new ways of doing or seeing things. As such, we are not merely the clerics of the derived wisdom but also the critics of the status quo. In this connection, I recommend Professor Robert Sterling's article in the September, 1973 Journal of Accountancy pointing up the fact that in our research endeavors we are willing to test and challenge the very underlying assumptions of our discipline; but when we turn to the writing of texts we stick to the traditional wisdom. Why? It helps sell books which generate more royalties.

Further, we are so flattered and importantly compensated by the "summer internships" with major firms and the consultative relationships with financial houses that we all too frequently fail to discern when our standards of independence and integrity have been severely compromised.

In short, let us recognize potential conflicts of interest within ourselves as readily and effectively as we can discern them in others.

In a broader, more far reaching vein, let us be committed to the complete education of professional persons--in fact, rather than by a platitudinous assertion in our institutions' catalogues. Let us by precept and example make clear that our profession is not just a way of doing things--it is a way of life, involving our total Weltanschauung. The very definition of "profession" subsumes a commitment to service. Probably of greater import, a professional person must first be a person--with the values, outlook, commitment, sensitivity, and comprehension presumed for such a total person. In brief, before we can have a professional person we must make certain we have a total person. Our educational objectives must be dedicated to assuring the development of such a total person; this commitment goes beyond numbers of credits and speed with which technique can be applied. I am, of course, calling for a major reappraisal of the content and thrust of our programs for the total education of tomorrow's professional accountants.

And Our Professional Organizations:

Proceeding to our professional organizations, especially the American Institute of CPAs, I urge, first, that it become such a professional organization rather than a trade organization overly protective of the material interests of its members and the captive of the few firms representing something of an oligopolistic force within our midst.

Especially in point, I urge that the Institute move to the really effective disciplining of those of our colleagues, whether they be identified with the one-man or ten-thousand-man firm; and if the latter, whether he be at the base or apex of the pyramid. To this end I urge that the AICPA reread the arguments advanced by the Wheat Committee report for the creation of an independent Financial Accounting Standards Board, and then recognize how these arguments can be applied even more compellingly to a corresponding dissociation of the profession's disciplinary process.

As for accounting firms, I would move to reduce their size and scope of activity. To begin with, I would deprive any firm committed to the independent attest function of the right to provide management advisory or consultative services, possibly even tax services, excepting as a direct incident to such attest function. I urge such a prohibition, first, because I firmly believe that such peripheral services contaminate the essential audit independence (and insist that all scholarly research heretofore published would support my view in this regard); then, too, I believe the giantism which presently characterizes our profession's firms is inimical to a true professional relationship within the firm--

it is inimical to the esprit required to pass the wisdom and standards of performance from generation to generation. A table of organization will not replace the human interaction between a master devoted to the totality of his profession and those who aspire to the long climb to the summit.

What counsel might I give to the Financial Accounting Standards Board, that new, most prestigious group within our professions' ambit? First, consistent with its power, prestige, and resources, I recommend that it avoid the "gnat-straining" kind of changes which are being urged on the Board by its many friends. Instead, I urge that the FASB move to clarify the broad, pervasive problems which are plaguing our profession and thereby give to us a firmer base on which to stand.

The kind of problem which might be envisaged as properly coming within the FASB scope is clarification of the meaning of the auditor's certificate. We are, of course, all intimately familiar with the ritualistic phraseology about "having examined" and "presented fairly" all in accordance with GAAP. This ritual, while firmly enshrined in our texts, has not been authoritatively defined by our profession and, as a consequence, has been capable of being interpreted or misinterpreted to suit almost any preference.

So vital was this question that in its 1965 report, the AICPA Select Committee to study the APB Opinions pleaded with the Board at the earliest possible time "to determine the meaning of the terms of art used in our certificate 'present fairly in accordance with GAAP.'" The Committee set forth a series of varying alternative interpretations of that phraseology. It asked rhetorically "What purposes and limitations attach to financial statements and to the auditor's opinion?" This question, the Committee went on, "is of first importance to the public and profession. . . . The Committee believes that an [official APB] utterance should be given top priority. It would be the subsoil on which subsequent pronouncements could be grounded, and understood . . . ." Until the profession has such an official utterance, the Committee asserted, "there is no point in beginning."

<u>Finding a Subsoil</u>:

Alas, almost a decade has now elapsed and there has not yet been the "official utterance" which the Committee asserted would be the "subsoil" for all subsequent APB pronouncements and without which "there is no point in beginning." Absent that subsoil, is it any wonder the profession is in a quagmire? Absent the defined compass point, is there any wonder we are drifting all over the turbulent seas? Absent the official pronouncement from the profession, there is little wonder that the courts, especially

Judge Henry Friendly in his landmark Continental Vending *opinion, provided the definition required for the protection of the total society--with resultant grief to many of our colleagues in the profession. Absent such an official utterance, we have such prominent spokesmen like John Burton and A. A. Sommer, Jr., providing the answer, consistent with Judge Friendly's views, that our statements must not only be fair in accordance with GAAP but they must be independently fair as we see the fair.*

It would appear that with these repeated assertions by responsible viewers of the accounting scene our profession would have come up with the "official utterance" urged by the Seidman Select Committee. Why hasn't it? I can only surmise and conclude that our colleagues like this "never-never land," where the public is encouraged to draw its own inferences (mythical though they might be) while permitting us, at least initially, to deny any paternity for the illegitimate statements. While the profession is thus hoping to perpetrate something of a hoax on the outside world, the ultimate hoax is all too frequently on the perpetrators themselves.

Back to the initial thrust of this recommendation: Let the FASB read and carefully consider the Select Committee's initial recommendation and then move to provide the official utterance, the subsoil, the point of beginning.

If, then, the Board still requires a major project, let it reflect long and agonizingly over the prevailing confusion regarding what I call the 3 R's in our underlying theory--Revenue, Realization, and Recognition. Here is a most pervasive problem embracing a multitude of general and special situations, e.g., contractors, manufacturer-lessors, land developers, franchisors, real estate operators, extractive industries, motion picture and television film producers, entities involved in foreign exchange turbulence, life and property insurers, banks, and finance companies.

In brief, what I am here suggesting are themes worthy of the rather expensive mountain structured in the bucolic Connecticut countryside. Don't permit the mountain to labor so long and assiduously just to determine the positions of the chairs in the musical chairs game--an indictment recently leveled against the reflective, foresighted economists in our midst.

To the Ultimate 'I':

Having thus given of my counsel to the SEC, the stock exchange, the security analysts and their organizations, the courts and the bar, to corporate managements and directors, to our col-

leagues in academe and the profession (including our firms and organizations), I conclude with what I sincerely believe to be the true and ultimate preachment, to the same Alpha and Omega to which I appealed when concluding Unaccountable Accounting, some-time ago.

> *In essence I am seeking to impose a "Nuremberg Code" on each of us engaged in our professional pursuit, a code whereby we commit ourselves to implement a standard of fairness, even though a contrary result could well be subsumed under GAAP. And we should adhere to the code in spite of "superior orders" or clients' directives. This is an awesome burden which I am imposing on the individual --but it is only through the acceptance of just such a burden that accountants will have a fair claim to professional recognition.*

APPENDIX H TO SECTION V

THE NUMBERS GAME: (EXPLETIVES DELETED)*

Watching the Franklin National Bank situation should have been rather like watching the tail end of a Monopoly game. You remember the scene: The hapless player (read Franklin) lands on Park Place (read Park Avenue). He is asked for enormous rent for his luxurious accommodations. So our unlucky player must tear down his hotels and mortgage his properties to raise cash. In a little over two years, Franklin National reduced its property holdings--from $35 million at the end of 1971 (just before it moved into its new headquarters at 450 Park Avenue) to $14 million at the end of 1973. In 1972 and 1973 it sold $24.5 million worth of buildings and leased them back.

The rest is history--a loss of as much as $39 million in foreign currency transactions and, according to Italian wheeler-dealer Michele Sindona, another loss of $5 million on securities transactions. The bank lost almost a quarter of its deposits in the first five weeks after its problems became public.

How did it all happen so suddenly? Only a month or so before the roof caved in, Franklin had released its 1973 annual report. The cover showed the sun in all its glory against a sky of vivid red, orange, and yellow. If ever there was a report bright with hope and promise, it was Franklin's annual report.

Nor was the narrative itself any less optimistic. "Franklin," Chairman Harold V. Gleason reported glowingly to stockholders, "is ideally suited by corporate temperament and tradition to adapt quickly to the vast revolutionary changes anticipated in the new local, national and world order."

Sounds like our bank did alright. Well, there was a disquieting increase in interest expense, from 50% of operating expenses in 1972 to 68.5% in 1973. But then all banks had that problem in 1973, and accountants Ernst & Ernst had given the report a "clean" opinion--no caveats; in their opinion the financial statements fairly reflected Franklin's financial condition at the end of 1973.

Alas, then, the stockholders had no warning?

*Reprinted by permission from Forbes, July 1, 1974, pp. 74-75.

Ah, but they did. Trouble is that few of them ever get to read a Form 10-K, that detailed document all nationally-traded corporations must file with the Securities & Exchange Commission and which--as we will explain later--is rather hard for the general public to come by although it is a public document.

Banks don't have to file 10-K's. They are specifically excluded from the requirement. But bank holding companies do. Franklin was a corporate horror story, worlds removed from the glossy, happy annual report. No rising sun in the 10-K. Strictly a falling star. Any stockholder who read and understood it might well have bailed out.

Item after item in the 10-K pictured a company unable to keep up with the treadmill it had jumped onto, and seemingly too weary even to step off.

For a start, the 10-K showed that the rise in yield on loans lagged behind the rates the bank had had to pay to acquire the funds. "Indeed," the 10-K continues, "at times during 1973, the rates paid for such funds exceeded the yields earned on such loans." In other words, there were times when Franklin lost money.

There was an item entitled "Federal Funds Borrowed" and another entitled "Other Liabilities For Borrowed Money." These represent highly volatile, very short-term money borrowed by banks, sometimes almost literally overnight. Franklin's annual report showed an increase of 72.5% in the purchase of such funds. What it did not show was that the average interest rate Franklin had to pay on those funds was 8.88%, a rate higher than the average yield it earned on <u>any</u> form of loan outstanding.

Overall, the spread--the difference between the average yield earned and the average rate paid--was a beggarly 0.94%, down from 1.91% the year before, which was no great shakes itself. If a stockholder had studied these figures he should have been alarmed as interest rates climbed this year. (The overnight rate recently was 12.38%.) But he would have looked in vain for such information in the annual report. It was only in the 10-K.

Then the 10-K got to loan losses. The valuation reserve, as the 10-K (but not the annual report) explains, "is the only portion of the reserve available for loan charge-offs." If more loans go sour than the valuation reserve can handle, the balance must come straight out of earnings. Franklin's valuation reserve declined from $20 million in 1969 to $10 million in 1973. In the same period, its loan almost doubled, from $1.5 billion to $2.8 *billion. The 10-K writers thought this contrast important enough to emphasize. The annual report didn't mention it at all.*

In fact, what the annual report did say on the subject was positively misleading. A footnote in the 1973 annual report states that the year's provision for bad debts actually exceeded by $1 million the minimum amount, which is based on a rolling five-year average of loan-loss experience. Sounds very conservative.

A glance at the 10-K quickly killed this assumption. In mentioning the same transaction, the 10-K pointed out why the loan write-off exceeded the formula. The reason was that actual loan losses had also exceeded by $1 million what the formula covered. So, there had been nothing conservative about the bank's accounting. The annual report seemingly tried to make a virtue out of necessity by concealing the reason for the additional charge.

None of these facts--nor many more in the 10-K--came as much of a surprise to the hard-nosed money managers of the big investment houses. With reams of information at their fingertips, they had long since pulled out. "You won't find any sophisticated investors in Franklin National," says Harry Keefe of Keefe, Bruyette & Woods, the bank stock specialists. "People who can read a balance sheet were out of there long ago."

The Franklin's report is a tremendous contrast to that of the Security National Bank of Long Island, itself no shining knight when it comes to performance. Security's report is the more commendable because it is not a bank holding company and therefore is not required to file a 10-K. It had the same kinds of problems as did Franklin--negative spreads at times, bad debt losses--but it laid them out clearly in its annual report. And Security's auditors, Arthur Young & Co., gave a qualified opinion to the financial statements because of potentially uncollectible loans due from companies in reorganization. Franklin had such doubtful debts, too, yet Ernst & Ernst did not even require disclosure of them, much less qualify their opinion. The potential losses are mentioned only in the 10-K.

How could Ernst & Ernst have given a clean opinion to such a grotesquely optimistic annual report? How could they have failed to mention the fact that the semiannual examination of the bank, conducted by the Comptroller of the Currency as required by law, had begun in November and had shown no signs of ending at the end of January when the auditors' letter was signed?

We called Ernst & Ernst to ask. They begged off any explanations on the grounds that Franklin was still a client, everybody was being investigated and comment would be inappropriate. So we called Franklin.

We spoke first with Treasurer John Sadlik. After ducking a few questions about the discrepancies between the annual report and the 10-K, Sadlik referred us to the public relations department. "Whatever the differences are, I'm not in a position to comment on them, and I'm not going to discuss them with you," he harrumphed.

Arthur G. Perfall, senior vice president for public relations, was only a bit more helpful. "The annual report does not and is not intended to duplicate the 10-K," he pontificated. "The annual report contains the material which we, and our counsel and our accountants, feel is required and germane." If Franklin made decisions the way it apparently expected investors to make investment decisions, no wonder the bank was in trouble.

Dear reader, this isn't really an article about Franklin National. It is really a sermon on the way all too many major corporations regard their annual reports: as a public relations document rather than as an honest accounting to stockholders.

"Let 'em read the 10-K's," some managements may say. Easier said than done. To get a copy one must either write to the SEC, which will provide one for a fee, or ask the company. It can be time-consuming. We asked Franklin for a 10-K and, after mentioning our affiliation with FORBES, were sent one within a day. But an associate who did not mention FORBES was still waiting a week later.

Any wonder the public has deserted the stock market?

APPENDIX I TO SECTION V

COMPANIES VS. AUDITORS: WHY ARE SO MANY COMPANIES FIRING THEIR ACCOUNTANTS?*

by

Arlene Hershman

Last month financially plagued Memorex, the computer peripherals company, announced it was firing its accounting firm, Arthur Andersen, because of a disagreement on how to account for a new lending agreement the company had made. About the same time, restaurant and motel operator Prime Motor Inns ditched its accountant, Peat, Marwick, Mitchell & Co., grumbling to the press that the accounting approach the Big Eight auditor preferred would have chipped almost 10% from the company's nine-month earnings figures. And a few days later, Philadelphia insurer Fisco told its shareholders that its auditors are partly to blame for the company's $26 million profit loss this year.

Is the honeymoon over? It seems only yesterday that a company and its auditors were the very picture of a cozy twosome, with scarcely a family squabble to mar their rapport. No more. The company-auditor relationship has become a virtual battleground, and some of the battles are coming out into the open. Companies are denouncing their auditors in press bulletins and to stockholders, and some are even suing them. James J. Ling's Omega-Alpha, for one, has asked $115 million in damages from two auditing firms because of alleged errors in the financial statements of a company it had bought.

The accountants, for their part, are refusing to buckle under. In letters to the Securities and Exchange Commission, and in press releases, they are giving their side of the story and defending their actions vigorously.

What the battle boils down to basically is the meaning of that ubiquitous term: "generally accepted accounting principles." Back in the late Sixties, it will be remembered, those principles were stretched considerably as companies--with the help of their auditors--were able to write their own ticket to account for such

*Reprinted by perrmission from Dun's Review, July, 1974, pp. 33,35,36.

things as mergers, sales on installment contracts, and what constitutes an extraordinary item. But those easygoing ways brought down the wrath of both stockholders and the Securities and Exchange Commission on the accounting profession, and cost auditors millions of dollars in settling class-action suits. The result is a new conservative stance by the profession.

Unfortunately, in a chancy business year like 1974, some companies are loath to go along with that conservatism. They are leaning hard on their auditors to allow practices that accentuate the positives and minimize the negatives. . . . And when the auditors refuse, more and more companies are firing them. "Auditors and companies are disagreeing more these days," comments one SEC staffer, "because the companies want to do what the auditors taught them in the late Sixties, and now the auditors, afraid of expensive lawsuits, are saying no."

Many companies, needless to say, feel that the auditors' stiff-necked stance is not justified. While they sometimes go along with the auditors' decisions, they make it clear that they are doing so under protest. Says SEC chief accountant John C. ("Sandy") Burton: "Four or five companies in the last year have asked us to back them up in accounting disputes with their auditors."

Take the case of Milgo Electronic. The Miami maker of telephone electronic devices had its first disagreement with its auditors a year ago. The CPA, Arthur Andersen, disagreed with Milgo's estimate of how much money the company should set aside from earnings for refurbishing equipment out in the field. Because they could not come to terms, the auditors put qualifying words in its certification of Milgo's financial statement for the year.

This year Milgo came in with record sales and earnings. But the results were not nearly as good as they could have been because the auditors insisted on changing numbers that pared some 10 cents a share off earnings--even though Milgo claims its estimates of reserves the prior year had proved accurate. Milgo went along, although it disagreed with the decision. Says Charles C. Weston, financial vice president: "Although the company feels strongly this year, as it did last year, that its reserves are adequate, it reduced its earnings in order not to have a qualified auditor's report two years in a row."

One big reason for the auditors' more conservative ways is the SEC's new assertiveness as watchdog over the profession. Under chief accountant Sandy Burton, the SEC has increased its disclosure requirements. Schedules showing amounts and timing of lease obligations, for example, are now part of the annual reports. Most important of all, the SEC is claiming the right to review an auditor's procedures for examining books.

In the past year, the SEC has told two national auditing firms, Touche Ross and Laventhol, Krekstein, Horwath & Horwath, to institute tighter controls--or else. An industry joke going the rounds, as reported by one accountant: "The Big Eight firms have offered to donate an accountancy chair to any university if Sandy Burton would only agree to sit in it."

Investors, of course, stand to benefit from these disputes. More reliable statements mean fewer chances for over-blown earnings or assets statements. And information about the nature of the company-auditor disagreements, when they are reported, provides early warning signals for sophisticated investors.

Reading the Small Print:

Most fallings out between companies and auditors are more likely to appear in the footnotes of annual reports or SEC filings than in the headlines. Here, any change in auditors--the SEC requires that companies report them--and qualifications of financial figures by auditors are revealed.

The SEC reports are particularly interesting because the agency requires a company to spell out any disagreements it may have had with its auditors in the last eighteen months. And if an auditor is fired, it must send the SEC a letter giving its version of the squabble. These give both the SEC's investigators and savvy investors material to examine closely.

For experience has shown that when a company fires its auditors, it often telegraphs bad news for investors. A few years ago, for example, the SEC reports revealed that four computer lessors went shopping for new auditors who held more agreeable principles about the value of their computer equipment. Major losses owing to new, lower valuations of the equipment followed. In other cases, both U.S. Financial and food company Westgate-California went through Byzantine auditor changes before their troubles came to light. "We discovered U.S. Financial's problems out of these reports," says Sandy Burton, "which we think is a real plus."

Auditors enter qualifications in a company's annual report when they have doubts about the reliability or certainty of some numbers or when the accounting principles used are not consistent from year to year. They tell precisely what it is they are questioning, or what is different. Both auditors and regulators agree that qualifications are meant to be warnings to investors.

When opinions are qualified because the auditors had questions or doubts about the reliability of the numbers, the SEC and the New York Stock Exchange look twice too.

Auditors only qualify a statement when a change in the numbers in question would have a material impact on the company's financial picture. Some auditors claim they use a 5% difference in earnings or assets as material, but there is no industry standard. While qualifications do not always result in the auditor's worst fears being realized, it is a common practice to assume that such uncertainties often foretell future write-offs, write-downs, or other subtractions from earnings. "I like auditor's statements that qualify certain transactions," says corporate gadfly Lewis Gilbert. "It tells a shareholder what to focus on."

Investors who read the qualifications and footnotes in Pitney Bowes' 1972 annual report, for example, were tipped off six months before the company took a major write-off. S. D. Leidesdorf, auditor for Pitney Bowes-Alpex, a company subsidiary that made electronic point-of-sale register systems, qualified the subsidiary's financials because of skepticism regarding its ability to recover its promotional, research and development outlay.

Price Waterhouse, auditor for Pitney Bowes, also took cognizance of Leidesdorf's uncertainties in its certification of the parent company's financial statement. Price Waterhouse envisioned a loss of $13.7 million for the subsidiary at worst. Unfortunately, as Pitney Bowes announced regretfully last November, the loss came to $37 million, or $2.85 a share. The stock traded in the low teens during the six-month interval between the release of the annual report and the announcement of the write-off. Smart investors who read the numbers had time to get out before the stock plummeted to 7 after the announcement.

Many major companies had qualifications on their 1973 audit statements. The outcome of lawsuits caused qualifications on the reports of Johns-Manville and Federal Mogul, among others. Auditors qualified the reports of White Motor Corporation and B. F. Goodrich because of uncertainties about the value of contracts. And Eastern Air Lines' report had a whole paragraph hinging on its ability to get fare increases, sell off equipment, and postpone deliveries of equipment.

More to Come?:

Uncertainty is so pervasive, there is a strong belief among auditors, regulators, and companies that the number of qualified statements will increase dramatically this year. Audit partner

Edward Weinstein of Touche Ross reflects the thinking of many auditors when he says: "My gut feeling is that this year we are going to see a lot more qualified statements."

The auditors, moreover, are questioning managements' numbers in areas that were once simply accepted at face value. Pension cost uncertainties as related to plant shutdown is one area. For example, Federal Mogul, manufacturer of a wide range of bearings and other metal vehicle and machinery components, got hit with a suit last June by the United Auto Workers, seeking benefits for employees who will be out of jobs because of the company's closing of two plants in Detroit. The union's demand for $16 million in benefit payments resulted in a qualification in Federal Mogul's 1973 report--underlining the auditor's uncertainty of the suit's ultimate outcome. Its fears were realized in May, when the company settled for $5 million--a sum roughly equivalent to 20% of Federal Mogul's 1973 pretax earnings.

A similar situation existed at steelmaker H. K. Porter. Its auditors had qualified the 1971 annual report on the grounds that it was uncertain how much more allowance, if any, was necessary for pension outlays arising from plant closings. The company's attorney, in fact, contended that the piper perhaps would not have to be paid at all. The uncertainty about the payments dragged on for two years. But apparently Porter saw the matter differently this year. With the approval of its new auditors, Ernst & Ernst (Arthur Andersen was replaced after qualifying Porter's statements two years in a row), it subtracted some $1.7 million from its 1973 earnings to pay the pension bills--a bite equal to 25% of the company's pretax profits.

An even stronger warning flag to investors is the auditor's "going concern" qualification. For with this the auditor states that he is uncertain about the company's ability to stay in business. The qualification hinges on, say, the company's ability to raise the money to pay its creditors in the following year. Two recent examples: Sequoyah industries and Curtis Electro Corporation both of which were subject to "going concern" qualifications and have applied for reorganization under bankruptcy proceedings this year. "Companies contend," says S. D. Leidesdorf's Barry Burris, "that the qualification is a self-fulfilling prophecy."

Investors are also picking up the trail of problems in reading the public reports to the SEC on changes in auditors. Unfortunately, these documents are not as helpful as they should be, as the SEC itself admits. Part of the problem is that the SEC's instruction for reporting disagreements are subject to varying interpretations. As a result, many disagreements are never reported. And often the real reasons for a change are difficult to discover.

Take the case of Leader International. Ernst & Ernst gave the American Exchange-listed light-equipment and homes fixture maker a qualified report in 1972. When the company switched auditors the next year, however, it listed no disagreements with Ernst & Ernst. Rather, it claimed the change was motivated by the need for a smaller auditor that could give its books closer attention. Apparently, the greater watchfulness did not clear up the difficulties that Ernst & Ernst had wondered about. In November, Leader filed for reorganization under Chapter 11.

Leader's lapse in not reporting disagreements is typical of a large number of companies. An analysis of the SEC files of auditor changes shows that disagreements are reported by either the company or the replaced auditor in only some 10% of the cases. However, the SEC accounting staff has discovered that the percentage almost triples if the tabulation is revised to include all cases in which the change was preceded by a qualified report.

Who's Winning?:

There is no question that the current situation is a confusing one. Even experts differ on what constitutes a disagreement between company and auditors. A qualification in the strictest sense means only that the auditor is uncertain--not that he necessarily has another figure in mind. H. K. Porter, for one, contends that the qualifications of its reports for two years "were simply the results of misunderstandings." In Arthur Andersen's stricter reading of the SEC regulation, it requested that Porter notify the SEC about their differences that led to the qualifications.

Moreover, reading the self-serving contentions of the company and the auditor in these disputes sometimes multiplies the investor's confusion. Mutual Oil of America, an oil production and exploration company, had a disagreement with Ernst & Ernst about accounting for the assets and liabilities of partnership deals it operates. When the auditor refused to go along with the bunching of the partner money with the company's, Mutual simply went out and found another auditor who agreed with it.

Investors, therefore, have to be agile to avoid being caught in the cross fire. While the requirement that disagreements be spelled out to the SEC may intimidate some companies from jettisoning their auditors hastily, management still holds the upper hand. If an auditor intimates that he would qualify a report, the company can still retaliate by firing the auditor.

The trouble with this kind of warfare, observes Touche Ross' Edward Weinstein, is that it is between two countries with atom bombs. "As long as they threaten each other, they have a lot of power," he says. "But once they start throwing bombs, they run the risk of being wiped out."

The SEC's Burton reads the current scene as a definite sign that the auditors' attitudes have changed permanently for the better. He believes that the accounting profession will increasingly fulfill its watchdog role over management and provide investors with more reliable financial reports. Though Burton warns that this change will come slowly over a period of years, he says, "I think the accounting profession can do the job."

Others are not so optimistic. Despite the current flowering of qualified statements for Big Board-listed companies, accounting critic Ted O'glove believes that auditors should have qualified a lot more reports this year than they did. "Where was Ernst & Ernst on the Franklin National Bank?" he asks. "Management still has the whip hand because it can fire the auditors."

Privately, even many auditors are skeptical that the current falling out heralds the beginning of a permanent change in the relationship between the CPAs and the companies they monitor. Rather, they believe that the marriage is merely feeling the strain of difficult times. When business is healthier, they expect the auditors to revert back, at least to a degree, to the rubber-stamping of management's notions. "The accounting profession," one auditor observes, "is reacting not out of any moral fervor or new realization of its role, but out of concern for its own health and well being."

If that is so, then Sandy Burton may have to get even tougher on the auditors.

APPENDIX J TO SECTION V

ARTHUR ANDERSEN & CO. ESTABLISHES PUBLIC REVIEW BOARD*

by

Harvey Kapnick

We are pleased to announce that our firm is establishing a Public Review Board. As indicated in the attached statement relating to the operations of this Board, a public accounting firm has a significant responsibility in the private sector of our economy not only to clients but also to investors and creditors and to the public generally. We are dedicated to fulfilling this responsibility and to improving the effectiveness of our free enterprise system in the public interest. We believe that the establishment of this Board is a constructive and beneficial step that should enhance the efforts of our firm to carry out its function in the business and financial community in the best possible manner.

The general purpose of this Board is to review the professional operations of our firm, including the manner in which our firm is managed and financed, the scope of our practice, and how the quality of our work is controlled.

Initially there will be five members of the Board, who will serve on a part-time basis. We are announcing the formation of this Board at this time because of the current interest in this subject. As additional members are selected, they will be announced at that time. The present members are as follows:

William L. Cary--Dwight Professor of Law at Columbia University; Counsel, Patterson, Belknap & Webb; former Chairman of Securities and Exchange Commission

James Don Edwards--Research Professor at University of Georgia; Past President of American Accounting Association; Member of AICPA Study group on the Objectives of Financial Statements

Newton N. Minow--Partner, Sidley & Austin; former Chairman of Federal Communications Commission

*Reprinted by permission from Arthur Andersen & Co., Executive News Brief, Vol. 2, No. 8, June, 1974.

George Romney--Chairman of National Center for Voluntary Action; former Chairman of American Motors Corporation; former Governor of Michigan; former Secretary of Housing and Urban Development

Randolph William Thrower--Partner, Sutherland, Asbill & Brennan; Chairman, American Bar Association Planning Committee; former Commissioner of Internal Revenue Service

Newton N. Minow will act as the initial Chairman.

The broad and diverse backgrounds of the members of the Board give them unique qualifications to evaluate our firm from the standpoint of the public interest, with particular reference to the performance of our professional services.

The members of the Board will establish their own program for reviewing and considering the operations of our firm. They will have access to all information that is necessary to accomplish their objectives.

The Board will be expected to submit comments and suggestions from time to time to the management of our firm. Also, it is contemplated that the Board will make an annual report that will be published by the firm.

We believe that this Board will bring an outside viewpoint to our professional practice, particularly with respect to our public responsibilities as independent accountants and auditors.

Harvey Kapnick
Chairman

STATEMENT OF GENERAL PURPOSE, ORGANIZATION, AND FUNCTIONS OF PUBLIC REVIEW BOARD OF ARTHUR ANDERSEN & CO.

General Purpose

A public accounting firm has a significant responsibility in the private sector of our economy not only to clients but also to investors and creditors and to the public generally. Arthur Andersen & Co. (referred to hereinafter as the firm) is dedicated to fulfilling this responsibility and to improving the effectiveness of our free enterprise system in the public interest. The establishment of a Public Review Board (referred to hereinafter as the Board) is intended as a constructive and beneficial step to assist the firm in its efforts to meet its responsibilities to the public and the business and financial community.

The general purpose of the Board is to review the professional operations of the firm on a continuing basis. This includes the manner in which the firm is managed and financed, the scope of its practice, and how the quality of its work is controlled. The Board also will consider the performance of professional services by the firm that are related to the public interest.

The members of the Board will have access to all information in the firm that is necessary to accomplish their objectives. They may visit any of the offices and talk to any of the personnel. Full cooperation in furnishing requested information and in providing essential data will exist at all times.

The members of the Board will have freedom in establishing their own program for reviewing and considering the operations of the firm, and they will be furnished with whatever staff assistance they consider to be necessary.

This Board should bring an outside, independent viewpoint to the professional practice of the firm in its service to clients, investors, and others who have an interest in the public responsibilities of the firm as independent accountants and auditors.

Organization and Functions

Membership and Compensation

The Board will consist of individuals who have not been members or employees of the firm, with one of the members designated as chairman. The members of the Board will be consultants rather than employees of the firm. They will be persons of outstanding reputation in business, public service, education, or the professions. They will be appointed by the Chairman of the firm, and approved by the Board of Directors of the firm.

The duration of the term of each Board member will be two years, subject to renewal for additional two-year terms. The firm will pay the Board members an annual compensation for their services and reimburse them for their expenses.

Meetings

The responsibilities of the Board members are expected to require about fifteen to twenty days of work during each year for

Board members other than the chairman and a few days more on the part of the chairman.

The Board will hold an initial meeting in Chicago at the convenience of the members as soon as practicable after the Board members are appointed. This initial meeting shall be essentially an orientation session, at which time the Board members will meet members of the management of the firm.

Subsequent to the initial meeting, it is expected that the Board will meet at least quarterly. Some of the meetings may be in offices in the United States other than in Chicago and possibly in offices outside the United States. The times and circumstances of these meetings will be within the Board's discretion, subject only to having the necessary arrangements made by appropriate firm personnel. Also, individual Board members will visit various offices of the firm from time to time.

The Board will include within the scope of its review the educational processes of the firm. This review will include a visit to the Center for Professional Development at St. Charles, Illinois.

Further detailed procedures of the Board will be determined by its members.

Review of Quality and Manner of Performance

One of the functions of the Board will be to review the general quality of the work of the firm in carrying out its professional practice. As part of this function, the members of the Board will review firm policies, standards, and procedures with respect to the firm's professional practice, including auditing and financial reporting, and will make comments and suggestions to the management of the firm as to improvements that in its judgment should be considered. However, the Board will have no responsibility for making or implementing policies or procedures of the firm.

The members of the Board will review the results of the internal review program conducted by the firm relating to its professional practice.

Liaison with the Firm

The Chairman of the firm's Committee on Accounting Principles and Auditing Procedures will have the responsibility for making the necessary arrangements and for performing the liaison function with the Board in all matters involving the firm.

A partner of the firm will be designated to act as Secretary to the Board, to handle correspondence, scheduling, and other matters as determined by the Board. Additional staff assistance will be furnished to the Board as required.

Confidential Nature of Information

Each Board member will agree to be bound by the same requirements of confidentiality with respect to information, including any related to clients, as are partners of the firm.

Reports by Board

The Board will make whatever proposals for improving the quality of the firm's professional performance that it believes to be appropriate. These proposals are to be transmitted to the Chairman of the firm.

Periodically, the Board will render reports to the Chairman of the firm summarizing the Board's conclusions and recommendations with respect to the firm's professional practice.

The Board in carrying out its function will also render an annual report that will be published by the firm.

INDEX BY AUTHOR

INDEX BY SUBJECT

(Authors included in other index except when they are referred to by others.)

A

B

C

D

G

H

I

J

K

L

M

N

O

P

Q

R

S

V

W

Z